Parenting in
the Zombie Apocalypse

Contributions to Zombie Studies

Parenting in the Zombie Apocalypse

The Psychology of Raising Children in a Time of Horror

STEVEN J. KIRSH

CONTRIBUTIONS TO ZOMBIE STUDIES
Series Editor *Kyle William Bishop*

McFarland & Company, Inc., Publishers
Jefferson, North Carolina

LIBRARY OF CONGRESS CATALOGUING-IN-PUBLICATION DATA

Names: Kirsh, Steven J., author.
Title: Parenting in the zombie apocalypse : the psychology of raising
    children in a time of horror / Steven J. Kirsh.
Description: Jefferson, North Carolina : McFarland & Company,
    Inc., Publishers, [2019] | Series: Contributions to zombie studies
    | Includes bibliographical references and index.
Identifiers: LCCN 2019018878 | ISBN 9781476673882 (paperback :
    acid free paper) ∞
Subjects: LCSH: Parenting—Psychological aspects. | Terror. |
    Psychic trauma in children. | Children and violence. | Zombies—
    Psychological aspects.
Classification: LCC BF723.P25 K49 2019 | DDC 649/.1019—dc23
LC record available at https://lccn.loc.gov/2019018878

BRITISH LIBRARY CATALOGUING DATA ARE AVAILABLE

ISBN (print) 978-1-4766-7388-2
ISBN (ebook) 978-1-4766-3653-5

Front cover image © 2019 Shutterstock

Printed in the United States of America

*McFarland & Company, Inc., Publishers
    Box 611, Jefferson, North Carolina 28640
    www.mcfarlandpub.com*

For Sudha, Michelle, Daniel, and Emily

Table of Contents

Preface

I love zombies and have for going on 40 years. Like many kids growing up in the 1970s, my formal introduction to the Zombie Apocalypse started with the holy trinity of horror films by George A. Romero: *Night of the Living Dead,*[1] *Dawn of the Dead,*[2] and *Day of the Dead.*[3] The decapitations, eviscerations, and dismemberments captivated me. The bloodier, the gorier, the better. Fast forward a decade or so and not much had changed. I still loved the zombie genre and all of the bone-crunching and blood-spurting carnage it depicted. By this point, I had received a Ph.D. in developmental psychology, landed a tenure-track job at Washburn University, and started teaching courses on the fundamentals of psychology and child development. In part because of my training and experiences in the classroom, and in part because of the countless hours I spent watching and reading about humans killing zombies and zombies killing humans, the mindset of the survivors started to intrigue me more than brain splatters, tumbling intestines, and arterial sprays (impressive as they were). And so it went for more than another decade. During that time I started teaching at SUNY-Geneseo, penned two original academic texts, *Children, Adolescents, and Media Violence: A Critical Look at the Research* and *Media and Youth: A Developmental Perspective*, and co-authored a third, *Psychology for Living: Adjustment, Growth, and Behavior Today*.

Even as I was writing about the effects of consuming media on youth, I maintained my voracious zombie appetite. By age 50, I had taken in the Zombie Apocalypse in just about every medium imaginable: television, movies, video games, books, comic books, apps, dice games, and podcasts. In each instance, I visualized myself in the shoes of the living. Without fail, I always ended up in the tattered shoes of the living dead. C'est la vie. That is life and undeath in a world overrun by the living dead. At least the

1

Zombie Apocalypse was not real. But when has a little thing like "reality" ever stopped a college professor from teaching a course on the subject?

After much reflection and soul searching, I decided the time had come to merge my knowledge of the undead with my understanding of parenting research and child development. Much to my delight, not to mention surprise, the College agreed. The result was an honors seminar entitled "Parents vs. Zombies." Students in the class read articles about contemporary parenting strategies and discussed the advantages and disadvantages of continuing to use them once the walking dead roamed the earth. The course addressed the following question: "What does the existing body of social science research teach us about raising youth when parents fear both the living and the dead?" Two years later, I was able to teach "Parents vs. Zombies" a second time. After seeing, once again, the utility of using the Zombie Apocalypse to relay the challenges that parents face in the real world, I decided to write an academic book on the topic. This book.

Parenting in the Zombie Apocalypse investigates issues related to parenting through the lens of the "hypothetical" Zombie Apocalypse. Given that an undead rising has yet to occur, there is no direct research on parenting in the land of the living dead. At first glance, the lack of real-world research would seem to make the "academic" part of this book a bit difficult to pull off. However, there *are* studies about parenting in war zones and areas of violent crime. There *is* research related to infant and maternal mortality, parenting while grieving, the effects of food insecurity, and living without modern conveniences. And there *are* theories related to parenting. In fact, there are many of them. So, while it is true that research on parenting during the Zombie Apocalypse is lacking, there are plenty of theories and real-world studies applicable to it.

Throughout the book, I illustrate or introduce key psychological concepts with examples from zombie-laden films, books, comic books, and so on. Familiarity with zombie media and lore, however, is not a prerequisite for reading this book. Despite the longevity of the zombie genre (and much to my dismay), many people are still unfamiliar with its most popular offerings, such as the Romero films mentioned above or AMC's television series *The Walking Dead*. With these people in mind, I have written *Parenting in the Zombie Apocalypse* such that a novice to the genre will still be able to understand the exemplified concepts. For those interested in exploring the Zombie Apocalypse for the first time, or for veterans looking for something new to read, Box P.1 presents a list of some of my favorite zombie-filled books, each with a summary in 15 words or less.

Box P.1: *Zombie Literature of Note*		
If you like ...	**Title and author**	**Bite-size summary**
Star Wars	*Death Troopers* by Joe Schreiber	*Star Wars* meets zombies.
Star Trek	*Night of the Living Trekkies* by Kevin David Anderson and Sam Stall	Zombies at a Star Trek convention!
Batman and Superman	*Ex-Heroes* by Peter Clines	Superheroes vs. zombies.
Young adult novels	*Rot & Ruin* by Jonathan Maberry	Teenage hormones vs. zombies vs. bad guys.
Blogging or the TV show *Jackass*	*Feed* by Mira Grant	Blogging about zombies, politics, and conspiracies.
Victorian novels or martial arts	*Pride, Prejudice, and Zombies* by Seth Grahame-Smith and Jane Austen	A retelling of the classic story set in a zombie-infested 19th-century England.
Mash-ups	*Zombies versus Aliens versus Vampires versus Dinosaurs* by Jeff Abugov	Have your cake and eat it too.
Couples therapy	*Married with Zombies* by Jesse Petersen	Forget date night—nothing brings a marriage together like killing zombies.
Dark comedies or Christmas songs	*I Saw Zombies Eating Santa Claus* by S. G. Browne	A little girl mistakes a sentient zombie for Santa.
12-step programs or cooking shows	*Breathers* by S. G. Browne	Even the undead need counseling.
Seal Team Six	*Patient Zero: A Joe Ledger Novel* by Jonathan Maberry	Tactical operations, terrorists, and zombies.
Reading your sibling's diary	*Day by Day Armageddon* by J. L. Bourne	A soldier's journal during the Zombie Apocalypse.
Saying "BRAINNNS"	*My Life as a White Trash Zombie* by Diana Rowland	Mystery and intrigue surround a newly "born" brain-eating zombie.

One of my favorite techniques for facilitating the understanding of course material is to have students identify psychological concepts in books or animated films. Students find such assignments enjoyable and valuable, and report that they help them connect to course content. I hope that this book helps the reader in the same fashion, resulting in a greater understanding of and appreciation for the fascinating and complex nature of human development and the role that parents play in it. Nevertheless, for many, a book on parenting during the Zombie Apocalypse seems ridiculous. Zombies are not real, after all. But as mentioned above, when you take the zombies out of the Zombie Apocalypse, you are still left with impoverished conditions, violent surroundings, and parenting under conditions of extreme physical and emotional duress. In today's world, the reality is that hundreds of millions of parents and children live in adverse, apocalyptic-like environments. Thus, in addition to being a book about parenting in a fictitious world overrun with the living dead, *Parenting in the Zombie Apocalypse* underscores the point that real-life parenting often occurs in harsh and untenable conditions. By exploring parenting among the dead, one can learn about parenting among the living.

I want to thank the Edgar Fellows Honors Program at SUNY-Geneseo for green-lighting "Parents vs. Zombies," the course that inspired this book. I am also indebted to my colleagues Drs. Jennifer Katz, Christine Merrilees, Monica Schneider, and Colin Zestcott for listening to my musings on parenting during the Zombie Apocalypse and providing feedback on draft chapters of this book. I am incredibly grateful to SUNY-Geneseo alumni Meghan Barrett ('16), Julia Cameron ('18), Pamela Emengo ('16) and Sean Maclean ('18), whose enthusiastic response to the honors course inspired me to make this book a reality. Finally, a special thank you to my dear wife, Sudha, who believed in this book from the first time I told her the idea. I couldn't have written it without her love and support.

Introduction

The Zombie Apocalypse will be unkind to everyone, but it will be especially cruel to children. Nowhere is this more obvious than in "Days Gone Bye," the very first episode of AMC's *The Walking Dead*.[1] The scene opens with Sheriff Rick Grimes attempting to scavenge fuel at a derelict gas station. As Rick moves between vehicles, he encounters a little girl who is no more than ten. She is facing away from him, wearing pajamas, a dirty robe, and bunny slippers. She picks up a teddy bear from the ground and wanders away. Rick calls to her, and she turns around. She is unmistakably dead. As she moves toward him, Rick raises his gun and reluctantly puts a bullet into her brain. As blood erupts from the back of her head, the little girl falls to the ground. So too does her teddy bear.

The odds of an adult surviving a Zombie Apocalypse are slim. Based on the spread of real-life infectious diseases, mathematical models estimate that a zombie plague will go from patient zero (that is, the first zombie) to an extinction-level pandemic in a matter of months. Just how bleak is the situation? Assuming a 90 percent chance that each zombie infects at least one person per day, a mere 100 days after the first zombie attack, fewer than 300 people in the world would still be alive.[2] Other models suggest that with military involvement 12 percent of the civilian population can survive a Zombie Apocalypse.[3] As you can see, the odds of living through an undead rising are not very good. Those odds get even worse for children. Depending on the presence or absence of caretakers and age, youth will have little to no chance of surviving a single encounter with a zombie, let alone the Zombie Apocalypse.

Reanimated corpses will not be the only threat to the lives of children. In addition to the presence of an unforgiving, unrelenting, and undead predator, a breakdown in society will accompany the rise of the living dead.

Governments will collapse; modern conveniences will no longer exist; and lawlessness, violence, and brutality will all increase. It will be survival of the fittest, at its most primal level.

What are parents to do? How are they supposed to raise children when they fear both the dead and the living? Throughout the book, I apply parenting research and relevant psychological theories to the Zombie Apocalypse. To help accomplish this task, I relay content from popular media offerings that depict undead risings. Fair warning: spoilers abound, especially for zombie-themed media involving children, such as *The Walking Dead* (television show and comic book) and Jonathan Maberry's novel *Rot & Ruin*.

Just How Long Will It Take for the World to Fall?

In Zombie town (https://mattbierbaum.github.io/zombies-usa/), you control the Zombie Apocalypse! See how the location of patient zero, the ratio of zombies killed to humans bitten, and the time it takes a zombie to travel one mile affect the fall of civilization.

Overview

I have divided the books into five major sections. Section One, "On Zombies," is purely foundational, as it introduces the reader to the essentials of the Zombie Apocalypse. In Chapter 1, "Welcome to the Zombie Apocalypse," I discuss the worldwide popularity of the genre and the psychology behind it. Theories and research from the fields of evolutionary and motivational psychology, as well as communications, are prominent. The second chapter, "A Zombie Primer," addresses the nature of zombie functioning. Can zombies think or feel emotions? How do they exist if their stomachs and intestines have fallen out? Do the undead remember their former lives or recognize their loved ones? These are just of few of the many zombie-related questions answered in this chapter. Also, I address the basics of zombie-human interactions, identifying strategies of survival for both young and old.

Of course, this chapter is decidedly hypothetical as (of yet) there are no real zombies on which to base my contentions. After playing numerous zombie-themed video games, reading hundreds of books, and spending countless hours on the various horror and zombie pages of Reddit, I finally realized that there is no canon for the living dead, and there is a distinct possibility that some readers may object to my views on zombie physiology and behavior. And that's OK. When discussing the psychology of the living, social scientists often disagree. Why should the psychology of the living dead be any different?

In Section Two, "The Nature of Childhood and Parenting," I introduce general theories related to childhood and parenting as well as relay the harsh reality of infant and maternal mortality. Chapter 3, "The Destruction of Childhood," discusses the nature of childhood and threats to its existence. In this chapter, I discuss the effects of stress on important developmental tasks and stages that affect parenting. As it turns out, the Zombie Apocalypse is not the only stressor that can reduce childhood to ashes.

In the fourth chapter, "Maternal and Infant Mortality," I relay the dangers of pregnancy and childbirth as well as the likelihood of newborns surviving past the first year of life. I rely on theory, empirical studies, and epidemiological findings associated with living in nations classified as *developed* (i.e., countries with high industrialization and high per capita income) or *developing* (i.e., countries with low industrialization and low per capita income) to support my zombie-related contentions.

In the fifth chapter, "Why Parent?," I evaluate the reasons for parenting in environments filled with adversity. I base my contentions on evolutionary psychology and terror management theory, the latter of which has nothing to do with terrorism, despite its name.

Section Three, "The Determinants of Parenting," discusses three classes of influence on caregiving. Chapter 6, "Characteristics of the Parent," focuses on the internal forces that shape the way parents parent, including their upbringing, personality, religious beliefs, sense of self, and the presence of mental illness (e.g., anxiety, depression, PTSD). Chapter 7, "Characteristics of the Child," addresses three areas of child and adolescent development that significantly affect parenting: behavioral self-control, emotional self-regulation, and aggressive behavior. I also discuss the challenges of parenting children with mental health disorders. In the third and final chapter, "Contextual Sources of Stress and Support," I review the broader social contexts (e.g., relationships with friends and family) that adversely affect parenting or, conversely, help it. I end the chapter by discussing the interaction of parent, child, and contextual determinants of parenting.

Section Four, "Parent-Child Relationships," addresses parenting techniques and other child-rearing issues that could potentially facilitate (or hamper) psychological well-being and survival in the land of the dead. In Chapter 9, "Attachment," I provide an overview of attachment theory, including the causes and consequences of secure and insecure attachments, and apply this information to the Zombie Apocalypse. In environments with a certainty of parental death, which pattern of attachment is most beneficial for youth? We shall see. In Chapter 10, "Parenting Styles," I discuss the advantages and disadvantages of various parenting behaviors and disciplinary techniques across development and under different environmental conditions.

The fifth and final section, "Moving Past the Horror," discusses the associations between trauma, grief, and resiliency. Death is a part of life and even more so during the Zombie Apocalypse. In Chapter 11, "Parenting and Grief," I review the stages of grief affecting parents and children. Then, I discuss the effects of parental loss on children's welfare, followed by the impact of losing a child on parental well-being. In the final chapter, "Post-Apocalyptic Resilience," the discussion shifts from parenting during the Zombie Apocalypse to raising children in a post-apocalyptic world. First, I present the real-world characteristics of children, parents, and communities that promote resilience. I then discuss this information as it relates to the post-apocalypse.

However, before youth can thrive in a post-apocalyptic environment, they must first survive an apocalyptic one. Ultimately, the battle for the continued existence of humanity comes down to the battle between parents and zombies.

SECTION ONE:
ON ZOMBIES

1. Welcome to
the Zombie Apocalypse

It is Christmas Eve and crawling toward you from the front of the fireplace is a man covered from head to toe in red. But the bloated figure does not want to eat the milk and cookies waiting on the countertop for jolly old St. Nick. Instead, he wants to eat you. Santa Claus is but a myth. Money in hand, you find a tooth under your child's pillow. As you lift it higher, you see another tooth, and another tooth and a few jawbone fragments scattered about the bottom of the bed. The Tooth Fairy does not exist. On Valentine's Day, you see a heart with an arrow through it; the rest of the body is nowhere in sight. You remind yourself to aim for the head next time, assuming there is a next time. You had better hide. Cupid is but a figment of the imagination. Nowadays, Halloween seems to happen nightly, but children no longer trick or treat for candy. They are the candy. Fairytales with happy endings no longer exist, for the monsters under the bed, in the closet, behind the door, and surrounding the house are very real. Welcome to the Zombie Apocalypse!

On the Popularity of Zombies

Zombies, or some incarnation of them, have been with us for centuries. The Vikings believed that *draugr* emerged from their graves with superhuman strength and cannibalistic hunger. During the middle ages, *revenants*—human corpses made of skin and bones—wandered the graveyards of France hunting down those that dared to enter their domain. In Japanese mythology, the giant skeletal *gashadokuro*—a creature created

9

from the bones of those who starved to death—captured its human prey and bit off their heads. According to 17th-century Chinese folklore, a reanimated corpse known as *jiangshi* hopped around with its arms out-stretched in search of food, which happened to be the *chi* (life force) of the living. In many Native American cultures, *windigos*—transformed humans that smelled of death and decay—feasted on the corporeal. Ironically, the term "zombie" derives from Haitian voodoo culture (and the West African word "nzombi"), in which magic reanimates the dead bereft of intelligence, self-awareness, and souls. It was not until the 1960s, and the success of George A. Romero's cult classic *Night of the Living Dead*, that the modern version of the zombie—with its decaying flesh and mindless propensity to bite, infect, and kill—came into prominence.

Although the inevitable apocalyptic event involving the reanimated dead has yet to occur, the fictional ones are a mainstay of various entertainment mediums. For years, AMC's *The Walking Dead* was the number one rated television program for adults 18–49. Recently, season 8 of the show averaged around eight million viewers per episode.[1] The comic book basis of the television series (also entitled *The Walking Dead*) typically sells between 50,000 and 100,000 copies per issue.[2] Zombie-themed books, such as Max Brooks' *The Zombie Survival Guide* and *World War Z: An Oral History of the Zombie War*, became *New York Times* best sellers, each selling more than million copies.[3] On film, Romero's *Night of the Living Dead* makes most "top 10" lists for horror,[4] and the movie adaptation of *World War Z* was a box-office smash, garnering more than $540 million worldwide.[5] Zombie-themed video games, such as *Dead Rising* and *Left for Dead*, are highly sought-after as well. Leading the video game horde is Capcom's *Resident Evil* series, which has sold more than 84 million copies worldwide.[6] Newer entertainment mediums are not immune to the pull of the zombie virus either. The radio-serial podcast *We're Alive*, which chronicles the trials and tribulations of a group of survivors during the fall of civilization and the rise of the dead, has had more than 50 million Internet downloads.[7]

Even the Atlanta-based Centers for Disease Control and Prevention (CDC) has capitalized on the popularity of zombies. To help people get ready for the 2011 hurricane season, the CDC published a Zombie Apocalypse preparedness guide on its website, which included a downloadable graphic novella, *Preparedness 101: Zombie Pandemic*. On the accompanying "Zombie blog" was the following quote from Assistant Surgeon General Ali S. Khan: "The rise of zombies in pop culture has given credence to the idea that a zombie apocalypse could happen. In such a scenario, zombies would take over entire countries, roaming city streets eating anything living that got in their way. The proliferation of this idea has led many people to wonder, 'How do I prepare for a zombie apocalypse?'"[8] Information on preparedness for "real emergencies" followed. The zombie posting was so popular that the usually low-traffic CDC preparedness website soon crashed. Included on the website were printable posters that featured the eyes of a menacing zombie peering over a piece of wood. The tagline for the poster was "Get a Kit, Make a Plan, Be Prepared." The CDC knew the following to be true: if you prepare for zombies, then you are ready for just about any calamity that may come your way.

For some, fictional adaptations of the Zombie Apocalypse are not visceral enough. As a result, on hundreds of college campuses, and in communities on every continent (save Antarctica), people gather to play the live-action game Humans vs. Zombies, which is essentially a game of tag where the zombies are always "it." During the game, zombies (identified by an orange bandanna worn around their heads) attempt to tag participating humans (who wear the same bandanna around an arm or a leg). Once touched, infected participants transfer their bandannas from their arms or legs to their heads, signifying that they are now members of the ever-growing zombie horde. Humans defend themselves against the undead with foam darts, marshmallows, or balled-up socks. Although an on-target projectile will incapacitate a zombie for 15 minutes, zombies can only die from starvation. To avoid death, zombies must repeatedly tag a human within a repeating 48-hour window. Humans win the game when all of the zombies starve. Zombies win when there are no humans left to tag.[9]

When out and about, do not be too surprised if you see a horde of "zombies" shambling toward you. In all likelihood, you have just run into a zombie walk, run, or pub crawl. They are often done in support of a charity, and participants in zombie walks (and the like) dress up in their favorite zombie-themed costumes (replete with realistic-looking blood and gore) and roam en masse through the streets. Zombie walks can range in size from a few hundred to several thousand. According to Guinness World Records, the largest gathering for a zombie walk occurred in Minneapolis, Minnesota, in 2014 with nearly 15,500 participants.[10] Of note, before the start of a zombie walk, organizers often warn participants to be on best their best undead behavior and not attempt to scare, startle, or touch the surrounding crowd. Over the past decade, zombie-themed entertainment have contributed $5 billion to the worldwide economy.[11] Like it or not, the living dead have overrun pop culture.

For many, the longstanding and widespread regard of the zombie is somewhat surprising. After all, zombies are far less appealing than other nightmarish creatures. Vampires have sex appeal and swagger. Zombies are nothing more than a putrid display of rotted flesh. Upon transforming in the light of a full moon, werewolves possess unbridled power and fierceness. Zombies are only as strong as the anatomical limitations of the sinews and muscles that remain intact. Missing from the skill set of the zombie are the cleverness of the witch, the enchanting song of the siren, and the wrath of the wraith. Zombies are dim-witted. They cannot sing, only moan. And their aggression comes not from vengeance, but from a primal desire to hunt, infect, and kill. Despite these misgivings, zombies are as popular as ever. The question is "Why?" Many psychologists believe that the answer lies in our evolutionary past, and, in particular, two atavistic fears: (1) the fear of predation and (2) the fear of contagion.

The Fear of Predation

For most 21st-century industrialized societies, the odds of running into a creature that can readily kill you with a venomous puncture, an oxygen-depriving constriction, or by tearing into your flesh and causing exsanguination are quite low (unless you live in Australia). In fact, according to the World Health Organization (WHO), the leading causes of death globally are (1) heart disease; (2) stroke; and (3) lower respiratory infections.[12] Of course, people do die from animal attacks and insect bites every year, but those are far less common than the other hazards mentioned above.

For the most part, modern conveniences afford humans the opportunity to die without becoming the prey of a hungry predator. Nevertheless, evolution has genetically sensitized us to such threats, a phenomenon referred to as *prepared learning.* In the *environment of evolutionary adaptedness*—the setting in which particular characteristics evolved—hominids attuned to predators and situations that foster predation were more likely to survive and reproduce than those that were not. As a result, their genes, and the corresponding characteristics that sensitized people to fear predation, passed from generation to generation, and they are still present today. When the undead inherit the earth, humans will drop a link on the food chain, becoming the prey of a relentless predator. Zombies, then, tap into our innate fear of predation.

The Fear of Contagion

As the fear of predation indicates, survival in an unforgiving world requires attention to detail. But predators are not the only threat to human life. Parasites, bacterial and viral infections, and countless other contractible diseases can kill just as readily as a predator. Currently, upward of one million people die each year from *vector-borne diseases*—illnesses caused by pathogens and parasites in human populations—such as Zika, malaria, and dengue fever. Of note, transmission of vector-borne disease occurs from animals to humans as well as between humans. Common vectors of contractible diseases include mosquitoes, sandflies, ticks, and aquatic snails. Just how problematic are vector-borne diseases? WHO estimates that worldwide 2.5 billion people are at risk for infection from dengue fever alone![13]

Given the potential for death, humans have evolved to fear contagion and avoid vectors of pestilence. How did evolution accomplish this? In part, through the emotion of *disgust*—defined as feelings of revulsion to something unpleasant. Our senses of smell (e.g., a fetid odor), taste (e.g., a putrid flavor), touch (e.g., something uncharacteristically warm, mushy, or slimy), and sight (e.g., secretions, decay, or disfigurements) can lead to feelings of disgust. In many ways, disgust is humanity's first line of defense against pathogens. Feelings of disgust reduce the chance that people will drink, eat, or touch vectors capable of transmitting harmful, and potentially deadly, diseases. Without a doubt, zombies are disgusting. The living dead activate nearly all of the senses that can elicit disgust. The undead have a foul odor, ooze vile fluids, appear decayed and disfigured, and are slimy and mushy to the touch. I'm pretty sure they don't taste too good either.

As you can see, we fear zombies because they are disgusting creatures that can effectively hunt and kill humans. And, when they are displayed in front of us, we become attuned to them for the same reasons. Although atavistic fears of predation and contagion can explain our visceral response to the living dead, they cannot explain why zombies engender such worldwide popularity. However, the tenets of the uses and gratifications perspective and self-determination theory can.

The Uses and Gratifications of Zombies

According to the *uses and gratifications perspective*, people use media, in all of its varied forms (e.g., such as movies, television, and comic books), for the rewarding experiences they engender and the needs that they meet. As it turns out, zombie-themed media fulfill a variety of needs, including escapism, social comparisons, catharsis, fear reduction, companionship, sensation seeking, morbid curiosity, and vicarious experiences.

It is important to note that zombie entertainment can meet one or more of the needs above at any given point in time. In other words, needs are not mutually exclusive. Moreover, the needs met can change from one use to another, even if the media consumed does not. For example, one week a gamer may play *H1Z1* for companionship, whereas the next week the same gamer decides to play to escape the pressures of school.

ESCAPISM. *Escapism* is an attempt to "leave" reality by replacing current thoughts and feelings with different (and hopefully more entertaining) ones. For instance, to get relief from the drudgeries associated with family and work responsibilities, to alleviate loneliness and boredom, or to feel good, people read books about the Zombie Apocalypse, view movies involving the undead, and play video games where they battle hordes of the living dead. When engaged in a fantasy world of zombies, the real one can be forgotten, at least for a short while.

Two psychological principles provide evidence for the escapist nature of zombie-themed media: psychological absorption and flow. *Psychological absorption* is a suspension in the typical integration of thoughts, feelings, and experiences. That is, the psychologically absorbed do not process, think about, or experience the world as they usually do. As a result, the world around them goes mostly unnoticed. Moreover, when absorbed in a task, the individual is intensely focused, less attuned to their current emotional state (including feelings related to anxiety), and seemingly unaware of the passage of time. For instance, when psychologically absorbed in a video game, players do not feel hunger or realize how late it is until after they have finished playing.

Like psychological absorption, when in a flow state, the individual focuses intensely on the task at hand, and the passage of time distorts (e.g., it flies by). However, unlike absorption (in which negative emotions, such as frustration, can leak through into consciousness), individuals in a flow state experience intense feelings of joy and unparalleled success while completing a task. When in a state of flow (a.k.a. being "in the zone") individuals maximize their physical and cognitive skills and meet difficult challenges with relative ease. Nevertheless, for most media-based experiences, psychological absorption is a more typical state than flow.

It is because of psychological absorption that escapism can intensify when playing video games, or watching video clips, that use *virtual reality* technology—an immersive three-dimensional environment involving stereoscopic displays. For example, in a virtual reality video game, the player *experiences* moving through a virtual environment, rather than *watching* a computerized character do the same thing. *Immersion*—the replacement of real-world sensory input (be it visual, auditory, or tactile) with sensations from the virtual world—is the hallmark of virtual reality. The more immersive a virtual reality environment becomes, the more realistic it feels. Thus, as immersion increases, so too does escapism. Why observe the Zombie Apocalypse from afar when virtual reality places you right in the middle of it?

SOCIAL COMPARISON. Starting in the elementary school years and continuing throughout the lifespan, people begin to evaluate and compare themselves to others in a variety of areas, such as income, intelligence, athletic ability, and physical appearance. At times, people engage in what psychologists call an *upward social comparison*, in which individuals contrast themselves against those perceived to be better off than they are. An example is a couch potato measuring their physical fitness and agility against the participants on *American Ninja Warriors*. At other times, people employ a *downward social comparison*, in which they compare themselves to those worse off than they are, such as when the gainfully employed walk by the unemployed homeless. Not too surprisingly, upward social comparisons tend to make people feel worse about themselves. Case in point: viewing your friend's fantastic vacation photos on Instagram and reading about another friend's job promotion on LinkedIn may be a sad reminder of all of the things you have yet to accomplish in your life. So, when people want to feel better about themselves, they often make downward social comparisons, which, by their very nature, typically guarantee a favorable evaluation of the self. For some, especially those under stress, the attraction of an undead wasteland lies in the fact that the inhabitants of that god-forsaken world have it worse than they do, and, as a result, they feel better about their lives.

CATHARSIS. In Stephen King's classic horror novel *The Shining*, Jack Torrance, his wife, and his son spend the long winter months at the remote and isolated Overlook Hotel. Jack's primary responsibility as caretaker is to release pressure as it builds up inside the hotel's aging boiler. But, as Jack succumbs to the evil lurking within the premises, he slowly becomes murderous and maniacal and loses touch with reality, and, as Jack spends the last few hours of his life trying to murder his wife and son, he forgets to release the pent-up pressure in the boiler, which subsequently explodes into a ball of fire.[14]

According to Sigmund Freud, aggressive urges accumulate, just as pressure built up inside the Overlook's boiler. Aggressive desires left unchecked reach a fever pitch, ultimately resulting in violent outbursts. *Catharsis* is the process of ridding oneself of volatile pent-up anger and aggressive feelings. During the late 1960s, Bruno Bettelheim advocated for the therapeutic power of violent imagery, believing that reading fairy-tales replete with violence could purge aggressive desires and reduce aggression. Take, for instance, *Hansel and Gretel*, the fabled fable by the Brothers Grimm in which two young siblings outsmart the witch that has captured them. Rather than the witch murdering and eating the children, Hansel and Gretel burn the witch alive in her oven, courtesy of a push from Gretel. According to Bettelheim, reading *Hansel and Gretel* dissipates children's need to act aggressively. Similarly, modern-day proponents of catharsis contend that violent video game play and watching onscreen violence produce similar outcomes. After a long day at work, school, or taking care of loved ones, what could be more relaxing, ridding the body of both tension and anger, than decapitating a zombie or two in the video game *Left for Dead* or watching gooey disembowelments on *Fear the Walking Dead*?

Although the commonly held belief that venting, ruminating, and acting out releases pent-up anger and aggressive feelings, empirical data do not support this contention. Not only has research consistently failed to support the presence of a catharsis effect, but frequently the opposite is found. Instead of reducing aggression, releasing pent-up energy by hitting objects or yelling actually increases aggressive thoughts and feelings. Nevertheless, when attempting to vent feelings of aggression, people that believe in the benefits of cathartic behavior seek out violent media, including tales of the Zombie Apocalypse.

FEAR REDUCTION. Gerard Jones contends that, in the face of real-life violence, depictions of violent fantasy, such as those shown in comic books, television, movies, and video games, can help people calm themselves down, reducing both anxiety and fear. As Jones states, "Being shocked by an image within the safe confines of fantasy can help them learn not to be so shocked in reality."[15] In support of his argument, Jones relays the story of Andrew, who, in the aftermath of the Columbine massacre, became anxiously preoccupied with school shootings. But through repeated viewings of the violent and gory movie *Natural Born Killers*,[16] Andrew's fears related to school shootings soon diminished. It would follow, then, that the consumption of zombie-themed entertainment might produce similar results.

In contrast to Jones' contention, levels of fear and anxiety often increase following media violence consumption for children, adolescents, and adults. However, it is not as simple as that, for the motivation behind the use of violent imagery matters. For instance, individuals lower in empathy and higher in aggressiveness garner more enjoyment than others from frightening media. Additionally, adolescents watching violent movies to master their fears show positive emotions, but not negative ones (such as fear) after watching a violent film. For some, zombie-themed media may increase anxiety whereas, for others, it may lower it. It all depends on the characteristics of the consumer and the gratifications sought while using the media.

COMPANIONSHIP. The consumption of zombie-themed media can provide opportunities for camaraderie, promote friendships, and maintain relationships. For instance, it is quite common for people to gather (in real life or online) to watch and talk about the latest episode of AMC's *The Walking Dead* or play a video game, such as *Call of Duty: Zombies*, while chatting with one another during gameplay via headset. Moreover, zombie-themed media can aid relationships by serving as a focal point for casual conversation during its consumption or long after the media offering has ended. Twitter and Instagram posts, YouTube videos, and Reddit forums all aid in these endeavors. For example, on the subreddit r/zombies, more than 84,000 subscribers discuss any and all zombie-related issues, including questions related to surviving a zombie horde to recommendations for books, movies, and video games.[17]

Online interactions can get quite large. For example, the sixth season of *The Walking Dead* was the number one most-tweeted television series in the United States, averaging 435,000 tweets per episode.[18] Currently, the official *The Walking Dead* Instagram page has 6.6 million followers.[19] The massively multiplayer online game, *H1Z1: King of the Hill*, regularly has thousands of players at any given point in time.[20] Such large-scale social media use attests to the power of the Zombie Apocalypse to promote companionship.

Towards the end of the seventh season of *The Walking Dead*, speculation grew over which character(s) would meet their demise at the hands, and barbed wire-wrapped bat, of the newly minted villain Negan. As always, the Internet had something to say about this, namely "If Daryl dies, we riot." For some, Daryl Dixon was just a favorite character. But, for others, Daryl meant as much to them, if not more, than some of their real-life affiliations. Although unidirectional, such *parasocial relationships—*

defined as an unrequited, emotional investment in a real or fictional character—can create feelings of companionship. Adults with intense parasocial relationships even experience anxiety and depression when their favorite character dies or the network cancels the show. People engaging in strong and intense parasocial relationships tend to feel alone, as they often lack real-life friendships. Unfortunately, imaginary connections do not provide the same benefits to health and well-being provided by real ones.

SENSATION SEEKING. Much like riding a roller coaster or going skydiving, the Zombie Apocalypse can gratify the user's need for new experiences, excitement, and physiological arousal, a phenomenon psychologists refer to as *sensation seeking*. For example, teens with a history of watching horror movies state that they do so to "have fun," "freak themselves out," and "to be scared,"[21] all of which align with a high need for sensory input. Because of their immersive quality, video games, especially those that use virtual reality technology, are the perfect conduits for arousal. When playing survival horror games, such as *Resident Evil HD Remastered*, physiological responses, such as heart rate and blood pressure, quickly elevate. Fear builds up, so much so that it is quite common for people to let out blood-curdling screams during gameplay. However, it is not merely the rush from being scared that drives most players of survival horror games. Instead, it is the intense feeling of pleasurable relief experienced after gameplay ends—as Mark Butler calls it, a "post-horror high."[22]

MORBID CURIOSITY. The Zombie Apocalypse is replete with blood, gore, and human suffering. Zombie lore dictates that the only way to kill a revenant is to destroy its brain. Not surprisingly, zombie deaths typically involve the crushing of skulls or penetrating projectiles to the head, followed by a fountain of blood and brain matter. In addition to the graphic nature of zombie deaths, in the world of the living dead, human deaths are particularly gory, with arterial blood spray frequently accompanying the tearing of flesh. For both zombies and humans alike, disembowelments and dismemberments are commonplace. See Box 1.1 for a list of memorable kills by both zombies and humans.

The Zombie Apocalypse is not pretty, and it is not for the faint of heart. And that is why people like it. For many, the draw of a world overrun by reanimated corpses lies in the death, violence, and wanton destruction that it brings. Engagement with the living dead fulfills the need for *morbid*

Box 1.1: *Memorable Kill List*

Zombies Killing Humans

- A zombie inserts its fingers into the victim's eyes and mouth, pulling until the head vertically spits in two (*Dead Snow*, 2009).[23]
- A zombie breaks through a door and drags its prey towards its mouth, only to have a shard of wood slowly impale the victim's eye (*Zombi 2*, 1979).[24]
- A zombie bites into the arm, neck, or face of its victim, pulling away muscles and sinew in the process (frequently on *The Walking Dead*).[25]
- A zombie eviscerates a victim, eating the innards as it pulls them out of the still-screaming would-be zombie (*Shaun of the Dead*, 2004,[26] and just about every other on-screen adaptation of the Zombie Apocalypse).
- Zombified preteen Karen is seen kneeling over her dead father and eating his arm; she then kills her mother with a trowel (*The Night of the Living Dead*, 1968).[27]

Humans Killing Zombies

- A sledgehammer from a carnival strongman game is used to cave in the head of a zombified clown (*Zombieland*, 2009).[28]
- An airborne helicopter tips its rotor downward to mow through a crowd of fast-running quasi-zombies (*28 Weeks Later*, 2007).[29]
- A lawnmower is used to puree a house full of zombies (*Dead Alive*, 1992).[30]
- Acid eats away at the head of a zombie from the top down (*Diary of the Dead*, 2007).[31]
- Two moving cars connected by a steel cable carve, decapitate and halve the bodies of hundreds of zombies (*The Walking Dead*).[32]

---

curiosity—defined as the desire, excitement, and fear that accompanies the macabre. It is morbid curiosity that compels people to rubberneck as they pass a car accident, or watch (and re-watch) a YouTube video of some disastrous event. But, unlike sensation seeking, morbid curiosity (be it based in reality or fantasy) occurs because it helps people figure out the deadly mistakes and missed signals of danger that were the undoing of others. Morbid curiosity, then, allows people to gather critical information that could potentially increase their chances of surviving similar circumstances, even if those circumstances are fictional.

To meet the viewer's need for morbid curiosity, television shows, movies and the like tend to up the ante as the series or sequels progress. For instance, in the movie *Scream*, seven gruesome murders take place. In the sequels *Scream 2* and *Scream 3*, the body count rises to 10 in each film, and in *Scream 4*, 12 people meet their demise.[33] Before being stabbed to death in *Scream 2*, Randy states the three simple rules of horror sequels: (1) the killings become more elaborate (e.g., ingenious and gorier); (2) the body count always goes up; and (3) never, ever assume that the killer is dead.[34] The first two rules reflect the belief that, to create an emotional charge in those who watch a sequel, the level of violence depicted in the new film must supersede that of the previous movie. Why would this need to happen?

The answer lies in the psychological concept of *desensitization*—the decreased level of emotional responsiveness to vile, disgusting, or otherwise unpleasant stimuli. The more people consume violence and gore depicted on film or TV or in video games, the less it affects them. For example, after repeatedly viewing movie scenes replete with violence, viewers report feeling less sympathetic toward the victims in those clips. In the case of violent imagery, desensitization works in conjunction with morbid curiosity on its reconnaissance mission of detecting the downfall of others. It is much easier to focus on the cause of death when not distracted by the blood and gore surrounding the body.

VICARIOUS EXPERIENCES. Games and stories of the Zombie Apocalypse typically center on ordinary people doing whatever it takes to survive in a world full of horrors; it is coping under extreme and often inhumane conditions. The appeal of the zombie genre, however, not only lies in the resilience conveyed by the would-be survivors but also in the fact that the consumer can insert themselves into the narrative through the eyes of the characters. During *vicarious experiences*—defined as emotional or cognitive changes resulting from observing the behaviors, sensations, and feelings of others—the weak become strong, the fearful become fearless, followers become leaders, and the peaceful become stone-cold killers. The Zombie Apocalypse, then, allows people to experience the emotions associated with heroism, villainy, death, destruction, and mayhem without actually having to place their lives in danger or risk incarceration.

Moreover, the intensity of vicarious experiences, and hence their attraction, may be affected by the degree to which the user engages in *identification*—the process of feeling connected to a media character and adopting their identity and perspective. Two types of identification exist, similarity and wishful. In *similarity identification*, people identify with others based on the perceived similarity of salient features, such as hair color, tattoos, and body type. The list of potential similarities is endless, for it resides in the eye of the beholder. Not all characteristics need to match, just the ones the person deems most important.

In contrast, *wishful identification* occurs because the media user desires, in some way, shape, or form, to be like the character they are observing, regardless of the similarities and differences between the two. For example, a quiet, reserved, and physically weak child could wishfully identify with a loud, outgoing, and muscle-bound adult in a video game they are playing. Nevertheless, for both similarity and wishful identification the greater the sense of identification, the more powerful vicarious experiences become. Seeing similarities between oneself and the survivors of the Zombie Apocalypse may enhance the media consumption experience, potentially increasing its meaning, enjoyability, and, ultimately, attractiveness.

Zombies and Self-Determination Theory

Self-determination theory focuses on the factors that influence human *motivation*—a need or desire that energizes behavior and directs it toward a goal—including the impetus to watch, play, read, listen to, or otherwise consume media. According to self-determination theory, feelings of *well-being* (such as happiness and vitality) occur by meeting the psychological needs of autonomy, competence, and relatedness, and therefore the attraction of the Zombie Apocalypse may lie in the fact that it can meet each of these needs.

Autonomy refers to the sense of control that individuals feel when doing something they *want* to do, rather than something they *have* to do. Thus, choosing to consume any form of zombie-themed media, whether it be playing the video game *Death Road to Canada* or reading a comic book from the *Marvel Zombies* series, can potentially meet this need. *Competence* involves the successful completion of tasks, especially those that are challenging. Relevant examples include completing all levels of *Resident Evil*, knowing the details of every *Z Nation* episode aired and reading all of the books in Jonathan Maberry's young adult series *Rot & Ruin*. As these examples illustrate, certain types of media-based experiences (e.g., finishing a level of a video game) can create an immediate feeling of task-oriented competence. At other times, competence is demonstrated long after its consumption has taken place. For instance, knowing the difference between a "Newsie," "Irwin," and "Fictional" may only lead to feelings of competence during a ComicCon convention years after reading Mira Grant's novel *Feed*.[35] Finally, *relatedness* refers to a sense of connection with others. Social media, in all of its forms, can readily meet this need. Blogs, vlogs, posts on Twitter, Instagram, and Facebook, and so on all have the potential to promote relatedness, though trolls can negatively affect it. Moreover, playing zombie-themed video games online can foster relatedness through the camaraderie associated with playing as part of a team. As previously mentioned, such activities can also enhance real-life relationships with friends.

By meeting an individual's need for autonomy, competence, and relatedness, zombie-themed media becomes a source of *intrinsic motivation*—active engagement with tasks that are inherently satisfying. Thus, the motivation for their continued use comes from within. Stated another way, despite the depictions of blood, gore, and human suffering, people are attracted to zombie entertainment because of the satisfaction of consuming it. Comparatively, *extrinsic motivation*—the desire to engage in an activity because it is a means to an end and not because an individual is following their inner interests—is not based on an individual's need to feel competent and autonomous but on some external reward or outcome such as money, fame, or prestige. Whereas intrinsic motivation increases life satisfaction and enhances well-being, external rewards frequently do not. Thus, for many, stories of the Zombie Apocalypse are rewarding in and of themselves.

Final Thoughts

Many scholars contend that stories of the Zombie Apocalypse reflect cultural anxieties related to the fear of death, consumerism, runaway capitalism, government conspiracies, nuclear war, a lack of meaning in life, or just about anything weighing on the minds of the masses. For example, Frann Michel posits that "zombies can represent a rebellious underclass, as when they overrun the gated community of wealthy humans in *Land of the Dead*."[36] Greg Garrett states that the movie *Shaun of the Dead* explores how the living "can find themselves caught in a state that is not really life."[37] Mathias Clasen contends that "the modern zombie figure puts rotting flesh on the abstract skeleton that is ambivalence toward the global Other, that this is why the figure resonates loudly in many minds in this age of conflict and suffering broadcast globally and in HD."[38]

However, from a psychological perspective, the popularity of the Zombie Apocalypse does not lie in the *tropes* (i.e., familiar, reoccurring, or overused themes) represented on-screen or on the page. Instead, its popularity resides in the fact that (1) people are drawn to zombies because of biological imperatives related to survival and (2) zombie narratives meet a variety of human needs, ranging from the need for excitement to the need for companionship to the need to feel strong and powerful. Moreover, to those that enjoy them, television shows, movies, novels, podcasts, and video games of the Zombie Apocalypse are intrinsically motivating, thus their continued use is encouraged.

2. A Zombie Primer

The dead do not rise on their own, as something or someone needs to make it happen. Typical causes of the Zombie Apocalypse include viruses, diseases, and vaccines (see Box 2.1). Sometimes they are weaponized and sometimes not. On occasion, unfortunate accidents release the biohazard. On other occasions, terrorism is the culprit. In most zombie narratives, the zombie plague infects its human host before their demise. Death, in turn, activates the zombie catalyst, resulting in a reanimated corpse. As you can see, zombie bites serve two purposes: (1) to infect the uninfected and (2) to kill the victim through bacterial infection, blood loss, cardiac arrest, organ failure, and so on, thus triggering reanimation.

Box 2.1: *Causes of the Zombie Apocalypse*

- *Feed*[1]—Kellis-Amberlee virus (unintentionally created)
- *My Life as a White Trash Zombie*[2]—parasites
- *Left for Dead*[3]—a mutated strain of rabies
- *Patient Zero*[4]—prion disease (bioweapon)
- *Resident Evil*[5]—T-virus (bioweapon)
- *The Return of the Living Dead*[6]—toxic gas
- *The Walking Dead*[7]—no cause given
- *The Zombie Survival Guide*[8]—Solanum virus (source unknown)

Categories of Zombies

It is late at night, and you find yourself walking down a dimly lit alley. You hear a low, guttural moan. Then out from the shadows steps a zombie. Now, picture in your mind the face of the ghoul. For most, the typical zombie is a partially-decayed reanimated corpse. The skin appears ashen and bruised; the eyes are glazed

---

over with the irises barely visible; the clothing is tattered and torn; there are gaping wounds everywhere. When in motion, the zombie appears to lumber towards its victims with a singular focus: hunt, infect, and kill. However, different types of undead exist. There are the slow, shambling reanimated corpses on *The Walking Dead*[9]; the fast-running zombies with a keen sense of smell in the movie *World War Z*[10]; and, on the television show *iZombie*, passing-for-human revenants retain their vitality and acquire the decedents' memories upon eating their victims' brains.[11]

Of course, there are undead that fall somewhere in between the types of zombies mentioned above. In George A. Romero's *Land of the Dead*, semi-intelligent biters retain some memories from their former lives and demonstrate rudimentary, but volitional, motor skills.[12] Zombies pick up objects, hold hands, and attempt to play musical instruments. Big Daddy, the smartest of the undead bunch, even fires an automatic weapon with malicious intent. Let us not forget Ed, from *Shaun of the Dead*, whose video game acumen carries over from the living to the undead.[13] Zombies such as those found in *Feedback: A Newsflesh Novel* hunt in packs and use their brethren as decoys to lure their human prey into traps.[14] As these examples show, zombies can differ by appearance, speed, diet, coordination, and cleverness. Nevertheless, there are two main categories of zombies: stimulus-driven and intelligent.

Stimulus-Driven Zombies

Whether they are slow or fast, stimulus-driven zombies react to provocations in their immediate environment. Without emotion, they wander or remain motionless until a target presents itself. At that point, they become enraged. Then mercilessly, and tirelessly, they attempt to hunt, infect, and kill the uninfected. That is all they do. There is no planning, no scheming, no sign of proactive thought. A zombie's reason for being is to spread the cause of their affliction. In support of this mission, zombies will readily, though unknowingly, sacrifice their own undead lives, which is an excellent strategy from the perspective of the disease. All that matters is the continued dispersal of the contaminant; the hosts are expendable. For instance, the living dead's willingness to forfeit their second "lives" is one of the main reasons that defensive walls are no match for a zombie horde numbering in the tens of thousands. Imagine a legion of dead pressed against a wall. At some point, the forces exerted from the dead in the back crush the heads of the dead at the wall, who then fall to the ground in a heap. Over and over again, this scene repeats itself. Ever so slowly, a ramp of putrid flesh begins to form. Eventually, it breaches the top of the wall, at which point the zombies pour into the previously impenetrable fortress.

In traditional zombie fare, the contaminant that causes the dead to rise also stops the process of decomposition. In theory, a zombie celebrating the 500th anniversary of its reanimation would look just as dapper as it did on the day it was "turned." Still, gravity and other forces of nature affect the undead. Zombies weather when exposed to the elements in much the same way that leather becomes damaged when baking in the sun or when left outside for too long in the rain. Despite reanimation, the living dead cannot regenerate and they can succumb to injuries resulting from gravity, weather, or a well-placed ax. However, as long as the brain is still intact, a stimulus-driven zombie—even if it is just a bodiless head—will continue in its charge to bite and infect. Case in point: on *The Walking Dead*, after Hershel Greene's beheading at the hands of "The Governor," Michonne finds his (still undead) severed head attempting to gnaw at surrounding humans. It is not until Michonne puts her katana through Hershel's brain that his life as a revenant ends.[15]

Stimulus-driven zombies do not need to eat, as their bodies no longer convert food into energy. Nevertheless, they consume flesh, though they are not picky eaters. They will consume just about anything that is alive, including dogs, horses, cows, deer, and, of course, humans. In most zombie lore, only humans become revenants, and once the infected have "turned" the undead stop eating. Mission complete! A new zombie is born. If its ghastly body allows, the newly undead gets up, seeks out prey, and starts the cycle of undeath all over again. If the potential zombie cannot reanimate, well, then, it is an all-you-can-eat buffet. In extreme cases, which also seem to go against the rules mentioned above, zombies will mistakenly eat their own intestines. Imagine a serpent devouring its tail—a zombie Ouroboros, if you will.

Intelligent Zombies

Intelligent zombies are just like you and me: they hold jobs; get married; and fruitlessly try to get tickets to *Hamilton*. They even look like the living, although their characteristically blanched appearances often require make-up, color contact lenses and hair dye to complete the illusion. Unlike stimulus-driven zombies, who are either enraged or emotionless (there is no in between), intelligent zombies are sentient, expressing a wide range of human emotions.

Many intelligent zombies, such as Angel Crawford from *My Life as a White Trash Zombie*[16] and "Liv" Moore from *iZombie*, abhor taking human lives.[17] Their continued existence, therefore, is in direct conflict with their morality. Rather than killing to obtain food, many intelligent zombies work in hospitals, morgues, and funeral homes. Having ready-to-go meals delivered right to their office doors negates the necessity of taking human lives and prevents the accompanying guilt the murders would engender. For the intelligent zombie, finding meaning in its preternatural life matters more than the spread of the zombie plague. Because self-preservation supersedes the need to infect others, the intelligent zombie keeps a low profile, allowing few others to know its true nature.

Unlike their cognitively challenged counterparts, intelligent zombies must eat brain tissue to survive. Human flesh alone will not quell their cravings. Only human brain tissue satisfies the hunger pangs of the intelligent zombie in the much the same way that drugs sate the addict. The consumption of brains allows intelligent zombies to retain their human-like appearance and cognitive abilities, and, in some cases, gain beyond-human strength and agility. But beware, the longer intelligent zombies go without human brains, the more they turn into stimulus-driven zombies. As their beauty fades, so too does their ability to think for themselves. Side by side, a starving intelligent zombie is indistinguishable in look and behavior from a stimulus-driven zombie.

Given that the Zombie Apocalypse (as traditionally conceived) rarely includes the presence of intelligent zombies, the remainder of this book will primarily focus on stimulus-driven zombies and their mission to hunt, infect, and kill. Whether they are slow, fast, or intelligent, each type of zombie has its own set of characteristics. Check them out in the Box 2.2.

Quasi-Zombies

Not all "zombie" tales involve reanimated corpses. In some stories, biologically compromised *living* humans engage in zombie-like behavior. Such quasi-zombies bite their victims, tear into their flesh, crunch their bones, and eat their remains. For instance, in the movie *28 Days Later*[18] and its sequel, *28 Weeks Later*,[19] a rage-inducing virus is the source of a quasi-zombie uprising. In the same vein, in Stephen King's *Cell*, zombie-like behavior is the result of an electronic pulse delivered via mobile phone.[20] In each of the cases above, the murderous infected are alive until dead, and they do not reanimate.

Box 2.2: A Comparison of the Three Main Zombie Types			
	Stimulus-Driven: Slow	Stimulus-Driven: Fast	Intelligent
Can blend in with humans			X
Attempt to hide their existence			X
Hunting relies on senses	X	X	
Hunting relies on intellect			X
Predation is opportunistic	X	X	
Predation is planned			X
Horde activity	X	X	
Hunger leads to loss of intellect and body decomposition			X
Eat all body parts	X	X	
Eat only brains			X
Have beyond-human strength and agility			X
Can be easily outrun	X		
Outnumber humans	X	X	

Zombiism as a Neurological Disorder

Neurological disorders refer to dysfunctions of the brain, spine, and nerves located throughout the body. Symptoms of such maladies include pain, seizures, muscle weakness or paralysis, coordination difficulties, problems in sensation or perception, and cognitive deficits. Although most disorders of the nervous system are unrelated to zombiism, one is, albeit tangentially—*Cotard's Syndrome*, also knowing as Walking Corpse Syndrome. Some sufferers of Cotard's Syndrome think that they are dead. Others believe that they are rotting, missing body organs, or devoid of a soul. Many desire to hang out in graveyards or morgues to be close to deadness.[21] However, deadness is where the similarity between Walking Corpse Syndrome and zombiism ends, for those with Cotard's Syndrome do not hunt, bite, and attempt to kill the living.

Despite the fictional nature of zombiism, a neurologically-based diagnosis for it exists, *Consciousness Deficit Hypoactivity Disorder* (CDHD; see Box 2.3). The architects of CDHD, neuroscientists Timothy Verstynen and Bradley Voytek, contend that zombification changes the way the brain functions. Some parts of the brain become hypoactive (under-aroused), while other parts of the brain become hyperactive (over-aroused). Lack of oxygen to the brain and the zombie plague itself are responsible for these changes. Surprisingly, despite death and resurrection, some parts of the brain remain intact. Listed below are highlights of the functional and dysfunctional inner workings of the zombie brain.

Box 2.3: *Clinical Diagnosis for Consciousness Deficit Hypoactivity Disorder*

"CDHD is an acquired syndrome whereby patients present with a lack of intentional control over their actions, lethargic and fatigued movements (akinesthesia), loss of a sense of pleasure (anhedonia), general language dysfunction (aphasia), memory impairments (amnesias), and an inability to suppress appetitive actions such as eating or aggressive 'fight-or-flight' behaviors. Patients with CDHD often present with severe difficulty in recognizing familiar objects or individuals (agnosias) and persistent sleep disturbances reflected as chronic insomnia that results in a subsequent 'waking delirium' state. CDHD patients also present antisocial behavioral patterns (e.g., trying to bite or consume people) and these typically violent behaviors are strictly targeted at living humans. Indeed, a very strong pro-social behavior is expressed toward other infected individuals, as evidenced by the clustering and 'swarm intelligence' of groups of infected individuals. Subtypes: CDHD-1, also known as 'slow zombies,' present with more severe akinesthesia resulting in very slow and uncoordinated movements. CDHD-2, also known as 'fast zombies,' do not present with akinesthesia at all."[22]

A Brief Overview of the Brain

The brain consists of 80 to 100 billion cells (called neurons) and trillions of connections between those cells. Organized into different regions, networks of neurons perform similar functions. The brain stem, which is in the innermost region of the brain and connected to the spinal cord, regulates basic survival functions such as heart rate, blood pressure, and breathing. The cerebellum, located behind the brain stem, coordinates voluntary movement. Situated above the brain stem, the limbic system—comprised of the hippocampus, amygdala, and hypothalamus—is involved in feeding, emotion, and memory. The outer layer of the brain, referred to as the cerebral cortex, is responsible for higher mental functions such as thinking, planning, decision-making, and language.

Two hemispheres comprise the cerebral cortex, with each region consisting of four lobes. The frontal lobe is responsible for memory, thinking, planning, judgment, expressive language, and motor skills. The parietal lobe processes tactile information related to touch, pressure, and pain. The parietal lobe is also involved in shifting attentional focus between objects. The temporal lobe is responsible for hearing, language, and facial recognition. Although often discussed as part of the limbic system, the hippocampus is located in the temporal lobe. Finally, the occipital lobe processes visual information.

Hypoactive Brain Regions of Note

As previously mentioned, hypoactive areas of a zombie's brain are performing their functions slower than they should or not at all. Damage to the zombie's temporal lobe causes *face blindness*—the inability to recognize familiar faces. No amount of begging will enable the undead to identify their loved ones as anything other than the zombie equivalent of bacon. Regardless, pleading would be pointless, as the areas of the zombie brain responsible for language comprehension no longer work. Also, temporal lobe deficits greatly impair memory. Zombies have no recollection of their former lives—not their families, not their friends, and not even themselves. All memories cease to exist. And it is not just memories of the past that disappear. Damage to the temporal lobe, and, in particular, the hippocampus also prevents the creation of new memories. For the zombie, there is no past; there is only now, an endless now.

Parietal lobe deficits compel zombies to look at *all* objects and events that are attention-grabbing. Even when focused on something else, they *have* to look at new, competing stimuli. This phenomenon, called *disengagement deficit*, means that there is zero possibility of a zombie staying on task when a different stimulus appears. Take the case of an unlocked car filled with trembling, screaming teenagers surrounded by the living dead. As night falls, the teens realize that their fidget spinners light up when turning. Ever so slowly, they open the moonroof and toss their fidget spinners into the night. Although there is a waiting meal right before their undead eyes, the visual pull of the lighted-up fidget spinners is too powerful, and the zombies set out after them. You may be wondering why the zombies did not open the unlocked car door. Parietal damage makes those sorts of coordinator movements difficult, if not impossible, for zombies to enact.

Damage to the frontal lobes and resulting hypoactive functioning renders the suppression of impulsive behavior impossible, including violent urges. When attacking the living, the living dead act without any consideration for the consequences of their actions. When in pursuit of prey, a zombie will walk through fire, impale itself on a pole, or shamble off the end of a building, even if it means its demise. Hypoactive frontal lobes also result in the loss of higher-level thinking, reasoning, and decision-making capabilities. Zombies do not question the meaning of un-life; they are incapable of existential angst; and they do not have a mid-death crisis. Zombies are the simplest of beings: hunt, infect, kill ... repeat. Frontal lobe damage also renders speech impossible to produce or at best incomprehensible, hence the moan. Finally, although zombies can still register pain, damage to the frontal lobes eliminates the emotional impact of their discomfort. In other words, zombies do not care about the agony they are in, and, as a result, the behaviors causing it continue without interruption.

In addition to the cerebral cortex, other parts of the zombie brain are hypoactive. Degradation in sections of the hypothalamus prevents zombies from sleeping. Unlike their human counterparts (who when sleep deprived show deficits in concentration, reaction time, and decision-making), a lack of sleep has no impact on a zombie's performance. The living dead's pursuit of prey never stops, and it never rests. Being awake 24/7 increases the undead's chance of finding humans to hunt, infect, and kill. Finally, for slow-moving zombies, damage to the cerebellum produces severe movement difficulties, resulting in a wide stance and shambling gait as well as impairments in reaching and grasping. Of note, fast-moving zombies do not present with cerebellum deficits.

Hyperactive Brain Regions of Note

Located within the limbic system are the only two regions of a zombie's brain to become hyperactive: the amygdala and the hypothalamus. In humans, the amygdala is responsible for aggression as well as fight-or-flight behavior. When a threat or opportunity for conflict presents itself, people have two choices. They can (1) attempt to flee, thus avoiding a decidedly dangerous and potentially deadly interaction, or (2) stay and fight, which will put the self in harm's way. There is no such conundrum for the living dead, as there is no desire for personal safety. Continuous activation of the amygdala causes zombies to become enraged and hyper-aggressive.

Upon zombification, a few sections of the hypothalamus become hyperactive, while, as mentioned above, other portions experience hypoactivity. Together, these dysfunctional areas place the zombie in a perennial state of insatiable hunger. Zombies will eat an entire corpse (of those unable to reanimate), even if it means their stomachs burst during their dining experience.

Intact Brain Regions of Note

In the video game *Left for Dead*, avatars navigate an apocalyptic wasteland in search of rescue, dispatching hundreds of fast-moving zombies along the way. But not all of the bullets fired and Molotov cocktails thrown hit their marks. And if those projectiles hit the wrong vehicle, an alarm goes off, complete with flashing red lights and a deafening siren. The dinner bell just sounded, and a ravenous zombie horde is answering it.[23] As this example illustrates, the living dead are strongly attracted to sights and sounds that indicate the presence of prey. They can do this because the parts of the brain that process sensory stimuli remain intact during reanimation and thus continue to function normally. As long as their eyes, ears, and nose (i.e., their sensory organs) remain attached to their bodies, zombies can see, hear, and smell their prey just fine.

As previously mentioned, hypoactive cerebellar functioning causes slow-moving zombies to grasp, reach, and move about their environment awkwardly. Damage to the cerebellum makes it difficult for the living dead to make minor adjustments to their movements once they have begun. But what zombies can do without difficulty is start those movements. Because the motor cortex (which initiates commands for movement) remains intact, zombies can quickly lunge toward their prey with outstretched arms.

When Zombies Attack

Because of their neurological functioning, the undead are near-perfect vectors of disease. Areas of the brain related to hunting, infecting, and killing either remain intact or become hyperactive. In contrast, areas of the brain that might impede its spread become nonfunctional. The zombie knows no past, nor does it care about the future. It is a hyper-aggressive and fearless hunter that relentlessly tracks its prey. And its sole purpose is to bite, infect, and kill. It is a vector of disease and death. Nothing more, nothing less. The absence of rational thought makes conversation with the undead impossible. But, as Verstynen and Voytek point out, knowing the neurological limits of the living dead makes surviving among them possible.

THERE IS NO REASONING WITH A ZOMBIE. The most dangerous part of the Zombie Apocalypse is during the initial outbreak. Zombies are deceased, but they look diseased, not dead. The first course of action taken by physicians, friends, and family members will be to help the infected and plead with them to calm down and listen to reason. For most, this will be a fatal mistake, as there is no reasoning with the living dead. Although the zombie in front of them looks like the person they once knew, it is decidedly not that person. Stripped away is everything that makes a human unique: gone are their memories, personality, ability to express and feel emotions, and sense of self. The zombie is a disease, camouflaged in the shell of a person you once knew.

AVOID, HIDE AND RUN. In *Shaun of the Dead*, Shaun has a simple strategy for surviving the Zombie Apocalypse: kill his infected roommate, take his car, pick up his mother and girlfriend, go to the local pub to wait it out, and drink a pint or three.[24] All in all, it is not that bad of a strategy. The best way to prevent infection is to avoid the infected. Stimulus-driven creatures require stimuli to find their prey. Without sensory input, zombies will shamble along until a hapless human makes a mistake and triggers a zombie's hunting behavior. At that point, follow the number one rule of *Zombieland*[25]: "cardio" and run. Slow-moving zombies are no match in speed for even the slowest of runners. But unlike humans, zombies have unlimited endurance, so having a hiding place to wait things out will be of paramount importance. As shown in the movie *World War Z*, few people can outrun a fast-moving zombie. Surviving this type of run-in requires other survival techniques.

DISTRACTING THE DEAD. A zombie will stay focused on whatever captures its attention for as long as it continues to attract its attention. Case in point: the living dead will only attempt to break down doors when there are signs of habitation, such as movement in a window or the sounds of a crying and whimpering person. Without sensory input, zombies eventually go away. This phenomenon occurs, in part, because zombies lack *object permanence*—the understanding that objects no longer in view (smelled or otherwise sensed) continue to exist. For the living dead, out of sight is literally out of mind. This cognitive shortcoming, along with their marked disengagement deficit, renders them highly vulnerable to distractions. When faced with a single zombie, or even a horde, a well-timed explosion, firework, or friend yelling, "Over here!" can grab the attention of the undead long enough for it to forget all about nearby prey (which until just a moment ago had been standing right in front of them).

IF YOU CAN'T BEAT 'EM, JOIN 'EM. In the comic book version of *The Walking Dead*, Rick Grimes and company run into a group of nomadic survivors called The Whisperers. Their distinguishing feature is that they wear the skins of the undead over exposed flesh, such as their hands and face.[26] As long as they make little noise and limit their talking to one another, zombies consider them fellow predators rather than prey. Messier versions of this technique involve coating oneself in zombie blood and guts and lumbering around. As stimulus-driven hunters, zombies respond for signs of life rather than death, and, as a result, they can be easily fooled by disguise and mimicry. Just remember to keep calm and walk lamely.

WHEN YOU NEED TO FIGHT. Not only are mimicry and distraction useful when attempting to flee or hide from the living dead, but such techniques are also useful tools when the fighting the undead. Imagine being able to walk among the dead and then swiftly putt a spike into the back of a zombie's head. If done correctly, the surrounding undead will view you as one of their own, paying little attention to the crumbling corpse. Even when in close quarters, a handful of *bang snaps*—tiny, cherry-shaped explosives that make a "crack" sound when detonated—thrown at the wall behind a zombie would produce a loud enough sound to distract a zombie (who will turn toward the noise). With the zombie's head safely facing away from you, you can put a spike into the back of its head, or dispatch it by some other means.

Weapons and Children

During an invasion of the undead, access to weapons, and, more important, knowing how to use them effectively, is essential for survival. Max Brooks' *The Zombie Survival Guide* reviews a variety of weapons and combat techniques for use during the Zombie Apocalypse. According to Brooks, best-in-class weapons include steel crowbars (bludgeons), double-handed swords (edged weapons), crossbows (slings and arrows), trench spikes (hand weapons), and .22-caliber rimfire rifles or pistols (firearms). Given their lethality, and ability to maim, weapons training for children will be an essential part of growing up, For when a child (or adult, for that matter) dies (no matter the cause), they rise again and attack the living.

Always Remember, Safety First

When children find a gun lying about, they often begin to play with it as if it were a toy. All too often, accidental shootings follow. In the United States, approximately 1300 gun-related fatalities involving children and adolescents (under 18 years of age) and an additional 5790 gunshot wounds requiring medical attention occur annually. Around 6 percent of these deaths are unintentional; older children (aged 13–17 years) are twice as likely to die from accidentally discharged weapons relative to younger ones.[27] Moreover, around 80 percent of nonfatal firearm injuries result from children shooting themselves or from someone they know firing a gun.[28]

To prevent accidental shootings, the National Rifle Association's (NRA) Eddie the Eagle Gunsafe Program teaches children "what to do if they ever come across a gun." The four-step program is as follows: (1) *Stop.* Eddie the Eagle instructs children to stop and think about what they are supposed to do after seeing an unattended gun. (2) *Don't Touch.* Because accidental shootings occur when children handle firearms, the program admonishes children against touching weapons or moving the objects on which they lay (even an unhandled gun can discharge if it falls to the ground). (3) *Run Away.* After stopping and actively doing nothing, Eddie the Eagle tells children that they should run away from the gun. Placing distance between the child and the weapon reduces the likelihood that the child will shoot themselves or another person. Likewise, the further the child is away from the gun the lower their risk of being shot because of someone else's negligence. (4) *Tell a Grown-Up.* Finally, the program instructs children to tell a trusted adult about the gun, for only adults should resolve the dangerous situation and not other children.[29]

Children completing the Eddie the Eagle program can correctly relay the safety messages presented to them. However, during realistic conditions in which children find a replica gun (without an adult present), most children fail to heed the gun safety instructions they had previously demonstrated learning. Nevertheless, not only it is possible to teach young children that they should not play with found guns, but it is also feasible to have them demonstrate their knowledge in realistic settings. To accomplish this, researchers use an *active learning approach* in which children receive educational lessons on a firearm-related skill (e.g., gun safety) and then practice that skill via role-playing (i.e., children act out different scenarios involving finding a firearm).

Moreover, this program places children in realistic situations (e.g., they find an unattended replica firearm on the floor) where they can employ their new skillset. Importantly, when children make mistakes, even in realistic situations, an educator intervenes to explain what went wrong and what the children should have done instead. Not surprisingly, active learning approaches work best with repetition. Moreover, children as young as four years old consistently benefit from active learning approaches to gun safety. An active learning approach can teach children safety skills related to a variety of weapons, including axes, knives, swords, maces, and so on. During the Zombie Apocalypse, children and adolescents will need safety training for these weapons as well.

Weapons Training

As illustrated in *The Walking Dead* comic book, with the support of his father, Carl learns to fire a gun at age seven, though his mother dislikes the idea.[30] When should parents start teaching their children to use firearms? Although age and firearm restrictions vary by state, where legal, many firing ranges allow preschool-aged children to shoot weapons (with parental approval).[31] Aegis Academy, a corporation specializing in firearms education and training, provides the following recommendations for teaching children how to shoot guns.[32]

- Ages 3–7: Begin teaching firearm safety. At this age, children should be able to recite fundamental firearm safety rules, such as those supported by the NRA: (1) always keep the gun pointed in a safe direction; (2) always keep your finger off the trigger until ready to shoot; and (3) always keep the gun unloaded until ready to use.[33] Additionally, children should place their *toy* guns in lockable toy chests to emphasize the fact that "guns are not like other toys."

- Ages 5–7: Show children how to correctly clean and maintain firearms. Doing so teaches responsible gun ownership and reduces the mysterious and alluring appeal of weapons.

- Ages 7–10: Begin shooting real projectiles, but limit those to airsoft, BB, and pellet guns. Emphasize safety and responsible handling of weapons.

- Ages 8–14: Teach children to shoot live ammunition using a .22 caliber rifle or pistol. Focus on the fundamentals of aim, trigger control, and responsible gun ownership.

- Ages 12–18: Introduce low recoil defensive firearms, such as a 9mm and .223 rifle. At this stage, youth must master trigger control as well as learn to take personal responsibility for their safety and the safety of those around them.

- Age 14 and older: After mastering the 9mm and .223, introduce shotguns and larger caliber weapons.

In order to start shooting weapons, children and adolescents must be able to physically handle the gun, follow instructions, and demonstrate responsible behavior and impulse control. During the Zombie Apocalypse, Aegis Academy's age recommendations should not change much, as one of the limiting factors related to the use of shotguns and larger calibers is the body's ability to handle a weapons' *recoil*—the backward movement (kickback) of a firearm following discharge. The inability to handle a weapon's recoil can be especially problematic when using automatic and rapid-fire semi-automatic weapons, as the gun will continue to shoot even after kickback has begun. As a result, the muzzle will rise, placing those around the shooter and the shooter themselves at risk.

Games of the Zombie Apocalypse

Surviving the Zombie Apocalypse requires skill sets that most children and adolescents lack. But, once the initial slaughter has passed, weapons training, regardless of age, will be of paramount importance. In addition to such preparations, live-action games can help youth survive a plague of the undead. To be effective, however, these games must teach children and adolescents how to exploit the neurological weaknesses of zombies mentioned above.

Hide-and-Seek with Zombies. A zombie's neurology requires stimuli to trigger hunting behavior, so the ability to remain still, and quiet will be just as essential as combat training. Meditation exercises can help with this. When playing Hide-and-Seek with Zombies, use standard Hide-and-Seek game rules. For older youth and teens, use actual zombies instead of human stand-ins for added realism. Make sure to declaw (remove fingernails) and dejaw (remove teeth and lower jaw) zombies before game insertion.

MacGyver That Zombie. This apocalyptic zombie game bears the name of the famed TV character capable of escaping any dire situation by thinking outside of the box. During MacGyver That Zombie, children use a variety of household objects to create a weapon capable of piercing the skull and destroying the brain of a zombie. The first person finished shouts out the game's motto, "Everything is weaponizable!" and then runs over to a zombie's head placed in a vice to see if they can pierce or smash its skull.

Mimic the Zombie. Children will need to master zombie mannerisms, including their lumbering gait and uncoordinated attempts at reaching and grasping. Once children become competent on their own, add real zombies to the mix. The goal of this game is to move among the zombies without triggering hunting behavior. Teach children sign language for silent communication when among the dead.

Whack-a-Zombie. This game is just like Whack-a-Mole, only with live zombie heads (with teeth or lower jaws removed). By repeatedly smashing in the heads of zombies, youth become desensitized to the sights and sounds associated with killing the undead.

Zombie-in-the-Middle. Zombie-in-the-Middle is similar to Monkey-in-the-Middle, only with functioning zombies as "it" instead of children. The goal of Zombie-in-the-Middle is to save friends from the clutches of the undead through distraction. Start with a single zombie in the middle. Add additional zombies to the mix to help children and adolescents become expert distractors.

Zombie Tag. Zombie tag is similar to Humans vs. Zombies (see Chapter 1), only without weaponry. Just like the popular foam dart game, once tagged, players must join the ranks of the undead. The last human alive wins. Zombie tag is an excellent game for agility and cardio. For older youth and teens, use real zombies instead of playmates.

Final Thoughts

Nature is replete with real-life cases of "zombiism" in which the infected have no control over their behavior (although the cannibalistic behavior is notably absent). For example, *Gammarus lacustris* (a parasitic worm) takes control of fish, forcing them to leave the relative safety of the ocean floor and swim upwards toward the surface and predators. Another parasitic worm, *Leucochloridium*, infects the eyestalks of snails, which then begin to pulsate rhythmically in a manner consistent with a caterpillar's movements. In turn, such behavior attracts predators.[34] Similarly, rats infected with the parasite *Toxoplasma gondii* increasingly engage in fearless and reckless behavior. For example, infected rats lose their fear of cats, thus placing themselves in situations where prey should not be (i.e., near a cat). As the examples above show, zombie-like behavior puts the affected creature at risk for predation. However, during the Zombie Apocalypse, the zombies are the predators, not the prey, and their behavior is decidedly violent.

In addition to affecting behavior in rats, *Toxoplasma gondii* (which infects people via cat feces and eating raw meat or unwashed vegetables) may also alter aggression in humans. Relative to the uninfected, humans infected with *Toxoplasma gondii* receive a diagnosis of Intermittent Explosive Disorder (IED)—a failure to control aggressive impulses, resulting in recurrent behavioral outbursts—more frequently. Such outbursts can take the form of verbal tirades, acts of physical aggression (e.g., pushing, hitting) or even violent behavior (e.g., shooting or stabbing). Moreover, such angry and violent outbursts (as seen during instances of road rage) occur in response to relatively minor provocations (e.g., being "flipped the bird"). But, unlike the "rage" virus in *28 Weeks Later*, which causes a near-instantaneous descent into violence, *Toxoplasma gondii* is linked with long-term, and relatively small, changes in aggressive behavior, although the exact mechanism through which it contributes to IED is unknown. Nevertheless, with the link to aggressive outbursts already established, it seems plausible that a future mutation or weaponization of the parasite could lead to a short-onset rage-like virus.

Rabies comes the closest to causing the violent behavior of stimulus-driven zombies. Animals infected with rabies, such as foxes, raccoons, or dogs, become hyper-aggressive and attack humans. In some quasi-zombie tales, such as the movie *Rec*, and the video game *Left for Dead*, a mutated strain of the rabies virus causes the Zombie-like Apocalypse. However, as it exists today, rabies kills humans (around 59,000 per year worldwide),[35] but it causes neither hyper-aggressive behavior nor cannibalism.

In addition to infection diseases, synthetic "designer" drugs may bring about zombie-like behavior. For instance, a 19-year-old Florida teen killed a random couple in their home, then gnawed on the male victim's face. Similarly, while attacking a homeless man in Miami, a Florida man also chewed off parts of his victim's face. News agencies reported that the synthetic drug "Flakka" most likely caused the first attack,[36] whereas reports blamed "bath salts" for the latter.[37] However, in both cases, drugs tests failed to find traces of synthetic *stimulants* (i.e., drugs that increase in heart rate, blood pressure, and metabolism) in the bodies of the perpetrators.

Nevertheless, although rare, one potential side effect of powerful stimulants is *excited delirium*—a condition characterized by anxiety, hallucinations, insensitivity to pain, and hyper-aggression.[38] Thus, a weaponized drug (released into the air and water supply) that consistently causes excited delirium could bring about a quasi-zombie apocalyptic event.

Hijacking the brain to create quasi-zombies is one thing; reanimating the dead is quite another. As of yet, the living dead do not exist in nature. When the heart stops beating, CPR can bring a person "back to life," and warming the blood and internal organs of people found unconscious in frigid temperatures can revive the seemingly dead.[39] However, in both of these examples, people were only "mostly dead," to quote Miracle Max from *The Princess Bride*.[40] The Uniform Determination of Death Act defines death as "(1) irreversible cessation of circulatory and respiratory functions, or (2) irreversible cessation of all functions of the entire brain, including the brain stem."[41] Reanimation of the truly dead has yet to occur. Stories of the Zombie Apocalypse are just that—stories. But as Ian Malcolm from *Jurassic Park* says, "Life, uh, ... finds a way."[42] Or, in the case of zombies, undeath.

3. The Destruction of Childhood

Children grow up fast in the Zombie Apocalypse, or they do not grow up at all. The comic book version of *The Walking Dead* illustrates this fact quite well. Shortly after learning how to use a gun, seven-year-old Carl Grimes puts a bullet through the head of a "walker." Not long after, Carl shoots and kills family friend and former protector Shane Walsh, who at the time was threatening the life of his father.[1] Both of these acts represent firsts for Carl: the first time he takes an undead life, and the first time he takes a human one. It is the last time for neither. Carl survives his childhood. Other children in the comic books series are not as lucky. Not long after arriving at a near-abandoned prison, a sociopathic prisoner decapitates Hershel Greene's twin girls, Susie and Rachel.[2] After leaving the prison, and believing that reanimation is not such a bad thing, preschool-aged Ben kills his twin brother Billy. In turn, Carl kills Ben out of perceived necessity, as he feels that the adults in his group will fail to act appropriately.[3] Later, Carl witnesses the leader of a rival group, Negan, bludgeon his friend to death. Seeking vengeance, Carl hides in the back of a truck heading to their compound. Upon arrival, he unleashes the full force of a machine gun, killing five or six of Negan's men.[4] Carl is still a child at this point, years away from puberty. Adults killing children. Children killing children. Children killing adults. A palindrome of death, if you will.

Defining Childhood

The Zombie Apocalypse will bring death to the masses with certainty. Will it also bring about the end of childhood? To answer that question, a definition of "childhood" is in order. To an infant, childhood is the present;

to an adult, it is the past. To all, childhood is the earliest phase of life, characterized by immaturity, vulnerability, and dependency. Beyond these facts, defining childhood becomes complicated, for childhood can be age-related, law-related, task-related, stage-related, historical, and cultural. Some even view it as an arbitrary creation made by society. Depending on its definition, the Zombie Apocalypse may, or may not, lead to its destruction. Below, I present prominent definitions of childhood and discuss the chances of each conceptualization surviving the devastation wrought by the living dead.

Childhood as Defined by Age

Some scholars, especially those in the field of developmental psychology, define childhood as a function of chronological age. It is quite straightforward. Infancy refers to the period of childhood between birth and 12 months of age. Toddlerhood takes place between 12 months and 36 months. Early childhood (a.k.a. the preschool years) occurs between the ages of three and five. Middle childhood consists of children between six and 10 years of age. Early adolescence refers to youth ranging in age from 11 to 13. Middle adolescence takes place between the ages of 14 and 16, while late adolescence applies to individuals aged 17 to 19. Adulthood, then, begins at age 20.

THE EFFECT OF THE ZOMBIE APOCALYPSE. When defined by age, an invasion of the undead will have no detrimental impact on the existence of childhood. As long as books on child development exist and professors have someone to profess to, age-defined childhood will remain unchanged. Nevertheless, because the Zombie Apocalypse will require children to undertake behaviors typically carried out by adults, and because many child-centered environments (e.g., play gyms) and organizations (e.g., organized sports) will cease to exist, the activities and expectations *associated* with different age groups will change from their current configuration. For example, in contemporary society, adults typically perform security duties. However, during the Zombie Apocalypse, children in middle adolescence (and possibly earlier) will regularly take part in protective activities. For example, in Jonathan Maberry's *Rot & Ruin* (which is set 14 years after the Zombie Apocalypse), 15-year-olds take on positions of responsibility, such as testing fences for weaknesses, being on the lookout for zombies advancing toward the community, and even hunting and killing the living dead.[5]

Childhood as Defined by Law

In the United States, youth legally cross over from childhood into adulthood on their 18th birthday, as indicated by the right to vote and join the military. Nevertheless, federal law requires that individuals must be 21 years of age to drink alcohol. Individual states determine the legality of other "adult" behaviors, such as the minimum age of consent for sexual relations (which ranges from 16 to 18 years of age, with a few exceptions based on age differentials between participants)[6] and marriage (age 18 in most states).[7] Globally, the legal age for alcohol use, sexual consent, and marriage vary by country as well. Based on the legality of different behaviors, it becomes clear that childhood ends earlier for some activities than others, depending on where one lives in the world.

THE EFFECT OF THE ZOMBIE APOCALYPSE. The Zombie Apocalypse will end governance as we know it. Established federal, state, and local governments will all disappear. There will be no courts, no judges, no lawyers, and no laws. There will be no legal definition of childhood.

Childhood as Defined by Task Completion

To many, childhood is a journey. From infancy to adulthood, youth go from relative incompetence to competence; from dependence to independence; and from illogic to logic. Rather than relying solely on age as the defining feature of childhood, the journey perspective focuses on the tasks of childhood that, once accomplished, signify its end. Psychologists believe these tasks to be culturally universal, meaning that they occur in all societies. Regardless of whether a child is born in Japan, Germany, or Brazil, all infants need to develop emotional attachments to others, and all toddlers will attempt to master rudimentary skills and defend their autonomy with vigor. From the United States to India, early childhood is a time for learning right from wrong, and during middle childhood, all youth begin to compare themselves with others. Adolescents, be they in Nigeria or Australia, are tasked with figuring out who they are now and who they want to be in the future.

Additionally, theory dictates that developmental tasks unfold in sequence. Thus, specific tasks *must* be completed before other tasks can begin. According to this viewpoint, before developing personal values, children must first learn right from wrong. Similarly, the broadening of interests outside the family occurs before children create a sense of personal identity. See Box 3.1 for a list of the significant tasks of infancy, childhood, and adolescence.

Box 3.1: *Developmental Task Across Infancy, Childhood, and Adolescence*

Infancy
- Developing emotional attachments to others.
- Communicating physical, social, and emotional needs to others.
- Manipulating and moving about the environment.
- Adjusting to periods of separation from caregivers.

Toddlerhood
- Communicating through language.
- Acquiring the basics of self-control.
- Desiring independence (e.g., doing things for themselves).
- Learning that others may place limits on their behavior.
- Beginning to make choices, and prefer their decisions to others'.
- Attempting to master necessary skills, such as walking, kicking, and grabbing.

Early Childhood
- Learning the difference between fantasy and reality.
- Improving emotional and behavioral control.
- Becoming more compliant with rules.
- Connecting thoughts, feelings, and actions.
- Learning right from wrong.
- Learning social skills.

Middle Childhood
- Continued development of social skills necessary for friendship and peer acceptance.
- Developing and testing personal values and beliefs.
- Incorporating competencies and interests into the sense of self.
- Beginning to compare the self to others.
- Broadening of interesting to things outside the family.
- Learning social rules and norms for a variety of different situations.

Adolescence
- Developing a sense of self as an autonomous individual.
- Developing a personal identity.
- Adapting to pubertal changes.
- Adjusting to adult roles and expectations.

THE EFFECT OF THE ZOMBIE APOCALYPSE. The advent of the living dead should have little impact on childhood as a task-related phenomenon. Childhood will continue, as there is no reason to believe that the undead will alter the need for the completion of the major tasks listed above. Infants will still need to attach to caregivers. Toddlers must still learn the basics of self-control (lest they wander into the arms of a passing zombie). Preschoolers still will be required to connect thoughts, feelings, and actions. Youth in middle childhood will still need to learn rules and social norms (e.g., what to do if a friend sustains a zombie bite). Adolescents will still have to adapt to those awkward pubertal changes (e.g., yelling, "Watch out, zombie!" only to have their voices crack while doing so). However, as my parenthetical comments illustrate, the contexts and settings related to task completion will change during the Zombie Apocalypse. So too will the specific social mores conveyed during *socialization*—the process through which youth acquire the rules, standards, beliefs, and values of a culture. In the new world order, everything will be apocalypse-based and zombie-themed. For example, in *Rot & Ruin*, when teens turn 15, their schooling ends and they are required to get a job (such as fence tester, zombie spotter, or zombie hunter), or they will have their food rations cut in half.

Box 3.2: *The Fantasy-Reality Distinction During the Zombie Apocalypse*

Will the existence of zombies increase children's fear and belief in other monsters, such as vampires? Interestingly, the presence of zombies should have no impact on the *fantasy-reality distinction*, the ability to distinguish realities from non-realities (i.e., fantasy). What may come as a surprise to many is that as early as age three this ability is already in place, though not fully developed. For example, preschoolers are aware that cartoons are not real, and that imaginary friends are only make-believe. However, when errors do occur (and fantasy is mistaken for reality) widespread cultural acceptance and parental support accompanies the mistake. Rituals (such as leaving milk and cookies out for Santa Claus), evidence (e.g., finding money under a pillow from the Tooth Fairy), and testimony from others (e.g., a sibling verifying that the Easter Bunny does exist) help solidify the reality status of an entity.

Nevertheless, fantastical creatures can frighten children. As it turns out, *stating* that a creature is fantastical and *being sure* in that belief are two separate things. According to Jacqueline Woolley, "Children may understand that these entities generally are not real, but may be less good at saying 'it's not real' to themselves and comforting themselves with this knowledge."[8] For example, although children recognize cartoons as unreal at the end of the preschool years, their belief in fantastical beings in general (e.g., Santa Claus, the Easter Bunny, the Tooth Fairy) does not decline until age eight. Moreover, children make reality-based judgments on a case-by-case basis. By way of illustration, although a five-year-old child may believe that there are no monsters under their bed, they may be less sure about the beds at Grandma's house.

Although the major tasks of childhood will remain the same, the Zombie Apocalypse may affect the speed with which children go through these tasks. Del Giudice contends that during middle childhood two developmental strategies present themselves: slow and fast. *Slow strategies* involve a prolonged childhood, characterized by stable relationships with friends and family, prosocial behavior (e.g., helping others), high levels of self-control (e.g., not acting rash or impulsive), risk aversion (e.g., avoiding dangerous situations), and late-onset of sexual activity and reproduction. In most Western cultures, a slow strategy embodies the very nature of an ideal childhood. In contrast, *fast strategies* consist of early puberty, shortened adolescence, unstable family and peer relationships, high levels of risk taking, exploitative tendencies, and aggression as well as early sexual activity and reproduction.

In general, children in safe and predictable environments use slow strategies, whereas youth in dangerous and unpredictable environments employ fast strategies. Contingent upon environmental conditions, each strategy is thought to maximize the likelihood of survival (and later reproductive success)—a phenomenon known as *adaptive plasticity.* Whether caused by nuclear weapons, asteroids, aliens, or zombies, nothing destabilizes an environment like an apocalypse. Safe and predictable environments become neither safe nor predictable. As a result, youth in middle childhood during the Zombie Apocalypse should adopt fast strategies (even if they were previously using a slow strategy trajectory), effectively shortening childhood.

Childhood as Defined by Stages

Childhood does not occur in a vacuum. Instead, children grow up in the context of environmental, social, and cultural forces. Erik Erikson's theory of lifespan development, which proposes eight psychosocial stages of development from infancy to old age, focuses on the importance of relationships within the larger society to an individual's health and well-being. During each stage, the individual faces a polarity (i.e., a crisis), which pits a positive ability against a related vulnerability. At every stage of development, key social agents help the individual resolve the current crisis, with the resolution (be it successful or unsuccessful) influencing the outcome of the next crisis encountered. Thus, human development is both sequential and cumulative, with one's overall personality composed of the strengths and weaknesses acquired during each psychosocial stage. Of note, the resolution to each crisis is never set in stone. In the face of current life experiences, earlier resolutions (even those resolved years ago) may change for better or for worse.

The first five stages of Erikson's theory focus on psychosocial crises during infancy, childhood, and adolescence; I present them below. Box 3.3 details the remaining three adult stages of psychosocial development.

STAGE 1: TRUST VS. MISTRUST. The first psychosocial stage, *Trust versus Mistrust*, starts with birth and ends on the child's first birthday. Being completely helpless, infants must rely on others to meet their physiological needs (e.g., food, clothing, diaper changes, and so on) and their psychological desires for affection and emotional comfort. Having their needs consistently met leads infants to view the world as a safe place, and, correspondingly, trust the people around them. However, in the absence of appropriate care, infants become anxious and mistrustful of others (and the world). During this stage, the key social agent (responsible for the infant developing a sense of trust or mistrust) is the primary caregiver, typically the mother.

Trust vs. Mistrust in the Zombie Apocalypse. During the Zombie Apocalypse, parents will die, and for those that survive, meeting the physiological, psychological, and safety needs of their infants will become increasingly challenging. Because of parental loss, and not having their emotional needs met consistently, infants will develop a sense of mistrust about others and view the world as a dangerous place. The movie *Here Alone* shows the environmental conditions ripe for the development of mistrust. In the film, baby Hailey and her parents (Ann and Jason) find themselves in the middle of a Zombie Apocalypse. As shown in a series of flashbacks, not too long after escaping to an isolated forest, Jason dies, and Ann struggles to care for herself and her infant. If this situation were to continue, Hailey would resolve this crisis on the side of mistrust. However, before she can come to a resolution, Ann accidentally infects Hailey with zombie blood left on her clothes. To spare her child immense suffering, Ann feeds her infected baby a bottle filled with crushed aspirin, thus ending her life.[9] The world was indeed a dangerous place.

STAGE 2: AUTONOMY VS. SHAME AND DOUBT. Erikson's second psychosocial stage, *Autonomy versus Shame and Doubt*, occurs between one and three years of age. During this stage of development, toddlers strongly desire to be independent (i.e., be on their own) and self-reliant (i.e., do things on their own). Toddlers like to feed, wash, and put on clothes all by themselves. And they wish to develop mastery over these behaviors, repeating them over and over again. As parents (the key social agents of this stage) encourage children to walk, talk, and do things for themselves, children develop age-appropriate autonomy. However, when faced with restrictions of their actions or negative consequences for their behaviors, autonomy can quickly turn into *defiance*—active resistance to a demand indicated by the intensification of ongoing behavior, accompanied by anger and overall negativity—a tantrum, in other words. If parents are coercive or overprotective, children will experience self-doubt and feel ashamed of themselves.

Autonomy vs. Shame and Doubt in the Zombie Apocalypse. Nothing supports autonomy more than allowing toddlers to explore their environments independently. During the Zombie Apocalypse, nothing will result in more zombie-related deaths than allowing independent toddlers to explore their environments. When the undead arrive, the world effectively becomes a giant electrical outlet, and an unsupervised toddler has its finger extended looking for a place to insert it. To prevent premature death, parents will restrict their toddler's independent activities frequently, and with great fervor. And to ensure compliance (especially during periods of perceived danger) many parents will make their demands using a harsh and insensitive tone. Resultantly, a sense of shame and doubt will follow.

STAGE 3: INITIATIVE VS. GUILT. During the third psychosocial stage, *Initiative versus Guilt*, three- to six-year-olds readily explore their environments, initiate and plan new activities, develop friendships, and make judgments. Preschool-aged children know how to color, recognize numbers and letters, and engage in imaginary play. They also learn the activities and behaviors that bring them joy and those that bring less positive emotions, such as anger, sadness, and guilt. Support from family members (the key social agents of this stage), along with successful completion of activities, results in the sense of *initiative*—that is, knowing they can do things on their own. However, children that experience too many failures or conflicts with family members resulting in restrictions or punishment become passive and guilt-ridden, thus limiting their ability to take the initiative in the future.

Initiative vs. Guilt in the Zombie Apocalypse. Rather than being coerced or coaxed into starting an activity, preschoolers readily begin them on their own. During the Zombie Apocalypse, this could be problematic, especially when the dead are nearby and the need for silence becomes a necessity. Noisy activities will place young children's lives at risk and endanger the lives of those caring for them. Thus, preschooler-initiated activities likely to receive support from parents (and others) will be quiet, calm, and require few resources (such as toys or guardians). Children high in self-initiated self-control will receive fewer corrections and restrictions from parents, as will children better able to differentiate when they *can* do from what they *should* do. For these youth, developing a sense of initiative, even when surrounded by the undead, is still a possibility. In contrast, children requiring constant supervision due to their lack of impulse control, emotional reactivity, activity level, and poor decision making will find their initiative squashed, their conflicts with parents frequent, and a sense of guilt as the likely resolution to this stage.

STAGE 4: INDUSTRY VS. INFERIORITY. *Industry versus Inferiority* is the fourth crisis that children face. Between six and 11 years of age, children are required to master both academic (e.g., reading, multiplication) and social skills (e.g., entering and exiting conversations, conflict resolution). Not surprisingly, teachers and peers are the key social agents of this stage. Through hard work and perseverance, self-assured youth that succeed at developing various abilities at home, school, and play feel industrious. And the more competent youth become in dealing with their environments, the better they feel about themselves. However, frustrations and failures in academic and social settings evoke a sense of inferiority or worthlessness.

Industry vs. Inferiority in the Zombie Apocalypse. Traditionally, this stage occurs during the elementary school years, with meeting parental and teacher expectations related to educational content (e.g., reading, writing, and arithmetic) the key to developing a sense of industry. However, schools will close during the Zombie Apocalypse, and K–12 educational institutions will cease to exist. Nevertheless, educational activities will continue at home, albeit in a much scaled-down version of pre-apocalyptic times. After all, foraging for food, hiding from zombies, and defending one's home from human threats and the undead will leave parents and children little energy for educational pursuits.

Rather than school activities being the primary influence on the resolution of the *Industry versus Inferiority* stage, school-aged children will begin to measure their competencies in other ways. Of paramount importance will be skills related to survival, self-defense, weapon use, and the like. Children that are unsuccessful in developing such abilities (which may lead to ridicule from peers as well as punishment and disappointment from parents and other adults) will generate feelings of inferiority (assuming a zombie does not eat them). In contrast, success in these areas will result in the sense of industry, and a higher chance of surviving a plague of the undead.

STAGE 5: IDENTITY VS. ROLE CONFUSION. Throughout adolescence, roughly 12 to 18 years of age, individuals redefine their identities, incorporating the various changes occurring in their bodies, minds, and sexuality. Accordingly, during the fifth psychosocial stage, *Identity versus Role Confusion*, adolescents strive to answer the question "Who am I?" The more effective adolescents are in facing this crisis, the stronger their sense of personal identity becomes in a variety of areas, including sexuality, ethnicity, and career choice. However, when difficulties arise during the identity crisis, adolescents become confused about who they are now and who they want to be in the future. Peers are the key social agents at this stage as adolescents primarily explore their identities through real-world interactions with others. However, adolescents also explore their identities on the Internet. Once resolution takes place, childhood presumably ends.

Not satisfied with Erikson's conceptualization of an identity crisis, James Marcia expanded Erikson's two-solution model to a four-solution one. According to Marcia, two dimensions comprise an identity: exploration and commitment. *Exploration*—investigation related to different aspects of one's identity—ranges from low (i.e., little to no identity search) to high (i.e., regularly investigates various aspects of the self). Similarly, *commitment*—the obligation to the decisions made regarding the self—also ranges from low (i.e., readily changes their mind) to high (i.e., steadfastly sticks to their choices). Crossing commitment with exploration creates four identity statuses.

- *Identity Achievement*—high levels of both exploration and commitment.
- *Identity Diffusion*—low levels of both exploration and commitment.
- *Moratorium*—high levels of exploration and low levels of commitment.
- *Foreclosure*—low levels of exploration and high levels of commitment.

Identity achievement occurs after an active exploration of personal values and beliefs followed by a commitment to a self-chosen ideology. Identity-achieved adolescents know who they are and what they want to do with their lives. In contrast, adolescents in a state of identity diffusion struggle with their identity, but make no active effort to clarify it. In effect, they have given up. With no clear direction, identity-diffused youth are at risk of manipulation from others. Characterized by exploration without commitment, adolescents in moratorium frequently redefine who they are without truly investing in any single identity. Rebelliousness characterizes this state of being. Finally, foreclosed youth make strong commitments (which tend to be in line with parental expectations) without actively exploring their options. Although they are seemingly content with their decisions during adolescence, the lack of exploration may lead to regret later in life.

Identity vs. Role Confusion in the Zombie Apocalypse. How are adolescents supposed to figure out who they are and how they fit into the adult world when the world itself is undergoing a dramatic change? Most likely, they cannot. In support of this contention, consider the following: after resettling in Canada, adolescent Karen refugees from Myanmar (whose new lives held no resemblance to their former ones) exhibited high levels of identity crisis and role confusion, as well prolonged identity resolutions.[10] Similarly, the Zombie Apocalypse will tear out everything that teens hold near and dear to their hearts, both figuratively and (potentially) literally. Schooling options, gone. Traditional vocation and career options, gone. Customary dating opportunities, gone. Conventional hangouts with peers, gone. Clothing options, gone (all teens will be wearing "distressed" garments this season and in the near future). As a result of these changes, role confusion will abound.

Regarding Marcia's identity statuses, foreclosure will be commonplace when the dead rise, as the need to survive will force adolescents to commit to roles they did not choose for themselves nor had time to explore fully. Others will likely experience identity diffusion, as the fall of civilization and the uncertainty of living with the living dead will leave few options to commit to or investigate. However, after an extended period of adjustment to the new zombie-filled landscape, and a degree of predictability ensues, the possibility of a successful resolution to the identity crisis should increase. Youth will finally be able to see their role in the new world order and attain identity achievement. For example, let us consider teenage Carl Grimes from the comic book version of *The Walking Dead.* After years of struggling with his damaged appearance (he lost an eye to a bullet) and attempts to be like his lawman-father, Carl contentedly settles on blacksmithery as a profession.[11] However, for adolescents that try to fit themselves into a world that no longer exists, role confusion will remain.

Box 3.3: *Adult Stages of Psychosocial Development*

Erikson proposed three stages of adult psychosocial development. Below are the crises that adults face as they age and the likely effect that the Zombie Apocalypse would have on their resolutions.

Stage 6: Intimacy vs. Isolation.

During early adulthood, which begins at age 19 and lasts an additional 20 years, individuals strive to establish intimate relationships with others. A successful resolution involves the formation of satisfying, close relationships with peers of both sexes as well as an intimate relationship with another person. The inability to establish rewarding relationships with others results in a painful sense of isolation or loneliness.

Finding love in the time of zombies will be difficult. Maintaining that love will be even harder, as stress negatively affects relationship satisfaction. Stressed partners are unsupportive partners. And unsupportive partners don't stay together long. Chapter 6 discusses relationships issues with intimate partners in more detail.

Stage 7: Generativity vs. Stagnation.

Generativity refers to the ability to look beyond the self and to contribute to the welfare of others. It involves accomplishing things that make the world a better place. The successful resolution of this stage, which starts during middle adulthood (age 40 or so), results in productive community members. For those that fail to meet the challenges set forth for them by society, stagnation occurs, and the person becomes increasingly self-absorbed. During this period of aging, people begin to think about what they would like to do with the rest of their lives.

Adults that survive the undead rising long enough to participate in the rebuilding of civilization should develop a sense of generativity. After all, what better way to contribute to the welfare of others than to take an apocalyptic wasteland and make it more habitable for future generations? Nevertheless, for many, the challenges associated with living in a zombie-filled world will be overwhelming, leading to stagnation and self-absorption. Instead of looking out for others, stagnated adults will care only for themselves, although they will still be on the lookout for zombies.

Stage 8: Integrity vs. Despair.

During late adulthood (65 years and up), individuals experience a time of contemplation. Adults that reflect upon a fulfilling life develop integrity and feel happy with themselves. However, for those that view their lives as disappointing, meaningless, and filled with failure, despair follows.

Until the tide of undead turns, despair will overwhelm the elderly. How could it not? The Zombie Apocalypse will have destroyed nearly everything they worked hard to build. And virtually everyone they know will have died. The realization that they will not see a better tomorrow (or any tomorrow, for that matter) will be ever-present. In many instances, the wisdom they have attained will be meaningless to the new world order. Adding to their misery will be the fact that others may view them as a burden.

Childhood as a Social Construction

Many scholars, especially those in the fields of anthropology and sociology, view childhood as a *social construction*—a reality based on jointly shared beliefs and assumptions about the world. In other words, because children's roles, activities, and perceived value vary by culture and historical context, the definition of childhood varies by those factors as well. For example, during the early 1800s, 5- to 13-year-old British children frequently worked alongside adults, but by the late 1800s compulsory education had replaced work, in effect changing the nature of childhood. Similarly, cross-cultural studies indicate that for children in developing nations, childhood is less about education, and more about contributing to the family economy directly through work (e.g., fishing, foraging, hunting) or indirectly by caring for younger siblings. Necessity, it seems, plays a vital role in determining the activities and expectations associated with the construction of childhood.

As a social construction, childhood has no universal beginning. Many cultures, especially those with high rates of infant death, delay the onset of *personhood*—being fully human—from birth until a later point in time, which, as it turns out, could be months or even years later, depending on the culture. Often, a "naming" ceremony announces a child's transition from non-personhood to a valued, full member of society. Such delays purportedly provide parents and extended family members a degree of emotional distance from a child, who may very well die during infancy or early childhood. In other societies, children receive personhood after contributing economically to their families, which typically does not occur until middle childhood. In contrast, societies that place paramount importance on the psychological and emotional value of children (rather than on their economic viability) confer personhood at birth or earlier.

During the *juvenile stages of development*—ranging from infancy to late adolescence—tremendous change occurs physically, cognitively, socially, and emotionally. Although each stage is developmentally unique, they share one commonality: they all differ from adulthood. From this point forward, the term "childhood" will subsume all pre-adult stages of development. Similar to its beginning, the end of childhood (and thus the start of adulthood) is variable as well. In some cultures, teenage circumcision is a rite of passage into adulthood. In other societies, marriage signifies the onset of adulthood, although the age associated with it can vary greatly. In rural areas of Morocco and India, for example, marital unions can take place during middle adolescence. In contrast, in the United States first marriages tend to occur in the late 20s.

THE EFFECT OF THE ZOMBIE APOCALYPSE. As the previous review illustrates, it is impossible to identify childhood by a universally agreed-upon series of ages, tasks, or behaviors. When viewed as a social construction, childhood has no definitive beginning and no conclusive end. However, it is possible to evaluate childhood from a particular praxis and discuss the effects of the Zombie Apocalypse on the social construction of childhood from that vantage point.

When the dead rise, a social *destruction* of childhood will take place in developed nations. The conceptualization of childhood as being consumption-rich with access to a wide range of resources (e.g., the Internet, shopping malls, Wegmans), as well as being characterized by lengthy periods of education and enrichment activities (e.g., sports, music, drama, art), will cease to exist. In its place, subsistence living, fear, and a survival mentality will develop. At that point, the characteristics of childhood will be reconstructed, with delayed personhood and contributions to the family economy (i.e., survival) at its core.

In contrast, for youth in developing nations (along with children experiencing impoverished childhoods in developed nations), the Zombie Apocalypse may bring very little change regarding the social constructions of their childhoods. Food will still be scare, children will still be required to do labor (both domestic and otherwise) and pool resources for survival, education will still be lacking, and children will still be surrounding by significant dangers. The primary difference between pre- and post-apocalyptic life will be the frequency of death (which should increase), and the reasons for it.

The Contexts of Childhood

Regardless of its definition, childhood takes place in a variety of different settings, such as home, school, and playgrounds. Contexts such as these, in which children are directly involved, significantly affect their development. Consider the following: not only does bullying affect a child's current quality of life negatively, but it also places them in jeopardy for developing anxiety and depression years later. What is more, locations children never even step into, as well as broader cultural beliefs, also affect their course of development, albeit indirectly. Urie Bronfenbrenner categorized the contexts that influence youth—known collectively as *the ecological environment*—into four interrelated systems: microsystem, mesosystem, exosystem, and macrosystem.

A *microsystem* refers to the setting in which a child lives and interacts with others. Thus, when a child changes locations, so too does the microsystem. The term *mesosystem* refers to the linking of different microsystems over time, both of which involve the same child. For example, following a bout of bullying at school (microsystem #1), a teenager returns home (microsystem #2) and immediately picks a fight with their younger sibling. Thus, not only are the experiences within each microsystem influential in that setting but potentially in other settings as well. The third context of development, the *exosystem*, refers to the interaction between settings that directly involve the child (i.e., a microsystem) and those that do not (e.g., a parent's workplace, school board). For example, when work-related conditions over-stress parents, the home environment of their preschool children suffers (e.g., the parent is less sensitive and more hostile). In this case, a context unfamiliar to the child (i.e., a parent's workplace) influenced the child's life. The last of Bronfenbrenner's systems, the *macrosystem*, refers to the broader sociocultural context in which development takes place, including cultural, religious, and social class distinctions. More specifically, the macrosystem refers to the set of shared values, goals, practices, and attitudes that characterizes a group of people. In turn, these values, goals, and so on influence all other systems within the ecological environment, which correspondingly affect the child. As an example, children and adolescents brought up in cultures accepting of violence tend to be more violent themselves.

The Effect of the Zombie Apocalypse

As a theoretical construct, the ecological environment will be unaffected by the living dead. Microsystems, mesosystems, exosystems, and macrosystems will still function as major contextual influences in the lives of youth. What will change, however, are the particular settings that children grow up in, the types of interactions occurring between those settings, and the nature of both indirect and broader cultural influences. As an example, let us consider George A. Romero's classic film *Night of the Living Dead* and the ecological environment in which 11-year-old Karen Cooper finds herself. The setup for the story is as follows: A returning probe from Venus has exploded over rural Pennsylvania, spreading its contaminants across the countryside, and, as a result, the dead have risen.

Here are some pertinent elements from the rest of the story: Karen and her parents find shelter in the cellar of an old farmhouse after having their car overturned by reanimated corpses. In their escape, Karen suffered a zombie bite, to which she eventually succumbs. While in the cellar, Karen eats her father and guts her mother with a trowel. Finally, at the end of the film, Karen is undead and wandering the countryside as patrols of armed men exterminate any zombies they come across.

From an ecological environment perspective, both the overturned car and the farmhouse are microsystems. The fact that Karen ends up in the farmhouse cellar eating her father and killing her mother demonstrates a mesosystem influence, as the bite occurred in one microsystem (i.e., the car) but affected her behavior in another (i.e., the cellar). An example of an exosystem is the fact that although Karen was not involved in any of the decisions or settings related to the Venus probe, its explosion affected her nonetheless (via the dead rising and biting her). The fact that Pennsylvanian citizens banded together to eradicate the undead menace may reflect cultural values related to gun ownership, hunting, the importance of protecting one's family from dangerous outsiders, and the belief that governments try to cover up catastrophes, letting them run their course without providing aid.

Final Thoughts

The eight-year-old child laborer, who works 12 hours a day weaving carpets, could not care less about academic notions regarding the social construction of childhood. To the starving 10-year-old, age-related developmental tasks are meaningless. For teenage boys and girls in domestic servitude or sexual slavery, laws protecting children from harm seemingly do not exist, at least not for them. To the seven-year-old child conscripted into a paramilitary group, sedated and sent to the front lines, childhood is a myth. From a humanitarian perspective, childhood is neither a theory, nor a task, nor a legal determination. Instead, it is a right that has specific guarantees, including life, health, education, and protection from harm. Childhood is threatened when deprived of these guarantees, and when the deprivations are severe enough, ended. Save the Children Foundation has developed a list of "childhood enders," which, when present, mark the end of an intact childhood.[12] Examples of these destroyers of childhood include severe malnourishment, lack of education, child labor, marriage, sexual exploitation, pregnancy, and being a victim or perpetrator of extreme violence.

For youth with intact childhoods before the Zombie Apocalypse, the rise of the living dead will not only lead to the death of the masses but the destruction of their childhoods as well. Case in point: except for child marriage and teenage pregnancy, *The Walking Dead* has shown (or implied) most of the childhood enders listed above. Zombies and humans kill and injure numerous children. School is out of session and homeschooling is markedly absent. Children engage in labor as they help clear the zombie menace from their surroundings. Although the survivors seem adequately nourished, some survivors resort to cannibalism to stave off potential starvation. Implied sexual exploitation occurs several times throughout the series, most noticeably when a roving group of scavengers threatens to rape teenage Carl.[13] As cruel as the world of *The Walking Dead* seems, it is noteworthy that the program depicts most, but not all, of the real-world enders of childhood.

Currently, hundreds of millions of infants, children, and adolescents grow up in the presence of significant adversity. For instance, worldwide, 263 million children should be in school but are not. Nearly 170 million youth are child laborers, half of whom are engaged in dangerous work. Due to malnutrition, close to 156 million children experience stunted growth. Approximately four million girls get married under the age of 15, and nearly one million similarly aged girls give birth.[14] For these youth and others like them, childhood will not end with the Zombie Apocalypse. It is already over.

4. Maternal and Infant Mortality

No Doulas. No midwives. No doctors. Nothing is sterile. Nothing is even remotely clean. And nothing is stopping Judith Grimes from being born, except there is: the body of her mother, Lori Grimes. Without a Cesarean, Judith and Lori will both assuredly die. With the highly invasive procedure, done without anesthetic, and carried out by a friend with no medical training, Lori will die, but Judith will have a chance at life. Lori gives her that chance. The brutality and horror of this event—as shown on *The Walking Dead*—does not stop with Lori's death. In many ways, it starts there, for Carl, Lori's school-aged son, is the one who shoots her in the head to prevent reanimation.[1] A tough day for Carl, a tougher day for Lori. But overall, it is just a typical day in the life—and death—of a parent during the Zombie Apocalypse.

After the dead rise, billions will die. Of course, there will be survivors and life will go on, at least for a short while. Women will get pregnant, and children will be born. Nevertheless, there are risks associated with repopulating the earth, and zombies are not the only threats facing prospective mothers and their infants.

Maternal Mortality

Even with state-of-the-art medical care, childbearing places a mother's health at risk and at times results in her tragic death. *Maternal mortality rates*—the number of annual maternal deaths (per 100,000 live births) caused or aggravated by pregnancy and its management—quantify such occurrences. According to the World Health Organization, maternal mortality rates are lower for developed nations than developing nations. For example, for every 100,000 live births in the United States, 14 women die during birth or shortly after. The maternal mortality rate is nine in England, five in Japan, and three in Greece.[2] In the United States, non-pregnancy-related diseases, such as influenza and pre-existing medical conditions, account for nearly one-third of maternal deaths. Medical issues related to pregnancy (e.g., high blood pressure) and the process of birthing itself (e.g., bleeding or infection) account for the rest. Box 4.1 presents a list of potentially life-threatening medical conditions related to pregnancy and birth.

Box 4.1: *Medical Conditions Related to Pregnancy and Birth That Place a Mother's Life at Risk*

- *Gestational diabetes*—high levels of blood sugar—increases the risk of high blood pressure, miscarriage, and the need for a Cesarean section delivery.
- *Iron-deficiency anemia*—low red blood cell count—results in headaches, heart palpitations, dizziness, shortness of breath, leg cramps, and difficulty concentrating.
- *Preeclampsia*—high blood pressure and protein in the urine—increases the risk of stroke, organ damage, and seizures.
- *Hyperemesis gravidarum*—nausea and vomiting well beyond the period of "morning sickness"—can cause weight loss, dehydration, fainting, rapid heart rate, low blood pressure, and confusion.
- *Postpartum hemorrhage*—severe bleeding (most often at the site where the placenta attached to the uterus) following the birth of the baby—can cause maternal death.
- *Postpartum infections*—infections following childbirth—often occur at incision sites and in the uterine lining or urinary tract. Untreated infections can lead to sepsis (blood poisoning).
- *Prenatal or postpartum depression*—feelings of worthlessness, hopelessness, and sadness—increases the risk of suicidal thoughts and behavior.

In developing nations, where high-quality obstetric care is lacking and resources are low, maternal mortality rates are much, much higher. For instance, there are 1,360 deaths (per 100,000 live births) in Sierra Leone, 862 deaths in the Central African Republic, 856 deaths in Chad, and 814 deaths in Nigeria.[3] Overall, 99 percent of all maternal deaths occur in developing countries, the vast majority of which are preventable.

Undernutrition and Maternal Mortality

One preventable cause of maternal death is undernutrition, which takes two forms: *malnutrition* and *micronutrient deficiency*. Malnutrition occurs when calories expended exceed calories consumed. Compared to women who are not pregnant, expectant mothers require an additional 300 to 350 calories per day during the second trimester and around 500 added calories per day during the third. When food stores are in short supply, malnutrition becomes a real possibility, especially for pregnant women and their relatively higher caloric needs.

Micronutrient deficiencies occur when there is an under-consumption of essential micronutrients, such as vitamins and trace metals, even if the overall caloric intake is enough to maintain weight. Access to prenatal multivitamins can prevent most micronutrient deficiencies. Undernutrition can lead to a whole host of problems for expectant mothers, including iron deficiency anemia, which is a contributing factor in 20 percent of all maternal deaths.[4]

Unsafe Abortions and Maternal Mortality

Worldwide, an estimated 56 million women with unintended pregnancies undergo abortions annually, nearly 22 million of which physicians deem to be unsafe. Health professionals define an *unsafe abortion* as the termination of a pregnancy performed by individuals without appropriate medical training or occurring in a medically-compromised environment (e.g., unsanitary) or both. Standard methods for conducting unsafe abortions include drinking toxic substances (e.g., turpentine, bleach, or tonics mixed with animal manure), direct injury to the vagina, cervix, or uterus (using herbal remedies, coat hangers, twigs, or chicken bones), and blunt trauma to the abdomen.

In developing countries, where the vast majority of these procedures take place, unsafe abortions account for nearly 13 percent of all maternal deaths (primarily due to hemorrhage, infection, sepsis, and trauma to the genitals or bowel), and send more than seven million women to the hospital for treatment of abortion-related complications annually. Because unsafe abortions pose significant threats to women's physical well-being, health professions view seeking them as acts of desperation. Women choose to have unsafe abortions because of barriers put in place that obstruct their access to safer procedures, such as high cost, restrictive abortion laws, stigma, and reduced availability of service.[5]

The Human Threat to Mothers

Beyond the biological risks associated with childbearing, pregnant women may also face threats to their health and well-being from those closest to them in the form of domestic violence and one of its subvariants, reproductive coercion. *Domestic violence* refers to a pattern of abusive and threatening behavior by an intimate partner (or ex-partner) that causes physical, psychological, or sexual harm. Using a variety of violent (e.g., shoving, hitting, choking) and nonviolent (e.g., intimidation, manipulation, isolation, emotional abuse, financial control) tactics, abusers attempt to create vulnerabilities in their partners and achieve power and coercive control over them. In the United States, between 3 percent and 9 percent of pregnant women experience domestic violence. Pregnancy increases the odds of physical abuse by a factor of 4.1. Moreover, pregnant women and new mothers are 1.84 times more likely to be the victim of a homicide relative to other women. In fact, in the United States, homicide is the third most frequent cause of death among pregnant women. Worldwide, domestic violence during pregnancy is staggeringly high, with clinical studies reporting the highest prevalence in Egypt (32 percent), India (28 percent) and Saudi Arabia (21 percent).[6]

It is important to remember that domestic violence—whether it occurs during pregnancy or at another time—is about control and domination through fear and abuse. It is not "caused" by drugs, alcohol, or provocation. However, factors associated with an increased likelihood of becoming abusive in intimate relationships include an unplanned/unwanted pregnancy, stress, depression, and poverty.[7] Nevertheless, the responsibility for the abuse falls squarely on the shoulders of the abuser.

Reproductive coercion refers to abusive behaviors that interfere with a woman's independent decisions related to her reproductive system, choices, health, and timeline. Intimidation, manipulation, threats, and acts of violence are the tools abusers use to coerce or pressure their partners. The three primary forms of reproductive coercion are pregnancy pressure, birth control sabotage, and pregnancy outcome control.

Pregnancy pressure occurs when a person (e.g., partner, in-law) or government bullies or coerces a woman into becoming pregnant. As an illustration, in Margaret Atwood's *The Handmaid's Tale*, the ruling class forces fertile women of the underclass to become pregnant on their behalf. In today's society, tactics to force pregnancy include threats, or acts, of physical (e.g., bodily injury), psychological (e.g., withdrawal of love or abandonment), or economic (e.g., withholding finances to purchase birth control) maltreatment.

Birth control sabotage refers to unwanted interference with a woman's contraceptive use with the intent of causing her to become pregnant, for example, destroying her birth control pills or replacing them with placebos. Other examples include forcibly removing contraceptive patches and pulling out vaginal rings. Methods of birth control sabotage involving male contraception include refusing to wear condoms, poking holes in condoms, or secretly removing condoms during sex (commonly referred to as *stealthing*).

Finally, *pregnancy outcome control* refers to pressuring or coercing a woman into continuing or ending her pregnancy against her will. Behaviors used to enforce this form of reproductive coercion include making women feel guilty for their proposed reproductive choices, leading women to believe that there are no other options available other than to continue or end the pregnancy, and preventing women from having abortions through physical, psychological, or economic means.

In the United States, pregnancy pressure, birth control sabotage, and pregnancy outcome control almost exclusively take place within an intimate partner relationship. However, in other countries, family members also engage in reproductive coercion, often by controlling the use of contraception until the woman gives birth to a desired number of children or until a particular gender is born. For example, 6 percent of women living in Ivory Coast report experiencing reproductive coercion by their in-laws.[8]

Reproduction coercion places women's health at risk in a variety of ways. First, and as mentioned above, significant medical risks accompany pregnancy and birth. Second, the odds of experiencing physical abuse and homicide are higher for pregnant women relative to non-pregnant ones. Third, in part due to an effort to avoid reproductive coercion, abused women are less likely to tell intimate partners about their pregnancies. In areas of the world where safe abortions are difficult (if not impossible) to obtain, the only option left for terminating a pregnancy is to undergo an unsafe abortion, which, as previously stated, comes with a substantial number of risks to a woman's health.

The Effects of the Zombie Apocalypse on Maternal Mortality

Given a zombie's penchant to hunt, infect, and kill, devastatingly high mortality rates will accompany the rise of the living dead. Those rates should be even higher for expectant mothers, for the undead can cause death and destruction through both direct and indirect means. *Direct effects* refer to the immediate consequences of interacting with the undead, such as bites, dismemberments, and disembowelments. In contrast, *indirect effects* refer to consequences associated with living during a zombie invasion but occur without direct contact with the undead. For example, a zombie's bite will not cause iron deficiency anemia. Nor do the undead eat multivitamins. However, zombies will eat farmers and pharmacists. And in a world without farmers and pharmacists, there will be few vegetables rich in iron for expectant mothers to eat and only a limited supply of multivitamins for them to take. Under such circumstances, iron deficiency anemia is likely will follow. Below, I examine the impact of both direct encounters with the dead and the indirect effects of living in a world filled with zombies on maternal mortality.

THE DIRECT EFFECTS OF ZOMBIES ON MATERNAL MORTALITY. As previously discussed in Chapter 2, zombies stay attuned to their prey, and unless otherwise distracted, will hunt the closest human in their sights. Pregnant women waddle with a relatively slow gait. Doing so is a physical necessity. The downward pressure exerted from the growing fetus and the expectant mother's increasing body mass, along with the increased laxity of her ligaments due to hormones, causes her pelvis to widen, all of which leads to a broader stance. Additionally, bodily changes create looseness in the lower spine and shift the expectant mother's center of mass forward. To compensate, pregnant women bend their hips less and lean backward more while walking. Hence, the waddle. Not only does pregnancy reduce speed, but it also adversely affects balance. In fact, pregnant women have the same risk of falling as an average 70-year-old. When one is chased by the undead, one of the surest ways to avoid death is to be the *second* slowest person in the group. The odds of survival for faster individuals get even better when the slowest person is prone to tripping over their toes. Unfortunately, the pregnancy waddle and associated clumsiness make expectant mothers in need of a quick escape readily available prey.

THE INDIRECT EFFECTS OF LIVING WITH ZOMBIES ON MATERNAL MORTALITY. Even if pregnant women survive direct encounters with the undead, the indirect effects of the Zombie Apocalypse will still place their lives in grave danger. Not long after the dead rise, high-quality obstetric care, along with programs focusing on the prevention and treatment of injury, illness, and disease, will cease to exist. Most medical professionals will be dead or undead, most medicines and medical supplies looted. And most medications procured will not only be limited in number but also in shelf life. Previously sanitary conditions will quickly become unsanitary, increasing the spread of disease. As a result, once preventable and treatable medical conditions, including those associated with pregnancy and birth, will become increasingly difficult (if not impossible) to prevent and treat. Infection and blood loss during labor and delivery can kill just as readily as any zombie.

In some stories of the Zombie Apocalypse, those exposed to a zombie's fluids (through bites, blood spray, and the like) quickly become undead themselves, whereas in other tales of the undead, the zombie plague infects the living, who show no ill effects from the pathogen while they are still alive. It is not until death, regardless of the cause, that zombification takes place. For the latter type of Zombie Apocalypse, any medical condition (e.g., asthma, heart disease, cancer) is not only a liability to that person but also to everyone around them.

Case in point: on *The Walking Dead*, a teenage boy named Patrick dies from the flu, alone and at night. After reanimation, zombie–Patrick does what the living dead do best—hunt, infect, and kill.[9] After the ensuing carnage, members of Patrick's community finally realize that zombification can occur even if they do not receive a zombie bite. To safeguard the group, they isolate individuals showing flu-like symptoms. Another community member, Carol, hoping to halt the spread of the infection, murders two people suffering from the flu before the illness kills them. Subsequently, she burns their bodies, thus preventing reanimation.[10] As this example shows, concerns about death and zombification occurring unchecked may lead to the prophylactic killing (and corresponding destruction of the brain) of the moderately sick and not just the terminally ill. Thus, during the Zombie Apocalypse, complications during pregnancy or birth will not only be dangerous to mother and child but also to the broader community. In most instances, isolation, rather than execution, will be all that is necessary to give the mother a chance at recovery while at the same time providing for everyone else's safety.

As the apocalypse continues, food stores will be inadequate and new foodstuffs challenging to come by. For women unable to maintain their high caloric needs, malnutrition and micronutrient deficiencies will set in. Given the lack of available resources and the likelihood of complications and potential for death during labor and delivery, some women will choose to terminate their pregnancies. However, without the benefits, or availability, of modern medicine, unsafe abortions will become the norm.

Moreover, a lack of medical professionals will result in misunderstandings regarding the appropriate use of medications that prevent or terminate pregnancies. For instance, on *The Walking Dead*, Lori Grimes discovers she is pregnant with the child of her husband's best friend and partner, Shane. While hiding her pregnancy from her husband, Lori requests that a community member pick up some "morning-after pills" on his next supply run.[11] Not long after receiving them, Lori scarfs down a handful of pills, only to force herself to throw them up minutes later. However, even if the morning-after pills had remained in Lori's system, they would not have ended her pregnancy. Morning-after pills, such as Plan B One-Step, prevent pregnancy in one of three ways: (1) by preventing fertilization; (2) by temporarily stopping the release of an egg; and (3) by preventing a fertilized egg from attaching to the uterus.[12] What they do not do is terminate established pregnancies. For that, a different medication, such as mifepristone (RU-486), is required.

Mobility restrictions will prevent many pregnant women from foraging, making them dependent on others for food and additional necessities. The potential "burdens" associated with having a pregnant woman in their household or community may lead to cases of reproductive coercion in the form of pregnancy outcome control. Perpetrators of abuse will justify their behaviors by stating that preventing childbirth is for "the greater good."

Of note, it is doubtful that other forms of reproductive coercion, namely birth control sabotage and pregnancy pressure, will occur in the midst of an undead rising. As specified above, there will be individuals that only view pregnant women as liabilities, rather than contributors, to the community. As indicated below, the same will hold regarding the presence of infants. However, if on the off chance that humanity outlives the zombie menace, and enters a post-apocalyptic period involving the rebuilding of society, expect pregnancy-promoting forms of reproductive coercion to increase. "After all," they will say, "repopulating the earth is for the greater good."

Finally, the impoverished conditions, along with the lurking dangers of zombies, will place everyone under tremendous pressure and provide little hope for the future. The stress, depression, and impoverishment caused by the Zombie Apocalypse will likely lead to an increase in domestic violence, putting expectant mothers' lives at even greater risk.

Mortality of the Very Young

In the United States, *neonatal mortality* rates—death between birth and 28 days—indicate that for every 1,000 live births, 3.9 infants die. Congenital disabilities, premature birth, and maternal complications during pregnancy account for more than 40 percent of these deaths.[13] Typically, hospital births (with either midwives or physicians) have lower neonatal mortality rates than planned home births using midwives. Access to, and the availability of, emergency services at hospitals account for this difference.

Additional markers of childhood health include *infant mortality*, defined as death in the first year of life, and *under-5 mortality*, which refers to the death of children under five years of age. In the United States and other developed nations, infant mortality rates (based on 1,000 live births) are in the single digits, and under-5 mortality rates (per 1,000 live births) are similarly low. For example, in Japan, the neonatal mortality rate is less than one, while the under-5 mortality rate is two. By way of comparison, neonatal, infant, and under-5 mortality rates in developing nations are much higher, ranging from double to triple digits. In Angola, Central African Republic, Sierra Leone, and Somalia, the infant mortality rates are 96, 92, 87, and 85, respectively. The under-5 mortality rates for these countries are even higher: 157 in Angola, 137 in Somalia, 130 in the Central African Republic, and 120 in Sierra Leone.[14]

Biological Threats to Infants and Young Children

By age five, children from developing countries are 10 times more likely to die than youth from developed countries. According to the World Health Organization, 70 percent of under-5 deaths are the result of six conditions, all of which are currently preventable or treatable: neonatal conditions, respiratory infections, diarrhea, malaria, measles, and HIV/ AIDS. The inability to obtain health care and ineffective or delayed care-seeking behavior (e.g., waiting until symptoms are life-threatening) accompany the majority of these deaths.[15] Additional contributing factors to infant and under-5 mortality include malnutrition (which accounts for 50 percent of fatalities for children under five years of age),[16] an inadequate or contaminated water supply, unsanitary conditions, and living in an area of armed conflict. Worldwide, these percentages translate into nearly 15,000 deaths of children under the age of five every day.[17]

The Human Threat to Infants and Young Children

For centuries, and across the globe, parents have been putting their newborn children to death. Ancient Greeks, Romans, and Australian Aborigines murdered unwanted, deformed, and unhealthy infants. So too did the Irish Celts, Aztecs, Phoenicians, and Vikings. At times, the killings were ritualistic, and at other times, they were justified based on illegitimacy, availability of resources, practicalities, or economics. Rather than being considered assets, infants were liabilities. Unfortunately, the passage of time has yet to eradicate these viewpoints. However, to prevent killings, parents in some countries can place unwanted babies in protective boxes—called *baby hatches*—which alert nearby staff of an abandonment. Expectant mothers across multiple continents, including Africa (South Africa), Asia (India, Japan, Pakistan, Philippines), Europe (Austria, Belgium, Czech Republic, Germany, Hungary, Italy, Switzerland), and North America (Canada, United States), have access to baby hatches.

Nevertheless, in the United States, the third leading cause of death of children under age five is murder, preceded only by genetic/chromosomal abnormalities and accidents.[18] Worldwide there are 2.7 murders per 100,000 children under the age of five.[19] It is also worth noting that 75 percent of all under-5 deaths occur during the first year of life[20] and approximately 50 percent of children that die from child abuse are infants.[21]

Homicide in infancy occurs in three forms: *infanticide, filicide,* and *neonaticide.* Infanticide refers to the killing of an infant who has yet to reach its first birthday. Filicide happens when a parent commits infanticide, and neonaticide is filicide occurring within 24 hours of birth. Phillip Resnick has classified filicide into five different categories, each based on a different motivation. They are as follows:

- **Acutely Psychotic Filicide**—psychosis or delirium renders the parent out of touch with reality and not responsible for their actions. The parent kills the child without a comprehensible motive.

- **Altruistic Filicide**—in the face of a perceived horrifying and inescapable future, a parent kills their child to prevent its impending pain and suffering.

- **Fatal Maltreatment Filicide**—an abusive parent kills the child without intending to do so.

- **Spousal Revenge Filicide**—a parent kills their child with the intent of causing intense personal distress to the other parent.

- **Unwanted Child Filicide**—a parent kills an infant that they never wanted, or no longer wants, to rid themselves of the "burdens" associated with child rearing.

A few differences between filicide and neonaticide are worth mentioning. First, most women who commit neonaticide are young and emotionally immature single mothers. In contrast, parents that commit filicide tend to be older, in a relationship, and equally likely to be female or male. Also, concealment of the pregnancy and birth tend to accompany neonaticide, but not filicide.

Regarding the victims, gender bias does exist, but it also seems to be culturally dependent. For example, in China and India, parents are more likely to murder infant girls, whereas the opposite occurs in Australia, Canada, and Denmark. Nevertheless, globally, female filicide is far more commonplace than male filicide. This gender bias happens in part because there are far more patriarchal societies than matriarchal ones. As a result, the economic, social, and religious advantages (e.g., only males can light funeral pyres to release the souls of their parents) afforded boys lead many parents to perceive them as more desirable than girls. Homicide-related gender biases usually occur during the first three months of life, with fewer gender-based differences in murder rates occurring after that.

The Effects of the Zombie Apocalypse on the Mortality of the Very Young

As with maternal mortality, the undead can directly, and indirectly, reduce the life expectancy of the very young. Infants will not survive direct encounters with the undead, so their only chance of survival is for caregivers to keep them out of harm's way. As a result, placing infants in isolation, and in locations where others cannot hear them, will be of paramount importance. However, even isolation cannot adequately protect infants from the indirect effects of the Zombie Apocalypse. Below I address the direct impact of zombies on infant mortality as well as the indirect effects of living in a world inhabited by the undead.

THE DIRECT EFFECTS OF ZOMBIES ON INFANT MORTALITY. Babies have zero chance of surviving a zombie attack on their own. Compared to other species, the human infant is helpless at birth and incapable of caring for itself (let alone putting up a successful defense against an undead predator). Without human nurturance and protection, the infant will die—even without the threat of the living dead. It will be months before a newborn can fully support the weight of its head and a few more months after that before it can sit unsupported. Babies do not even begin move about the world on their own (through rolling, creeping, or crawling) until the second half of the first year of life, taking their first walking steps around the time they turn one. Even then, they are very, very slow, too slow to outrun the living dead. Nor do infants possess the agility to out-maneuver a zombie, nor the cognitive ability outthink one. Infants cannot physically defend themselves against the undead. What they can do, how-ever, is garner protection through their cries.

Infants cry because they cannot talk. They cry when they are hungry; they cry when they are uncomfortable; and they cry when they are in pain or in need of a cuddle. For just about every other unmet need, they cry. In fact, there are different types of cries for different needs. There are cries of hunger, cries that indicate fatigue, and cries specific to pain. Unfor-tunately, most parents have difficulty identifying the particular needs asso-ciated with their infant's cries. And when an infant's needs go unmet, its cries get louder and more distressed. If you have ever been around a dis-tressed baby, you know just how ear piercing its cries can be. The typical baby cry is around 110 decibels, which is just as loud as a car horn, snow blower, or power saw.[22]

During the Zombie Apocalypse, the infant cry is both a blessing and a curse, but mostly a curse. Crying is a blessing because it helps newborns and infants obtain the physiological requirements (e.g., food, clothing, clean diapers) needed for survival. Also, crying can result in soothing care from others, thus helpings infants allay their emotional needs (the effects of which I discuss in detail in the chapters ahead). Over the course of the first year of life, the newborn's general arousal states (contentment, alert interest, and distress/irritability) develop into organized emotions, includ-ing joy, anger, disgust, surprise, sadness, and fear. Of these emotions, both fear and disgust elicit protective behavior. During infancy, disgust is smell- and taste-based. Thus, when a baby expresses disgust, it is telling the care-giver that it has just smelled or eaten something that could potentially make it sick, so they should do something about it.

In contrast, fear elicits defensive behaviors from others. When a baby is fearful, adults will look for the source of that fear and take the required steps to protect the infant from harm. Around six months of age, infants become wary of unfamiliar people (which psychologists define as *stranger anxiety*) and may even cry in the presence of a stranger, whether the stranger is undead or alive. Unfortunately, stranger anxiety is proximity based, so if a baby is showing stranger anxiety toward a zombie, it means that the ghoul is likely in the room already. Moreover, parents should not expect their babies to be foolproof zombie alarms, as not all babies cry in the presence of an unknown entity—some babies look away, others coyly hide behind their caregivers, and some greet strangers with big smiles.

Crying brings the caregiver to the baby. That is a good thing. Unfortunately, during the Zombie Apocalypse, a baby's power saw-decibel-level crying will also bring the undead. Hence, the curse aspect of crying. And infants cry a lot. Newborns cry for about two hours per day, which increases to about three hours per day during the first six weeks of life, before decreasing to about one hour per day at three months. To make a difficult situation even worse, around six to eight months infants begin to show *separation anxiety*—distress at separation from a primary caregiver. Before the onset of separation anxiety, parents can readily hand their babies off to other caregivers without upsetting them. Likewise, parents can slip out of the room (leaving the baby alone in a safe and protected space, of course) to go to the bathroom or kill a wayward zombie, all the while the baby remains calm. Once separation anxiety starts, however, babies will not only cry at separations from primary caregivers, but they will also cry if their caregiver(s) appear to be leaving. And when they cry, they cry not with a whimper, but with a roar, which, of course, will attract the attention of any living dead nearby.

I would like to be able to tell you that separation anxiety is a short phase and that all parents need to do to avoid becoming a dinner bell for a nearby zombie horde is to isolate themselves for a few weeks or so. Unfortunately, I cannot. Separation anxiety does not even peak until 14 to 18 months of age, declining after that, but still presents for at least another year or so. Although parents can use techniques to reduce separation anxiety (e.g., leaving the infant with a familiar person; having pacifiers and toys available; reassurances of return), rarely is it eliminated. Separation anxiety dissipates when a child is confident that their departing parent will return. During the Zombie Apocalypse, such a belief will be hard to come by.

THE INDIRECT EFFECTS OF LIVING WITH ZOMBIES ON INFANT MORTALITY. Even without direct contact with zombies, living among the dead will adversely affect the health and well-being of infants. In this section, I describe the effects of living in the land of the dead on infants' mortality and general health. I also present the impact of the zombie apocalypse on infants' physical appearance and the resultant effect on parental behavior.

Health-related. As mentioned above, in developing countries, only six medical conditions (all currently preventable) account for 70 percent of under-5 deaths, with 50 percent of all deaths in this age group involving malnutrition. After the Zombie Apocalypse, infants and young children in developed countries that somehow manage to avoid death by the undead will now experience the world as though they were living in a developing country, with non-zombie related deaths primarily coming from disease and malnutrition. Also, after the dead rise, the same environmental conditions that adversely affect maternal mortality will wreak havoc on infant mortality.

To make matters worse, infants and young children will no longer receive vaccinations. Here is what the unvaccinated United States looked like during the 20th century. In 1921, 15,000 Americans died from diphtheria. During the mid–1960s, rubella caused 11,000 miscarriages and 2,000 infant deaths.[23] In the 1950s, polio caused 15,000 cases of paralysis each year.[24] Prior to 1963, measles hospitalized 48,000 people and resulted in 400 to 500 deaths annually.[25] Before 1985, Haemophilus influenzae type b (Hib) caused 20,000 infections and 1,000 deaths for children under five years of age. Finally, in the 1940s, there were 200,000 cases of whooping cough, with 9,000 deaths, each year.[26] Expect a return to pre-vaccination era levels of infection, only with much higher rates of death, as medical care for sick infants and children will be severely lacking.

Perception-related. Whereas the sight of a zombie makes people go "aghh," the sight of a baby makes people "aww." The behavioral response to an approaching zombie is to run away or to protect oneself from harm by any means necessary, violent or not. In contrast, people move toward babies rather than away from them. In both instances, the driving force behind the emotional and behavioral responses observed is the physical appearance of the creature in sight.

As discussed in the first chapter, zombies evoke disgust because of their diseased look. By way of comparison, the physical features of infants elicit positive emotions, protection, and caregiving activities from others, a phenomenon known as the *baby schema effect.* The physical features of infants that activate such behaviors include a large head, a high and protruding forehead, chubby cheeks, big eyes, a small nose and mouth, and a retracted chin. Psychologists contend that the baby schema effect evolved as a means of enhancing the survival of infants—that is, caregivers, as well as strangers, responded to distressed babies with the physical features mentioned above with the greatest amount of parent-like behavior.

However, there is a dark side to the baby schema effect. Adults not only rate cherubic infants—and their prototypical baby schematic features—as more likable than their less attractive age-mates, but also as friendlier, healthier, and more adoptable. Such attitudes could be problematic for infants living in an era where both parental death and malnutrition are commonplace. One of the likely outcomes of severe malnutrition is *marasmus*—a medical condition characterized by energy loss and emaciation. As the disease robs the infant's body of subcutaneous fat and muscle, the face of the infant with marasmus becomes thin and drawn out. Relative to those that are healthy, emaciated infants have fewer physical features in line with the baby schema effect. Thus, malnourished, orphaned infants will have more difficulty finding care—and hence a higher mortality rate—than orphaned infants that are otherwise healthy.

Infanticide. On the final episode of the Korean War–based television series *M*A*S*H*, a small group of Army medical professionals is attending to refugees and wounded soldiers on a bus. To avoid detection from a nearby enemy patrol, Hawkeye Pierce instructs those around him to remain quiet. Unfortunately, there is a crying baby on board the bus. Miraculously, as the enemy patrol approaches, the baby quiets, and the patrol passes by without incident. Hawkeye looks to the mother to thank her for soothing her infant, only to discover that it had not been soothing that silenced the baby. Instead, the mother had smothered her baby to death.

Substitute the word "zombie" for "enemy patrol" and the dangers of having a baby in the vicinity of the undead become apparent. During the Zombie Apocalypse, parents' ability to keep their infants (and other children) quiet will be of the utmost importance to their lives and the lives of everyone around them. In desperation, and to safeguard those they are with, some parents will resort to filicide. However, if the parent is unwilling to muffle a crying child with finality, others may decide to do so on their own. Alternatively, to reduce the likelihood of detection, some groups may proactively banish crying infants and their parents from protected enclaves. As Spock says in *Star Trek: The Wrath of Khan*, "Logic clearly dictates that the needs of the many outweigh the needs of the few."[27] Spock's self-sacrifice is one thing; sacrificing an infant for "the greater good" is quite another. During the Zombie Apocalypse, such gut-wrenching decisions may be unavoidable.

As depicted in many tales of the Zombie Apocalypse, scavengers make their way through a house devoid of life. Upon entering the master bedroom, they come across the lifeless bodies of a family, positioned neatly and lovingly across the bed. Their arms are crossed, their eyes are closed. A bullet hole graces each, and every forehead. In the face of an imminent zombie attack, it is likely that some parents would resort to filicide—in this case, altruistic filicide. To many a parent, a quick and painless death would be far more humane than dying at the hands and teeth of the living dead. Even without an imminent zombie attack, the onset of disease and famine, in the already bleak, horrifying, and seemingly inescapable undead landscape, will result in numerous instances of altruistic filicide. Under such adverse conditions, neonaticide will also grow in frequency, as parents deem more and more newborns unwanted or excessively burdensome.

Given the frequency of, and danger posed by, infants crying, along with the stress of living in an apocalyptic environment, fatal maltreatment filicide will also occur. Many of these deaths will be the result of *shaken baby syndrome*—brain injury resulting from forcefully shaking an infant or young child. Typically, caregivers that shake babies do not have a history of abuse. Rather, the caregiver loses control over their inability to soothe a crying child and shakes the baby out of frustration and anger.

Box 4.2: *The Period of PURPLE Crying Program*

The National Center for Shaken Baby Syndrome's intervention program, the Period of PURPLE Crying, focuses on educating parents about the causes of infant crying and the consequences of shaking. As indicated by the word "period," the program emphasizes that "crying has a beginning and an end."[28]

P—Peak of Crying. Crying increases through month two, then decreases in months three through five.

U—Unexpected. Babies start and stop crying for unknown reasons.

R—Resists Soothing. Some babies have difficulty being soothed, no matter the techniques tried.

P—Pain-Like Face. Babies may look like they are in pain, even when they are not.

L—Long Lasting. Babies can cry five hours per day or more.

E—Evening. Babies cry less in the morning than in the late afternoon or early evening.

Final Thoughts

Currently, rates of maternal and infant mortality vary widely across countries. However, as the dead rise, nations previously capable of preventing and treating most health-related threats to expectant mothers and infants will no longer succeed at either task, for when the Zombie Apocalypse arrives, the undead will un-develop developed nations. Although the living dead pose a significant threat to human life, they are nevertheless, predictable. They hunt. They infect. They kill. Repeat. Zombies are not prejudiced. Zombies do not discriminate against those they would eat based on the victims' race, creed, or religion. And zombies are neither malicious, nor spiteful, nor concerned about their futures. Humans, on the other hand, are all of these things and more.

To survive the Zombie Apocalypse humanity will not only need to endure the undead, famine, and pandemics, but also each other, the latter of which will most likely prove to be the most difficult. For instance, on *The Walking Dead*, Judith Grimes is a chubby toddler, seemingly unfazed by the apocalypse around her. In contrast, the comic book version of Judith Grimes dies under the crushing weight of her mother, who accidentally falls on top of her after being shot in the back during an incursion by a rival community. Lori dies as well.[29] Similar conflicts over land, dwindling resources, and so on will occur throughout the Zombie Apocalypse. And like *The Walking Dead* comic book, those altercations will have collateral damage in the form of dead infants and children.

It will not take long for neighboring communities to go from hospitable to hostile. For example, it had been three days since Hurricane Katrina devastated New Orleans and nearby cities in 2005, and large swaths of land were still underwater. Temperatures were soaring. For the citizens of the Crescent City, both food and water were running out, or, for many, already had. There was neither plumbing nor electricity. And in the city of nearly 455,000 people, government aid was seemingly nonexistent. With no help in sight, tens of thousands of people decided to flee New Orleans and head to the surrounding communities where they hoped to find food, water, and shelter. As thousands of evacuees crossed the Crescent City Connection Bridge towards Gretna, Louisiana, the Gretna police force brought their progress to a halt with the sounds of shotgun blasts fired over their heads. The mayor of Gretna, Ronnie Harris, stated that like New Orleans, Gretna (population 17,500) was also without essential services, running low on food and water, and had limited shelter available.

Up to this point in time, the Gretna police had bussed more than 5,000 evacuees to a rescue site. But Harris feared Gretna would soon be overwhelmed with refugees from New Orleans. Having seen images on television of looting and violence taking place in the Big Easy, Harris decided to stem the tide of evacuees entering his city. According to Harris, he walled off the bridge to Gretna with lines of police to protect his community.[30] Stated differently, Harris' decision to turn away everyone, regardless of whether they were sick, elderly, pregnant, or caring for an infant, was for "the greater good."

For those living through it, Hurricane Katrina was an apocalyptic-like event. But eventually, the government stepped up and provided needed resources to the remaining residents of the hurricane-damaged Gulf Coast. However, during the Zombie Apocalypse, the Crescent City Connection Bridge incident will repeat itself over and over again across the United States, only this time, there will be no government available to offer support and pick up the pieces.

5. Why Parent?

Parenting is challenging even under the best of circumstances, and the landscape of the living dead is far from ideal—it is genuinely treacherous. The encumbering undead; the self-serving and often violent living; limited stores of food; inadequate shelter; and the inability to treat illness, disease, and injury will threaten the lives of those living through the Zombie Apocalypse on a daily basis. Unfortunately, the presence of infants and young children will make survival all the more difficult. Although infants symbolize hope for the future and can bring great joy to those around them, the reality is that they and young children use up valuable resources and provisions as well as require near constant supervision and protection. And it will be years before they can make substantive contributions to their families and communities.

Additionally, due to their physical limitations and propensity to make noise, infants and young children restrict the mobility of those around them. Even when they are sheltering in place, their cries and ear-shattering tantrums can bring the undead right to their doorsteps. With so much danger about, and the ever-present likelihood of personal injury, death, and undeath just around the corner, why would anyone ever choose to parent? To answer this question, I will discuss parenting from two different theoretical perspectives: evolutionary psychology and terror management theory. First, however, I present reasons for parenting from a parent's perspective.

Reasons for Parenting from a Parent's Perspective

Be they teenagers or older adults, individuals enter parenthood for a variety of reasons. As discussed in the previous chapter, some become parents to meet the requests or demands of intimate partners, family members, and friends. Others feel that society, as a whole, pressures them to become parents. Some even contend that children's toys reflect expectations of future parenthood. For example, each year, toy merchants in the United States sell more than $3 billion worth of dolls.[1] Brands such as Barbie, Bratz, Lalaloopsy, and Monster High offer up dollies, figurines, and action figures for a range of ages from infancy to adulthood. Of course, no doll would be complete without the appropriate accessories, including clothes, cars, schools, houses, offices, pets, and so on. Some of the most realistic dolls are those in the Baby Alive collection by Hasbro. These replica infants crawl, babble, cry, sleep, drink, and eat. Some even poop and pee (diapers sold separately). Such realism allows children to mimic parenting behavior. Play, after all, helps prepare children for later life. Finally, parents, friends, relatives, and even strangers tell children that when they grow up, they too will be a mommy or a daddy.

Still, not everyone wants to have children. Around 20 percent of American women choose a childfree life.[2] Reasons for not having children (as opposed to delaying parenthood) include concerns about the personal restrictions childrearing imposes, such as less time and money available for leisure pursuits; an overall reduction in personal freedoms; difficulties in handling the fears and worries associated with parenting; and apprehension over providing children with substandard care. Nevertheless, societal pressure to reproduce is so intense that failure to conform to it willingly results in the stigmatization of childless adults as selfish, maladjusted, and leading an unfulfilled life. Others view the childfree choice as wrong and at times respond with *moral outrage*—defined as feelings of anger, contempt, and disgust directed at individuals that commit wrongdoings against others or the "fabric of society." Whether through positive cajoling or negative backlash, the implication is clear: society expects adults to have children.

Regardless of expectations, adults have their own reasons for wanting offspring. Some choose to parent for emotional and relational reasons, viewing the parent-child relationship as a source of joy, pride, and of course love. Many view parenthood as an opportunity to nurture others and to experience personal growth. Still others are more practical, desiring children to help ensure that when they are old and frail, someone will be there to take care of them. Also, children offer parents the potential for future economic benefits (e.g., working on the family farm) and social opportunities that could result in access to material resources (e.g., a dowry). Finally, the decision to parent involves the evaluation of one's health, financial circumstances, emotional maturity, career implications, age, religious convictions, the perceived need to do so, and the presence or absence of a supportive network.

Not only does society pressure individuals to have children, but at times it also dictates the maximum number of offspring they can produce. For example, in central Brazil, because of concerns over the availability of resources, the Tapirapé, an indigenous tribe of foragers, enforce a three-child per family policy through infanticide. Similarly, for nearly 40 years, China strictly enforced a one-child policy, which required women to use an intrauterine device as contraception after successfully birthing a child. The Chinese government also mandated that women undergo an abortion when pregnant with their second child. After a couple gave birth to two children, China forced at least one parent to undergo sterilization. Starting in 2016, China modified their policy to allow for the birth of a second child.[3] As it turns out, economics was the driving force behind the change, as decades of low birth rates meant that China would soon face a shortage of people needed to replace their aging workforce as well as too few young people to care for the elderly.[4]

Thus, in addition to deciding if, when, and how to have children, parents determine the total number of offspring they would like to have in their family constellation. Whereas some parents plan their pregnancies, others leave conception to chance. Nevertheless, the reasons for having children in the first place (e.g., expectations, economics, personal growth) apply here as well. Parents will also have additional children to reach a particular family size, to have a child of a specific gender, and because of personal beliefs or religious prohibitions against contraception.

The Effect of the Zombie Apocalypse

The Zombie Apocalypse will not alter the reasons for wanting to become a parent. The desire for positive emotional experiences, the need to love and nurture, aspirations for personal growth, having a future caretaker, and so on will still be there. It is just that the reasons for not having children will be more compelling, such as the high probability of children dying, starving, and suffering immeasurably. During the Zombie Apocalypse, even non-worriers will experience intense parenting-related fears. Providing substandard care (relative to pre-apocalypse conditions) will no longer be just a possibility; it will be an inevitability.

In fact, during the first part of the apocalypse, moral outrage may accompany getting pregnant rather than choosing to be childfree. The undead will have not just torn the fabric of society, they will have ripped it to shreds. And in the tattered remains, survivors will be concerned about the unwanted attention a crying infant will bring and the uncertainty and burden of providing for its needs as well as those of its mother (see Chapter 3). Much like the Chinese government of old, and the Tapirapé, the scarcity of resources may lead communities to impose reproductive limits with harsh penalties for violators. However, as the years go by and new pockets of society form, hopes for a brighter future will be dependent upon the creation of a new generation. At that point, the likelihood of a return to pre-apocalypse notions of moral outrage related to choosing a childfree life seems likely.

Evolutionary Psychology and Parenting

Evolutionary psychology attempts to explain human behavior (e.g., altruism, aggression) and mental processes (e.g., thinking, language) as products of *natural selection—*the process by which species adapt to threats and opportunities in their environments. Those well suited for their surroundings were more likely to survive and procreate than others. Over time, genes were either selected for (passed on to the next generation) or against (not passed on). Thus, inherited characteristics, referred to as *adaptations*, solved problems related to survival and reproduction better than other traits. For example, evolutionary psychologists contend that the fear of snakes is an adaptation, as it reduces the likelihood of snakebites and potential death due to infection or venom.

Reproductive Fitness

According to the evolutionary perspective, parents parent because, more often than not, doing so leads to *reproductive fitness—*the successful transmission of their genes to the next generation. The following quote by Bjorklund and colleagues embodies this viewpoint: "children are a parent's most direct route to genetic immortality."[5] Compared to other primates, the period of immaturity and dependency is much longer in humans. It is an adaptive necessity. An extended childhood allows for the development of the brain and higher mental functions (i.e., thinking, reasoning, language, and memory), the learning of skill sets, and the acquisition of knowledge related to the sophisticated social and cultural surroundings in which children live. Motivational drives connected to reproductive fitness helped ensure that parents provided the necessary resources for children to reach maturity and reproduce, thus assuring their own genetic legacy.

Not only do parents share 50 percent of their genes with their children, but they also share 50 percent of their genes with their siblings and 25 percent of their genes with each of their nieces and nephews. Similarly, grandparents share 25 percent of their genes with their grandchildren. The term *inclusive fitness* refers to the fact that not only does a parent's fitness benefit from raising their own children, but also from safeguarding the survivability (and presumed reproductive success) of those genetically related to them.

Parental Investment

Genetic immortality comes at a cost, or, as evolutionary psychologists call it, *parental investment*—defined as any behavior that benefits an off-spring that is in some way detrimental to the parent. The price of parenting a child takes many forms, including a reduction in the ability to invest in other offspring, limited mating opportunities, and difficulties in maintaining their bodies. Moreover, the costs associated with parental investment mean that parents must choose how to allocate their limited supply of resources. Ultimately, their decision affects the timing of pregnancy (taking into consideration the costs of pregnancy now versus in the future) and the quantity of offspring. Parents can raise many children, investing minimal resources (such as food, education, dowry, inheritance, and so on) in each. Conversely, parents can rear only a few children, with each child receiving a considerable amount of investment. Because an equal distribution of resources may not be the best strategy for inclusive fitness, parents will also need to decide how to allocate their finite resources.

Parents may say they love all of their children equally, but the concept of parental investment suggests otherwise. Evolutionary psychologists contend that parents invest in the offspring that they believe will produce the greater genetic return in the future, meaning grandchildren. To accomplish this feat, parents preferentially invest in their first-born children. At any given point in time during childhood, first-borns are closer to producing an offspring than later-borns. However, other factors influence parental investment as well, such as the sex of their child, cultural influences, and environmental conditions.

Given the nature of reproduction, in which females carry the fetus to term, the number of offspring produced by females over their lifetimes is relatively low. In theory, men (whose primary contribution to reproduction is insemination) should be able to sire more children than women can birth. However, because it takes one man and one woman to create a child, across the species and on average males and females will have the same total reproductive success. Nevertheless, in environments where females outnumber males, the average male is involved in more instances of successful fertilization than the average female. In contrast, when males outnumber females, every pregnancy is a reproductive success for a female, but some males will fail to produce any progeny. Now, imagine a situation in which parents have a son and a daughter. In circumstances where males outnumber females, parental investment in their daughters will be minimal as the odds of her producing offspring are already very high. In contrast, a large population of males means a highly competitive mating environment in which any advantage could improve reproductive success. In this situation, parental investment in their sons could be the difference between reproductive success and failure and, ultimately, the parents' level of reproductive fitness.

Beyond the total number of males and females in an environment, cultural factors also result in parental investment that is sex-biased. For example, in certain stratified patriarchal societies (such as Hungarian Gypsies), in which members hierarchically rank categories of people, higher-status males have greater success at finding wives than lower-status males. This phenomenon occurs because females are more likely to marry into higher social levels, whereas males tend to marry women of equal or lower social status. Thus, in lower-status levels, parents invest more heavily in their daughters than their sons. With the goal of improving reproductive fitness, sex-biased parental investment can also affect the total number of offspring produced. For example, daughters tend to participate in the caretaking of siblings more than sons, so having a first-born girl might encourage parents to have additional children, whereas such considerations are less likely to occur when the first-born child is male.

For parental investment to occur, there must be something to invest. In times of plenty, biased parental investment frequently takes place. When resources become threatened (as happens during times of pandemics, famine, and war), however, parental investment is reduced. Similarly, when environments are dangerous, and parents cannot reliably predict which of their children have the best chance of surviving long enough to reproduce, overall investment in children wanes, as does biased investing.

Alloparenting

In the environment of evolutionary adaptedness, mothers were the primary caretakers of helpless and semi-independent children. Parenting children alone would prove to be a substantial resource burden that had the potential to extend periods between pregnancies. Because of inclusive fitness, however, other family members (such as siblings, grandparents, and cousins) could be co-opted into helping feed, care for, and protect children that were not their own. Even though human survival and reproductive success required an extended childhood, the availability of non-parental care afforded mothers the opportunity to wean their young earlier and produce offspring at shorter intervals.

Given that singleton birth (as opposed to twins or triplets) is the norm for humans, parents with multiple offspring care for children at different stages of development. More often than not, such activities stretch parental resources. However, the upside to this breeding strategy is that not only can older children take care of themselves, but they can also help care for younger siblings. Anthropologists call this form of cooperative parenting *alloparenting*. In traditional societies, such as Hadza of Tanzania, females without infants of their own (e.g., grandmothers, siblings, and cousins) typically function as alloparents. Survival of the very young is often dependent on the presence of additional caregivers. Besides performing essential childcare duties, alloparents often supplement the diets of children in their charge. In times of scarcity, such provisioning can be the difference between survival and starvation, especially if the mother of an infant dies prematurely. For example, alloparents are more likely to provide care for weaned orphaned infants than non-alloparents. Sadly, for infants still breastfeeding, alloparenting does not increase their chance of survival following maternal death.

Stepfamilies

A stepfamily forms when two adults, one of whom has a child (or children) from a previous relationship, commit to one another (through marriage or cohabitation). Evolutionary psychology contends that reproductive fitness is the motivational force behind the parenting of genetically related offspring. In contrast, the *mating effect*—defined as the effort invested in acquiring and maintaining a mate—is the rationale behind parenting stepchildren. In other words, stepparents care for non-biologically related children for the sole benefit of keeping their intimate partner relationships intact. The well-being of stepchildren is secondary to that purpose. Accordingly, stepparents should direct greater parental investment toward their biological children relative to their stepchildren.

Evolutionary psychologists refer to this reproductive-fitness-protecting biased pattern of behavior as the *Cinderella effect*, aptly named after the fairytale character. In the animated movie version of the *Cinderella*, Lady Tremaine favors her biological daughters over her stepdaughter, Cinderella, who she relegates to the role of a scullery maid, treating her with disdain and cruelty.[6] Indeed, compared to their biological children, stepparents are more likely to neglect, abuse, and kill their stepchildren. Although the likelihood of such instances is higher in step-families, the overall incidence of stepparent abuse is still relatively low. There are more loving and caring stepparents than abusive ones.

Nevertheless, relative to a biological parent, children are more likely to experience a fatal accident when in the care of a stepparent. Some psychologists interpret this fact as evidence that unconscious evolutionary drives result in less vigilant supervision of stepchildren than biological children. Cruel as it may sound, from an evolutionary perspective, the death of a stepchild frees up resources to invest in biological offspring.

Adoption

In the United States, nearly 110,000 children are adopted annually. Of those, close to 70,000 infants and children are biologically unrelated to their adoptive parents.[7] Although the adoption of genetically related individuals improves parents' inclusive fitness, the adoption of genetically unrelated children yields zero genetic return. Nevertheless, the adoption of biologically unrelated children is prevalent today. Given that the investment costs of adoption outweigh the fitness benefits, how do evolutionary psychologists explain behavior that evolution seemingly should have eradicated? Some evolutionary psychologists contend that adoption is a misguided attempt at improving genetic fitness. According to this viewpoint, modern adoption is unique over the last few millennia and rare in the environment of evolutionary adaptedness.

Evolutionary psychologists contend that humans evolved in small tribes where the likelihood of genetic relatedness between individuals was relatively high. Thus, adoption in the environment of evolutionary adaptedness would, at the very least, have a modicum of benefit for inclusive fitness. Although we no longer live in genetically tight-knit communities, evolution has set that expectation in our genes. The adoption of unrelated individuals may be a vestige of our evolutionary past.

Like stepchildren, adoptive children share no genetic relatedness with their parents. However, unlike stepchildren, adopted children do not typically experience a deficiency of parental effort. Quite the contrary. Research shows that when adopted and biological children share the same home, adopted children receive the greatest amount of parental effort. This finding contradicts the contention that parents rear children solely to increase their genetic fitness.

Evolutionary Psychology and Parenting During the Zombie Apocalypse

Whether children are born before or after the undead rise, predictions based on the tenets of evolutionary psychology remain the same. First and foremost, parenting occurs in support of a genetic legacy. However, when the dead rise, the desire to procreate will become secondary to the motivation to survive. After all, dead parents and would-be parents cannot reproduce. As the Zombie Apocalypse progresses and survivors adjust to a world in which the dead roam, the drive to further genetic immortality will supersede concerns of survival. Women will once again begin to bear children voluntarily. However, the likelihood of both biological parents surviving well into the apocalypse seems slim and, subsequently, stepfamilies will form. Because stepchildren will compete for resources with biological children, and thus place the biological parents' reproductive fitness at risk, the Cinderella effect will become more prominent.

The motivation to bear children was, is, and always will be about reproductive fitness. However, access to resources (e.g., food, water, shelter, and so on) is crucial for survival and is therefore a vital determinant of parental investment. At the start of the Zombie Apocalypse, resources will be scant, famine a legitimate possibility, and skirmishes with other survivors seeking the same booty routine. Parents will find themselves with little to invest in their children and, consequently, will make few investments in them. Sad though it may be, parents will conserve resources for a time when offspring have a better chance of survival. The silver lining in this (blood-red) cloud is that birth order, sex, and culture will no longer affect parental investment. After all, there can be no biased investing when there is nothing left to invest.

When foodstuffs become more plentiful, and returns on parental investment seem likely, evolutionary-based biases will reappear. For example, parents will once again invest in their children based on the male/female ratios in their communities. However, the return of traditional culturally influenced parental investment requires that pre-apocalyptic cultural systems remain intact after the dead roam. They may not. Every survivor will have battled the undead, suffered immeasurable loss and struggled to live. Based on these commonalities, an ethos that cuts across traditional racial, ethnic, and status lines may coalesce into a survival culture. As a result, the effects of traditional cultural biases on parental investment will cease. Instead, parents will now invest in their offspring based on their perceived compatibility with the newly minted survivor culture. Under such circumstances, the meek will not inherit the earth, as evolutionary processes are difficult to circumvent.

Before the apocalypse, alloparents were critically important to the care and well-being of children as they provided them with comfort, protection, and supplemental provisioning (especially in times of need). During the Zombie Apocalypse, alloparents will continue to offer these benefits. However, unless family members live within proximity of one another, it seems unlikely that much alloparenting will take place. Travel between locations, even just a few blocks away, will be too dangerous to occur on a regular basis.

In the comic book version of *The Walking Dead*, Dale and Andrea take care of orphaned twins Billy and Ben.[8] Likewise, on AMC's *The Walking Dead*, Carol agrees to parent Lizzie and Mika Samuels following the death of their father.[9] On the same show, Rick parents Judith, a child he did not sire. In the video game *The Walking Dead*, Lee takes care of Clementine, a young girl he met by happenstance.[10] As these examples illustrate, during the early years of the Zombie Apocalypse, families comprised of unrelated adopted children will be far more common than the traditional *nuclear family* (defined as a family consisting of two parents and their biological children). Nevertheless, the rearing of adopted children does not fit neatly into evolutionary psychology's contention that the motivation behind parenting is reproductive fitness. However, other motives for parenting exist, as I will discuss below.

Terror Management Theory and Parenting

To quote the Red Queen from *Resident Evil*, "You're all going to die down here."[11] Did Alice and the surviving commandos from Umbrella Corporation's sanitation team really need reminding of the grave situation they were in: underground and under siege by a homicidal computer program? No, but telling them about it brought thoughts of their demise to the forefront of their minds, a phenomenon social scientists refer to as *mortality salience.* To explain how people function in the face of their impending death, psychologists rely on terror management theory.

Terror management theory sounds like a how-to-guide for defeating ISIS or an organizational framework for handling a terrorist attack. It is neither of those things. Instead, the "terror" in terror management theory is the fear of dying, and "management" refers to how people cope with that fear. According to the purveyors of terror management theory, Jeff Greenberg, Sheldon Solomon, and Tom Pyszczynski, humans, like a myriad of other species, have an instinct for self-preservation. However, humans are unique in that they are also consciously aware of the inevitability of their deaths. If not adequately dealt with, this paradox can lead to feelings of hopelessness and terror. Terror management theory posits mechanisms for preventing potential feelings of dread.

When faced with thoughts of their mortality, the first thing that people do is attempt to remove death-related thoughts from their consciousness. There are several ways to achieve this. One is to minimize the seriousness of the overall threat and the gravity of their current situation. In *Shaun of the Dead*, for example, Shaun and Ed think that the best approach to surviving a zombie outbreak is to grab their loved ones and head to the local pub for a few pints of beer. Another strategy is to deny that death can happen to them.[12] Dying is what other people do. It will not happen to them and it will not happen on this day. A third way is to be unconcerned about the possibility of imminent death. In support of this belief, individuals perceive potential causes of their demise as far away in distance (e.g., a different neighborhood) or time (e.g., years from now). For example, in *Land of the Dead*, the residents of a luxury high-rise apartment complex go about their lives unworried about the undead, for armed guards, two rivers, and a fence keep the zombies at bay.[13]

With thoughts of death out of their consciousness, or at the very least no longer the focus of their attention, people can go about their business, unfettered with concerns of their mortality. However, thoughts of death are still brewing below the surface of consciousness. If not managed, such death-related thoughts can lead to feelings of unmanageable anxiety. The solution here is obvious—become immortal. And I do not mean zombiism, as zombies are not eternal. Long-lived though they may be, they will eventually be claimed by exposure to the elements (even if decay or weaponry do not).

Terror management theory proposes two types of immortality: literal and symbolic. *Literal immortality* refers to the everlasting life of the spirit, soul, or energy force, but not the body, which will eventually die. However, the afterlife allows the essence of who we are to live on forever. For example, in Max Brooks' *World War Z*, a cult known as "God's Lambs," believing that the undead signified the Rapture, quickly infected its members to ascend to heaven.[14]

The second type of immortality is *symbolic*. By adopting a *worldview*—a belief system of a culture or community that provides values, morals, standards of goodness, and so on—individuals believe that even though they will eventually die, their worldview will continue on, thus providing a figurative form of immortality. The Whisperers from *The Walking Dead* comic book offer insight into the power of symbolic immortality. The Whisperers cover themselves with the processed skin of zombies. They travel among walkers, mimicking their movements and whispering to one another to avoid detection or trigger an undead feeding frenzy. Beyond these unique cultural components, the Whisperers live like pack animals, complete with an alpha leader. They are brutal to their enemies and each other, believing that only the strongest should survive. Their members are entirely committed to this worldview, striking down anyone that crosses their path.[15] Symbolic immortality can also occur by leaving one's mark on the world. We see this repeatedly on *The Walking Dead*, as indicated by the creation of communities such as the Hilltop, Alexandria, and the Kingdom. Each has been fashioned with the hope of re-establishing civilization, leaving a better world for those that follow.

In terror management theory, parenthood functions as a type of symbolic immortality. First, by passing on their genes to future generations, biological parents see themselves living on, symbolically. With any luck, their progeny will do the same. Terror managed. Second, and regardless of the genetic relationship with their children, parents also achieve symbolic immortality by enculturating children with their valued belief systems. When children carry forth their parents' worldviews (e.g., religion, philosophy of life), symbolically they take their parents with them. Also, the indoctrination of parental belief systems increases the parents' self-esteem. According to terror management theory, *self-esteem* occurs when individuals view themselves as valuable contributors to their championed worldviews. Terror managed yet again.

Detractors of evolutionary psychology point out that there is little evidence in the paleontological and archeological records about the mating and child-rearing practices of hunter-gatherer societies during the

Stone Age. They also contend that modern-day hunter-gatherers live in environments very different from those in the Pleistocene epoch, during which time the habitat provided far better hunting grounds.[16] Other scientists point out explanations for parenting behavior that has nothing to do with evolutionary adaptations. Take, for example, the Cinderella effect, which according to evolutionary psychology occurs in support of reproductive fitness. However, terror management theory can explain this effect as well, and without focusing on evolutionary processes.

Terror management theory posits that individuals will protect their worldviews when threatened, using deadly force if deemed necessary. Thus, if a parent perceives their stepchild as a threat to their worldview or an impediment to their literal and symbolic immortality, abusive behavior may follow. Moreover, the lack of genetic relatedness between parent and child allows parents to view their stepchildren as members of an *out-group* (i.e., a social group that one does not identify with). Stepparents could use differences in physical features, religions, ethnicities, or other things to validate this perception. In contrast, parents will view their biological children as members of their *in-group* (i.e., a social group that one identifies with)—in this case, kin. Aggressive defense of worldviews occurs more frequently against out-group members compared to in-group members. As a result, parents will treat their biological children better than their stepchildren.

In contrast to the evolutionary perspective, which predicts a Cinderella effect for adoptive children, terror management theory contends that by indoctrinating adoptive children into the parent's worldview, the parent's symbolic immortality and self-esteem will improve. Terror managed, and the likelihood of abuse assuaged.

Terror Management Theory and the Zombie Apocalypse

Nothing makes mortality salient like a Zombie Apocalypse, where people are literally staring death in the face. Therefore, mechanisms for banishing thoughts to the unconscious will be crucial for parents' survival and their ability to protect their children. With zombies on the attack, or marauders, for that matter, hesitation, even for a second, can be the difference between life, death, and undeath. Parents focusing on their own demise will hesitate, placing themselves, and their children, at risk. Under such circumstances, thoughts of mortality can quickly become a reality. Conversely, banishing thoughts of death from consciousness, rather than focusing on them, increases risk-taking behaviors. During the Zombie

Apocalypse, taking risks will be a necessity for incursions, defensive actions, scavenging, and foraging for food. When the dead rise, there will be no reward without risk.

As the prospect of imminent death subsides, but threats to mortality remain (after all, there are zombies about), the desire to have children will increase. Nevertheless, in the destruction wrought by the dead, new families will form, and children will fall under the protection of adults who may, or may not, be genetically related to them. This fact poses no problem for terror management theory, for unlike evolutionary psychology and its focus on genetic immortality, terror management theory's motivation for parenting is symbolic immortality, which the generational transmission of cultural beliefs accomplishes nicely.

Nevertheless, being in a stepfamily increases the risk of abusive parenting, although it far from guarantees it. There is no reason to believe that the risk of abuse by stepparents will be any different during the Zombie Apocalypse. If anything, stepparenting abuse will increase. According to terror management theory, mortality salience increases the likelihood of aggressive behavior. As already pointed out, the Zombie Apocalypse is a potent reminder of death.

Terror management theory makes it clear that humans need to be part of something bigger than themselves. Over time, communities will be reconstituted or begun anew, each with its own unique worldview. Some of these worldviews will be like Alexandria or the Kingdom, where a better life comes through cooperation, hard work, trade, and agriculture. Some of these cultural beliefs will be quite harsh, as is the case with the Whisperers, whose members value strength above all else. Although wearing zombie skin makes the existence of the Whisperers seem far-fetched, the mentality of the group is not. For example, in a shantytown located in northeast Brazil, poverty is crushing, and child mortality is high. But so are birth rates. This combination of factors has lead members of this community to view the death of children as likely and ordinary. Moreover, relative to healthy infants, community members treat infants deemed weak with less compassion and care. In a world where infants die often, such emotional detachments presumably make the death of a child easier to handle.

Final Thoughts

There are four main ways to become a parent during the Zombie Apocalypse. First, there are those that will begin the apocalypse with children already in tow. As society falls, and chaos ensues, many of these parents will die trying to protect their children. Some families will endure forced breakups, as torrents of people, hordes of zombies, or governmental regulations separate parents from their children. Such experiences will lead to the second way of becoming a parent, taking over the role of sole caregiver from family, friends, or even strangers. Others will become parents because their intimate partner was already rearing children. The final type of parents are those that give birth after the start of the apocalypse or conceive children in the midst of it. However, not all conceptions during the Zombie Apocalypse will be the result of consensual sexual relations.

When it comes to *sexual violence*—sexual activity without freely given consent—the historical record is clear. In war-torn regions of the world, the rape of women and girls resulting in pregnancy is prevalent. In 2016, there were 80,000 teen pregnancies in Guatemala (2,500 of which involved 10- to 14-year-old girls). Rape caused the majority of these pregnancies.[17] For years, Boko Harem militants have invaded villages, abducted women and girls, and submitted them to forced "marriages" and repeated sexual violence, the ultimate goal of which was to impregnate their victims.[18] During the Rwanda Genocide of 1994, assailants raped close to 250,000 women, resulting in an estimated 20,000 children.[19]

In armed conflicts between ethnic groups, rape-conceived pregnancy is the weapon of choice, especially where paternity determines ethnic group membership. For instance, during the Bosnian War (1992–1995), Serbs systematically and repeatedly raped tens of thousands of Muslim and Croatian women for the primary purpose of *genocide*[20]—defined as acts committed against another group (based on ethnicity, religion, or the like) with the intent of completely eradicating it. When used as a military tactic, rape-conceived pregnancy (1) subjugates, humiliates, and shames its victims; (2) creates terror in would-be victims; (3) generates dissent in communities, as victims of rape and their children are ostracized by those around them, including family and friends; and (4) can result in ethnic genocide, as community and family members view infants born of rape as having their fathers' ethnicity, and not their mothers'.

Rape-conceived pregnancies also occur in countries not currently mired in civil war or armed conflict. In the United States, more than 32,000 children are rape-conceived annually, one-third of which are birthed.[21] However, in contrast to war-related rape (in which the victim and perpetrator rarely know one another), acquaintances, family members, and current or former partners perpetrate seven out of 10 rapes in the United States.

For sexual violence involving juveniles, perpetrators know their victims 93 percent of the time.[22]

Although there is no definitive profile of a rapist, there two constellations of factors associated with the perpetration of sexual violence. The first grouping consists of *unhealthy sexual behaviors, experiences, or attitudes*. Risk factors include multiple sexual partners, early initiation of sex, impersonal sex, sexually aggressive peers, peer pressure to have sex, and victimization during childhood. The second constellation focuses on *the presence and acceptance of violence*. Here, the risk factors associated with perpetrating sexual violence include previously engaging in sexual violence, having sexually violent acquaintances, and knowing people that support sexually violent activities. However, this grouping also includes risks associated with violence in general, such as gang membership, positive attitudes toward the use violence, a history of delinquency, and *hypermasculinity*—which is characterized by a callousness toward women and the belief that violence and dominance are manly.

Parenting Rape-Conceived Children

Some mothers bearing rape-conceived children commit infanticide. Such was the case during World War II following the rape of thousands of Chinese women in Nanking by Japanese soldiers. In virtually all armed conflicts where military tactics involve rape, reports of infanticide follow. For others, the inaccessibility of safe abortion and religious/moral beliefs that preclude abortion as well as pregnancy outcome control measures initiated by family members result in women bringing their rape-conceived children to term. In armed conflicts involving ethnic genocide, militants will even hold women captive until abortion is no longer a viable option. During the Bosnian War, the Serbs did just that.

Women who raise war-related rape-conceived children often find themselves living in near isolation, in impoverished conditions, traumatized by their ordeal, and treated as pariahs in their communities. For example, young women impregnated by Boko Haram militants are subject to harassment and beatings upon returning home, as the local population views them as being under the influence of their former captors.[23] Others see women braving rape-conception as having their honor tarnished, which in turn dishonors the culture. In such communities, giving birth to a rape-conceived child is an act worthy of public and private rebuke. Traumatized through rape, devastated by their treatment from family and community members, women bearing raped-conceived children are at risk for a host of physical ailments (e.g., HIV, chronic pelvic pain) and psychological disorders (e.g., anxiety, major depression, posttraumatic stress disorder).

Women rearing children conceived by rape often act ambivalently toward them. To the mother, the face of her rape-conceived child is a constant reminder of the trauma she previously endured as well as a harbinger of the cruel treatment by family and friends that she will continue to face. As a result, many mothers find it challenging to establish loving bonds with their rape-conceived children, thus adversely impairing the parent-child relationship.

At the hands of their mothers, rape-conceived children undergo neglect, abuse, and unpredictable behavior (which can be frightening at times). Similarly, community members discriminate against and stigmatize rape-conceived children. Children born of rape become secondary victims of their mothers' trauma. As Andrew Solomon states, "To the mother, he is an incarnation of the rape; to the world, he is the rapist's heir."[24] Despite their pain and torment, many victims of rape will eventually see beauty in their children's eyes. For some mothers, it will take years to reach that point. For others, however, that point will be unobtainable, and the eyes of their children will remain the eyes of their rapists.

Sexual-Violence in the Zombie Apocalypse

The Zombie Apocalypse will make the entire world an active war zone. Battles will rage against the undead and the living. Whereas the undead pose no threat for sexual violence, one cannot say the same for the human combatants. Skirmishes between communities based on ethnic, religious, or other group memberships inevitably will occur. In areas of the world with a history of using rape-conceived pregnancy as a military tactic, there is no reason to believe that the advent of the walking dead will alter its use. If anything, the Zombie Apocalypse will present an opportunity to complete objectives started hundreds or even thousands of years ago.

Surviving the Zombie Apocalypse requires that individuals engage in copious amounts of violence, both toward the living and the dead. Violence will become a way of life, its use accepted and expected. This gladiator-like mentality will emphasize the importance of violence and dominance to survival. The combination of hyper-masculinity, pro-violent attitudes and behaviors, and a history of violent actions will increase the likelihood that men will become perpetrators of sexual violence—a mentality that will last long after humanity has scoured the planet of the zombie menace.

For both evolutionary psychology and terror management theory, explanations for the parenting of children conceived by sexual violence are the same as those used to explain the parenting of children conceived without it. The former focuses on reproductive fitness, whereas the latter emphasizes literal and symbolic immortality. However, neither theory captures the trauma experienced by the victims of rape, nor the pain and suffering resulting from it, for both mother and child.

SECTION THREE: THE DETERMINANTS OF PARENTING

6. Characteristics of the Parent

On *The Walking Dead*, preteen Lizzie Samuels is in a bit of a predicament. You see, Lizzie's father has just died from a walker bite, and the task of preventing his reanimation is hers. However, Lizzie is unable to kill her father. In her stead, another member of the community, Carol, "quiets" him. Later, after finding Lizzie and her sister Mika along a fence line, Carol gently points out to Lizzie that they need to talk about her inability to insert a shiv into her father's brain. Carol warmly tells Lizzie that she is weak and that the difference between life and death in a world full of zombies is acting fast and trusting your gut.[1] Tough love for Lizzie.

In contrast, Rick's reaction to finding out that his wife has died during childbirth is far from parental. As young Carl (whom, unbeknownst to Rick, has just shot his mother in the head to prevent reanimation) stoically stands in from of him, holding back both tears and the slightest hint of emotion, Rick starts to sob. He neither physically comforts his son nor provides words of consolation to a boy desperately in need of both. Instead, Rick picks up an ax and heads toward the dead to take vengeance upon them. No love for Carl. As these vignettes illustrate, Rick and Carol approach the parenting of grieving children very differently. The question is "Why?" The answer lies in the determinants of parenting.

According to Jay Belsky's *process model of parenting*, three primary factors influence parenting behavior: parent characteristics (e.g., personality, religious beliefs), child characteristics (e.g., temperament, developmental status), and contextual sources of stress and support (e.g., social settings, interpersonal relationships). By understanding these determinants, and the factors that influence them, the effects of the Zombie Apocalypse on parenting becomes more evident. In this chapter, I focus solely on parent characteristics. In subsequent chapters, I address the remaining determinants of parenting.

Parent Characteristics

Parenting stress occurs when the perceived demands of caring for children overwhelm a parent's available psychological, emotional, and physical resources. In most instances, parenting stress adversely affects childrearing, which then leads to unfavorable outcomes for children, such as emotional and behavioral problems. The process model of parenting provides a framework for understanding the many and varied determinants of parenting and the resultant parenting stress experienced. Characteristics of the parent that influence parenting stress and child-rearing include personality, psychological functioning, and the parent's upbringing. I discuss each below.

Personality

Personality—an individual's characteristic pattern of thinking, feeling, and acting—is one of several factors that differentiate one person from another. When faced with the same circumstance, say, an approaching zombie or two, personality affects how an individual will respond. For example, whereas those with fearless and bold personalities will likely run toward the undead menace, individuals low in these characteristics will undoubtedly run away from them. Likewise, for personalities that require the constant approval of others, the prospects of living in a world without Twitter and Instagram "likes" may be more frightening than living with the living dead. In contrast, less self-centered individuals may look forward to the challenge of a technology-free life.

It is not that personality dictates that a person always acts the same in every situation; it is just that some behaviors, thought patterns, and so on, occur more frequently than others. Nevertheless, the circumstances people find themselves in do affect the way they act, think, and feel. For instance, in a small gathering of friends, a person may be gregarious, but while attending a large house party, that same person may act more reserved. Such *behavioral signatures*—differing patterns of behavior that are context dependent—lead people to behave consistently in similar situations (small vs. large gatherings) even though their actions may transform (e.g., outgoing vs. reserved) as the circumstances they find themselves in change.

Psychologists contend that a constellation of different behavioral signatures comprise personality.

Although behavioral signatures may be beneficial under one set of circumstances, they may be equally harmful in others. Take, for example, Carl Grimes, who in *The Walking Dead* comics responds to personal threat with unabashed fierceness and brutality. When one is attacked by the living dead, a behavioral signature of violence without restraint can be advantageous. After all, destroying a zombie by bashing in its head is not overkill. It is a necessity. In contrast, when one is attacked by the living, violence without constraint can be disastrous. As an example, Carl's violent tenacity almost lead to the death of two teenage boys who had attacked him and a friend. Although Carl was in the right to defend himself, he continued to pummel his attackers with a shovel long after they lost their ability to fight back.[2]

THE BIG 5 PERSONALITY TRAITS. *Traits* refer to predispositions that influence behavior across a variety of contexts. Psychological research indicates that five traits account for the majority of variations in personality. Those traits are openness, conscientiousness, agreeableness, extraversion, and emotional instability (also known as neuroticism). Collectively, psychologists refer to these traits as *the Big 5*. Below, I discuss each of the Big 5 traits in the context of parenting during the Zombie Apocalypse.

Openness. The first of the Big 5 traits, *openness*, centers on an individual's creativity, curiosity, and flexibility of thought. Parents low in openness are unimaginative, pragmatic and close-minded, and they enjoy routine. On the other hand, those high on this trait are curious about the world, enjoy new experiences, and relish intellectual endeavors. Although parents high in openness tend to be creative and imaginative, too much openness can result in parents over-focusing on providing their children with novel experiences without sensitivity to the children's current needs or desires.

During the Zombie Apocalypse, the ability to adapt to rapidly changing circumstances means that parents high in openness will have an easier adjustment to the new world order than those low on this trait. Without the traditional creature comforts, resources, and protections of the pre-apocalyptic world, creativity will be an asset, and most likely a requirement, for the adequate care of children.

Conscientiousness. Conscientiousness, the second of the Big 5 traits, is the degree to which a person can control impulses that impede the successful completion of goals or tasks. Characterized as irresponsible and disorganized, parents low in conscientiousness act without thinking or considering the ramifications of their behaviors. In contrast, highly conscientious parents are careful, focused, reliable, organized, and capable of keeping their impulses in check. Additionally, parents high in conscientiousness provide their children with orderly and structured environments devoid of chaos. However, too much conscientiousness can result in over-controlling, intrusive behavior.

When the dead rise, conscientiousness will be the difference between life and death for both parents and their progeny. Carelessness, irresponsibility, and disorganization will end up placing families in situations they are not prepared for and cannot handle. And for many youth, having an over-controlling intrusive parent will keep them out of harm's way, at least for a short while, thus improving their overall chances of survival.

Agreeableness. The next trait, *agreeableness*, addresses an individual's ability to maintain positive social relationships through generosity, warmth, and cooperativeness. Whereas parents low in agreeableness are insensitive, critical, untrusting, and uncooperative, parents high in agreeableness are good-natured, helpful, forgiving, and empathetic. Moreover, parents high in agreeableness respond appropriately to the emotional vicissitudes of their children and display considerable amounts of warmth when interacting with them.

Being surrounded by death and the undead and experiencing the destruction of the only world they have ever known will challenge the emotional well-being of youth. Whereas parents high in agreeableness will be able to help their children cope with the dystopian world they now face, those low on this trait will find comforting their children difficult. However, in an untrusting and violent world, the characteristics of being critical, untrusting, and uncooperative may provide a survival advantage for parents low on agreeableness.

Extraversion. The fourth trait, *extraversion*, refers to how sociable, assertive, and emotionally expressive a person is. Extraverted parents are outgoing, talkative, and affectionate. In contrast, parents low on extraversion are withdrawn, quiet, and reserved. Relative to their less extraverted counterparts, parents high in extraversion are loving, optimistic, energetic, and stimulating. Nevertheless, parents extremely high on this trait can at times become *power assertive* (i.e., imposing their will through punishments) when interacting with their children.

Although psychologists consider power assertion a negative parenting characteristic, surviving an invasion of the walking dead may necessitate parenting behavior such as this. Children and adolescents may not always appreciate the danger they find themselves in and therefore require parental monitoring and correction to assure their safety.

Emotional Instability. The final of the Big 5 traits, *emotional instability*, focuses on an individual's emotional lability and reactivity. Whereas parents low in this trait are even-tempered and relaxed, parents high in emotional instability are easily distressed, moody, anxious, self-pitying and emotionally unpredictable. Parents high in emotional instability manage their children (whether they are infants or adolescents) in an intrusive, insensitive, harsh, and unresponsive manner. Moreover, highly neurotic parents attempt to control their children's activities through power assertion.

As previously mentioned, during the Zombie Apocalypse, power assertion may at times benefit a child's survival. However, emotional volatility will not only adversely affect a parent's ability to cope with her current predicament, but it will make it more difficult for them to meet their children's emotional needs effectively, or their survival needs, for that matter.

PERSONALITY CHANGE. Although personality is relatively stable over time, it can change. Case in point: on *The Walking Dead*, Morgan first encounters Rick after his son, Duane, mistakes Rick for a walker and hits him on the head with a shovel. Conscientiously, Morgan cares for the unconscious Rick but cautiously ties him to a pair of bedposts until he can be sure that the undead have not bitten him. Rick recovers and heads off to find his family, parting with Morgan and Duane on good terms.[3] The next time Morgan and Rick meet, Morgan tries very, very hard to kill Rick. Mind you, this was not a personal vendetta. The death of Duane at the hands of his undead wife had left Morgan a broken man. At this point in his life, Morgan was trying to destroy everything, alive or undead. Once again, the two men part ways.[4] Later, Rick and Morgan meet up in a different community.[5] Far from being murderous, this incarnation of Morgan will only destroy the dead, refusing to kill the living, no matter the circumstances. Morgan then moves in with a separate group of survivors where he forges a parent-like relationship with Benjamin, a teenage boy he is instructing in the martial arts. Following the boy's murder, Morgan's belief regarding the sanctity of human life changes. He will once again slay the living just as readily as the dead.[6]

Stressful Life Events and Personality Change. The ebb and flow of Morgan's use of violence illustrate the fact that *stressful life events*—adverse experiences occurring during one's lifetime—can lead to significant changes in personality. In addition to catastrophic events such as famine and war, stressful life events include common life transitions (e.g., moving out of the family home), meaningful life changes (e.g., becoming a parent), intense emotional experiences (e.g., loss of a parent; end of a relationship), and threats to health and well-being (e.g., being diagnosed with cancer). Regardless of the specific causes, one thing is clear: extreme events generate changes in personality. For instance, a break-up with an intimate partner increases emotional instability, the death of a spouse reduces openness, and getting a job for the first time improves conscientiousness. Although positive events have the potential to influence personality, when a change occurs, more often than not the precipitating event is aversive. Nowhere is this more evident than in the relationship between trauma and emotional instability. When an individual experiences the loss of a loved one, survives a life-threatening illness or accident, is assaulted (be it physical or sexual), or witnesses the victimization or death of another, neuroticism increases.

It terms of supporting a child's psychological well-being, the ideal personality for parenting is high in openness, agreeableness, extraversion, and conscientiousness and low in emotional instability. Additionally, the continued effectiveness of parenting relies in part on a parent's ability to maintain an advantageous personality profile (or one close to it). However, as just mentioned, stress can modify personality, resulting in the reduction of characteristics beneficial to parenting and an increase in those detrimental to it. Thus, as long as parents live in low-stress environments, all is well. However, as stress ramps up emotional instability will increase, while openness, conscientiousness, and agreeableness will all decrease. It goes without saying that when the dead rise so will stress. The Zombie Apocalypse will bring with it not one, not two, but all of the adverse stressful life events mentioned above.

It seems as though living in an apocalyptic environment filled with the dead will adversely affect all parents. As it turns out, that may not be the case. In and of themselves, traumatic and stressful life events do not always lead to changes in personality. More important than the nature of the stressor is how the individual perceives it. Some interpret adversity as something to endure. Others view adversity as an opportunity for personal growth. Whereas positive attributions benefit personality, negative ones are detrimental to it. For example, when parents interpret stressful events to mean that their family life is getting worse (regardless of its veracity), emotional instability increases and extraversion decreases.

As the old saying goes, when life gives you lemons, make lemonade.

But what are parents to do when life gives them zombies? Perhaps through religious, cultural, and personal values, parents will be able to find meaning in the desolate world they now face. Terror management theory predicts this to be a distinct possibility (see Chapter 5). For those that see beauty beyond the pain, and hope in the face of adversity, positive personality transformations may occur, such as increases in openness, agreeableness, and conscientiousness. In turn, such changes would benefit parenting, resulting in warmer, more structured, and flexible caregivers. Nonetheless, most parents will likely interpret the death, destruction, and cruelty of the Zombie Apocalypse negatively, resulting in emotional instability and difficulties in raising their children.

Physical Causes of Personality Change. Along with environmental stressors, traumatic brain injuries can affect personality, and typically, the observed changes are not for the better. During the mid–1800s, the scientific world became acutely aware that the brain housed personality when Phineas Gage had an unfortunate accident while clearing rocks to make way for a new rail line. An errant spark caused a hollow packed with explosives to detonate prematurely, rocketing an iron rod out of it. The upward trajectory of the rod tore holes through Gage's left cheek, eye socket, and left frontal lobe before exiting via the top of his skull. Gage's personality, characterized as even-tempered before the accident, underwent a dramatic modification. He became indulgent, uninhibited, and "profane" in social situations.[7]

Gage's unfortunate accident shows the adverse effects of traumatic brain injuries involving the destruction of brain tissue on personality. However, brain tissue does not need to be obliterated in an instant for personality to change. A *concussion*, in which the brain bounces around or twists within the skull, can cause short-term changes in personality. Following a concussion, many individuals suffer from *post-concussion syndrome*. Lasting weeks, months, or even longer, symptoms include cognitive impairments in memory, concentration, and thought. Patients may also experience depressed mood, irritability, and anxiety.

Although a complete recovery from a single concussion is probable, repeated concussions can lead to long-term and often devastating alterations in personality. *Chronic traumatic encephalopathy*—a progressive neurodegenerative disease caused by concussive trauma—results in marked increases in aggressiveness, depression, impulsivity, irritability, and suicidal behavior.[8] Eventually, chronic traumatic encephalopathy leads to *dementia*, whereby individuals undergo a cognitive decline so severe that it dramatically interferes with their ability to function from day to day, rendering them unable to care for themselves.

Since 2000, more than 383,000 members of the United States Armed Forces have sustained traumatic brain injuries ranging from mild concussions to penetrating shrapnel wounds. Recreational activities gone awry, accidents during military training exercises, and bodily damage suffered in active combat caused the majority of the aforementioned head traumas.[9] During military engagements, blast exposure is the predominant cause of traumatic brain injuries. Outside of military service, 153 civilians die from complications associated with traumatic brain injuries every day. That number translates to nearly 56,000 deaths per year. Accidental falls are the primary cause of traumatic brain injuries in civilian populations, accounting for roughly half of all visits to the emergency room involving head trauma.[10]

During the Zombie Apocalypse, the lack of medical care will make surviving a penetrating brain injury nearly impossible. On the bright side, the destruction of brain tissue accompanying such injuries should prevent zombification. Traumatic brain injuries rendering a person unconscious or severely dazed will often prove deadly, as surviving such an incident will require others to protect the disoriented and unconscious from the undead.

Mild concussions associated with battling the living and the dead, not to mention accidental falls resulting from living in a world of destruction, will be commonplace. Although developing chronic traumatic encephalopathy will still be possible, the likelihood of repeatedly surviving an encounter with a zombie after experiencing a head injury seems low. Zombies will eat the injured or turn them into fellow members of the living dead, long before chronic traumatic encephalopathy can develop.

Given that virtually all survivors of the Zombie Apocalypse will participate in combat, parents will also undergo their share of traumatic brain injuries. As a result, those with head trauma may experience short-term personality changes that adversely affect their caregiving. That is, they will begin to parent in a manner consistent with individuals high in emotional instability and low in agreeableness and conscientiousness.

Psychological Functioning

Psychological functioning refers to a person's overall sense of well-being and ability to accomplish daily tasks and long-term goals. Psychological functioning can be positive or negative, with the former referring to effective thought processes, positive self-attributes, and healthy social interactions, while emotional and behavioral problems characterize the latter. Below, I review several aspects psychological functioning critical to parenting during the Zombie Apocalypse, including the presence of the mental illness, the ability to regulate thoughts, emotions and behaviors, and the parent's generalized beliefs about the world.

PARENTING WITH MENTAL ILLNESS. In the United States, close to 44 million adults have a mental illness.[11] Worldwide that number jumps to 1.1 billion.[12] Currently, mental health professionals recognize hundreds of different psychological disorders. Here, I briefly introduce anxiety disorders, major depression, and post-traumatic stress disorder (PTSD) as they will frequent the Zombie Apocalypse, affecting both parents and non-parents alike.

Anxiety Disorders. As a healthy response to stress, whether it is going on a first date, starting a new job, or walking down a darkened alley, virtually all of us experience some level of *anxiety*—the unpleasant feeling and vague sense of unease that something terrible could happen. Although some anxiety can be energizing, at extremely high levels it can become immobilizing. In such situations, anxiety can prevent people from leaving their homes, interacting with others, or venturing into unknown places. For individuals with anxiety disorders, settings and conditions cause feelings of anxiety that are far out of proportion to the actual danger present. For example, whereas many people are anxious around live snakes, those with *ophidiophobia*—an anxiety disorder characterized by an intense, irrational fear of snakes—may hyperventilate and panic when viewing a picture of a snake (let alone a live one). Finally, for some, anxiety is everpresent, even in the absence of any specific danger or perceived threat.

Chronically anxious parents feel on edge most of the time. They find it hard to concentrate or make decisions due to concerns that something terrible is going to happen, even if they have no idea what that "something" is. Anxious parents can also suffer from *panic attacks*, during which they experience feelings of inescapable doom. During a panic attack, anxiety skyrockets to an intolerable level, causing cold sweats, dizziness, elevated heart rate, and difficulty breathing. Most panic attacks last between 15 to 30 minutes and occur in response to a specific situation, such as a zombie attack. At other times, the panic attack just happens, and there is no particular instigator.

The conversations anxious parents have with, and around, their children frequently focus on their own or their children's anxieties. Also, anxious parents try to inhibit their children from engaging in developmentally appropriate activities that seem "risky," such as climbing trees or jumping onto boulders. More so than other parents, anxious parents also attempt to shield their children from potentially anxiety-provoking circumstances. Parental anxiety related to protecting children from physical pain or disappointment is the hallmark of *helicopter parenting*. Considered over-controlling, over-protective, and over-perfecting, helicopter parents over-focus on their children, believing that as parents, they are principally responsible for their children's successes and failures. In addition to "protecting" children from general feelings of anxiety, helicopter parents believe that without their intervention some form of dire circumstance will likely befall their children. They think that parental vigilance is always required.

Post-Traumatic Stress Disorder. PTSD develops in response to a terrifying, life-threatening event, such as a natural disaster (e.g., flood, fire, or Zombie Apocalypse), armed conflict, physical attack, sexual assault, or severe accident. At times, the experience of being in a trauma causes the disorder, while at other times merely witnessing one is enough to develop PTSD. Given the nature of their jobs, police officers, soldiers, firefighters, rescue workers, and medical personnel experience PTSD at rates higher than the general population.

The symptoms of PTSD include reoccurring memories of the trauma, frightening dreams, and *flashbacks*, during which the affected person relives the traumatic event, including the emotional states that it caused (e.g., fear, shock, horror). Reminders of the trauma are especially likely to activate a flashback, and those with the disorder actively avoid them. Individuals with PTSD often experience an emotional numbness toward life and feel alienated from others. Angry outbursts, hypervigilance, and irritability punctuate their interpersonal interactions. At night, those with PTSD have difficulty sleeping, and during the day they experience problems in concentration. Although anyone can develop PTSD, the likelihood of developing it is higher for individuals with a history of trauma.

Parenting with PTSD is difficult. The emotional numbness directed at others includes those in the care of people suffering from PTSD. Compared to other parents, those with PTSD are more neglecting and more psychologically and physically aggressive towards their children. Moreover, parents with PTSD report great distress and dissatisfaction in their role as parents, often viewing their children negatively.

Major Depression. Major depression refers to intense and unrealistic sadness, accompanied by feelings of worthlessness. Additional symptoms of this disorder include decreased energy, loss of interest in daily routines, bouts of crying, and pessimism. Furthermore, some individuals with major depression experience *suicidal ideation* (i.e., thinking about or planning suicide) or attempt suicide. For some, the symptoms of major depression are manageable, and they can continue their daily routines, including their jobs. For others, however, the symptoms of major depression are severe enough to impede their ability to function at work and home, and at times lead to hospitalization.

The causes of major depression are many and varied. Biological susceptibilities, non-traumatic events, and daily hassles, along with negative or traumatic social and cultural experiences, can jointly, or independently, cause depression. Although major depression tends to run in families (suggesting an inherited biological vulnerability) it frequently occurs in people with no family history of psychopathology.

Major depression adversely affects a parent's ability to handle parenting stress, often disrupting the parent-child relationship. For instance, depressed mothers tend to interact with their children in a hostile and rejecting manner. As depression sets in, many parents become less available to their children, and the interactions they do have are often devoid of positive emotions. Overall, depressed parents are ineffective at parenting, engaging in more negative exchanges than positive ones.

Mental Illness in the Zombie Apocalypse. The Zombie Apocalypse is replete with risk factors for mental illness, including death, violence, impoverished conditions, emotional duress, and abuse (to name a few). Thus, for the majority of parents, the rise of the dead, the fall of society, and the wanton death and destruction that accompany both will lead to increased levels of anxiety, depression, and PTSD. Because of apocalyptic-related depression, parents who were previously warm and affectionate will now increasingly become hostile and rejecting. For anxious parents, the Zombie Apocalypse means that it will be nearly impossible to shield children from the horrors of the world. Helicopter parenting will become the norm. After all, the likelihood of something dire happening to children when out of parental sight (or in it, for that matter) will rise steeply. For parents of the apocalypse, PTSD will be hard to escape. There will be just too much trauma (both witnessed and experienced) to avoid, and, as a result, parenting will suffer, becoming more numb, punitive, neglectful, and aggressive.

SELF-REGULATION. *Self-regulation* refers to the degree to which a person can regulate their attentional focus (e.g., ignoring distractors and staying on task), behaviors (e.g., inhibiting impulses), and emotions (e.g., remaining calm in the face of strong feelings). Not surprisingly, parents with greater self-regulatory abilities govern their children more effectively than those low in these qualities. For example, parents low in self-regulation have difficulty planning, organizing, and completing parenting-related tasks. Also, they tend to respond negatively and harshly to the misbehavior of their children.

Conversely, parents high in self-regulation have excellent impulse control, participate in lengthy bouts of caregiving/supervising activities, respond more positively to their children's negative emotions, and implement discipline consistently. Additionally, parents high in self-regulation require children to do chores and other less-than-enjoyable activities, even if the result of their demands induces a negative emotional state in their children. Such parents play the endgame, realizing that in the long run, more harmonious and cooperative interactions will follow.

Exposure to stress adversely affects parents' ability to manage their own attentional focus, behavior, and emotional states. In turn, these self-regulatory difficulties reduce the effectiveness of their parenting. The challenges of the Zombie Apocalypse, such as fending off the dead, foraging for food, calming distressed children, and preventing harm from befalling those in their care, will likely overwhelm parents' abilities to self-regulate. As a result, the aforementioned problematic parenting behaviors related to low self-regulation will occur more frequently.

SOCIAL AXIOMS. *Social axioms* are basic premises and generalized expectations about the world. Examples of social axioms include believing that powerful people tend to exploit others; that failure is the beginning of success; and that faith in the Almighty helps people understand the meaning of life. These examples reflect three universal social axioms that affect parents on a daily basis: social cynicism, reward for application, and spirituality.

Social Cynicism. *Social cynicism* refers to the general mistrust of people, a pessimistic view of human nature, and the belief that exploitation occurs frequently. Social cynics put themselves and their self-interests first. They are concerned about being victimized and remain vigilant when around others. Social cynicism is prevalent in dangerous environments, as the dog-eat-dog (or zombie-eat-human) nature of the world requires it. To the social cynic, you are either the windshield or the bug.

Although social cynicism may promote survival, it is detrimental to the parent-child relationship, as anxiety and anger are residual effects of its presence. Furthermore, parents high in social cynicism attempt to influence their children through intrusive and overly assertive means. Given that social cynicism increases in response to unfavorable conditions, the Zombie Apocalypse, and the associated horrors perpetrated by the living and the dead, will lead to a dramatic rise of individuals high on this axiom. Nevertheless, the survival advantage associated with social cynicism may outweigh the adverse effects it has on parenting.

Reward for Application. Opposite this viewpoint is the *reward for application*, a belief that good things follow planning, hard work, and becoming well informed about the challenges ahead. Adults high in this characteristic approach parenting in the same manner that they would approach defending a house from a zombie horde, with foresight, research, and a belief that hard work can accomplish anything. In effect, such parents view their children's problems as solvable problems. Indeed, parents high in the reward for application caring for children with HIV provide better care for their chronically ill children than other parents.

The reward for application axiom is similar to the psychological concept known as *locus of control*, defined as the degree to which one believes that they control their personal outcomes. Note the primary difference between these two constructs is that the reward for application social axiom refers to a generalized belief about others, whereas locus of control is specific to the self. Given their similarities, it is worth addressing the importance of locus on control on parenting here.

Parents with a high degree of internal locus of control believe that they can be a positive force in their children's lives, even when the children's personality and environmental influences (such as peers or media) support/promote behaviors contradictory to parental desires. In contrast, parents low in this characteristic believe that they can do little to aid their children's development in the face of the number, and power, of forces outside of their control. Such beliefs translate into different types of parenting. Individuals high in internal locus of control communicate better with their children, are more sensitive to their needs, and are more consistent in dispensing discipline relative to parents that are low on this characteristic.

Exposure to stress, especially if it is of the unrelenting and unremitting kind, has a detrimental impact on parenting. Likewise, stress adversely affects individuals' reward for application social axiom and their internal locus of control. Both decrease in the face of adversity, thus reducing parents' belief in their ability to effect positive change in the lives of their children. An undead uprising will similarly produce negative parental beliefs, and in turn, problematic parenting behaviors (e.g., inconsistent discipline, decreased sensitivity, poor communication) will follow.

Spirituality. Spirituality (also called *religiosity*) connotes a belief in a supreme being and that religion positively influences the inhabitants of the world. Psychologists recognize four distinct aspects of religiosity, all of which have the potential to change parenting practices: religious affiliation (e.g., Christianity, Judaism, Islam), public religiousness (e.g., attendance at religious services), private religiousness (e.g., praying by oneself), and religious coping (e.g., using religion to help deal with the physical, psychological, social, or emotional demands of a stressful event or situation).

Religious affiliation affects parenting through their specific religious doctrines. At times, this may involve public religiousness—for instance, attending services at a church, mosque or synagogue. On other occasions, prayer or religious rituals take place in more private settings, such as the practice of thanking God before a meal at home. Additional religious ceremonies may involve small social gatherings, such as the reading of the Haggadah during the Jewish holiday of Passover.

Beyond the observance of religious practices, religion influences the manner in which parents socialize their children. For example, parents high in *biblical conservatism*—defined by biblical literalism, a belief in original sin, and a punishing attitude toward sinners—expect strict obedience from their children and justify the use of spanking (and other forms of physical punishment) on religious grounds. Although the adage "He who spares the rod spoils the child" does not appear in the Bible, there are several verses in the Old Testament in the same vein. Proverbs 23:13–14 states, "Do not withhold discipline from a child; if you punish them with the rod, they will not die. Punish them with the rod and save them from death." Likewise, Proverbs 22:15 admonishes, "Folly is bound up in the heart of a child, but the rod of discipline will drive it far away." Similarly, many religious parents justify the use of their aggressive or violent actions against others using the "eye for eye, tooth for tooth, hand for hand, foot for foot" verse put forth in Exodus 21:24.[13]

Of course, parents also use religious teachings to promote compassion, kindness, and *sociomoral development*—defined as helping others in needs, comforting others in distress, and making reparations after wrongdoings. As stated in the New Testament, Luke 6:31, "And as you wish that others would do to you, do so to them." Parents with a strong belief in the *sanctification of parenting*, defined as viewing parenting as an expression of God's will, are especially likely to promote sociomoral behaviors through their words and deeds. Moreover, parents high in this characteristic believe that in the service of God, parenting requires personal sacrifice, and, as a result of this belief, those that sanctify parenting often handle the stress associated with their children's behavioral problems effectively.

In the face of hardship, be it physical, emotional, or otherwise, individuals high in religiosity use their faith to help cope with their current predicament. However, Kenneth Pargament and colleagues contend that there are two subtypes of religious coping, positive and negative, and that their effects on parenting are vastly different.

Positive religious coping centers around a spiritual connection and a secure relationship with God, along with the belief that there is meaning in life. Conversely, an insecure relationship with God, a struggle to find significance in life, and a gloomy and threatening view of the world characterize *negative religious coping*. In the face of difficult circumstances, parents struggling with spiritually feel more parenting-related stress than those engaging in positive religious coping. Additionally, parents with a positive relationship with God feel more competent in their parenting abilities. Box 6.1 presents Kenneth Pargament and colleagues' breakdown of the various types of positive and negative religious coping.

Box 6.1: *Kenneth Pargament and Colleagues' Forms of Religious Coping*

Positive Religious Coping

- *Benevolent Religious Reappraisal*—based on the tenets of one's religion, stress is reappraised as advantageous.
- *Collaborative Religious Coping*—partnering with God to problem solve and gain control over a situation.
- *Religious Forgiving*—forgiving others and letting go of negative emotions through connectedness with religion.
- *Seeking Support from Clergy or the Congregation*—utilizing clergy and members of one's congregation for comfort and support.

Negative Religious Coping

- *Punishing God Reappraisal*—based on the tenets of one's religion, stress is reappraised as a punishment for one's sins.
- *Self-Directing Religious Coping*—relying on the self, rather than God, when attempting to cope with a stressor.
- *Spiritual Discontent*—being dissatisfied with God or confused by God's actions.
- *Interpersonal Religious Discontent*—dissatisfaction with clergy and members of one's congregation because of their lack of comfort and support.

Although positive religious coping can help parents handle everyday hardships, the ability of faith to help those who have experienced a trauma (e.g., rape, assault, witnessing something horrific) is a bit more complicated. Whereas some respond to trauma with increased religious fervor, more commonly, others find their faith weakened. Furthermore, those holding strong religious beliefs before a traumatic experience are the most likely to lose their faith after it.

Psychologist Hagar ter Kuile contends that traumatic events often shatter the assumptions of the highly devout that God is protective and that their faith will shield them from harm. In such situations, disturbances in psychological functioning (increased stress, anxiety, depression, and so on) are likely to follow. However, trauma survivors living in spiritual communities tend to find that their religious beliefs and activities strengthen following a traumatic event. Additionally, rather than increasing, negative psychological functioning decreases in religious environments. Thus, living in a religious community may protect victims from having their faith-based assumptions shattered. In such cases, positive religious coping may provide newfound "meaning" to traumatic experiences, thus helping victims repair damaged aspects of their psychological functioning.

The Bible touts numerous cases of resurrection in which the dead return to a fully functioning human form and life, as seen in Lazarus, whom Jesus brought back to the living four days after his death. Zombies, however, do not rise as the result of holy resurrection. Nevertheless, the presence of zombies will have religious significance. In some tales of the apocalypse, God brings wrath upon the earth because of human failings; in others, God uses apocalyptic events to identify the faithful from the faithless. Even if God is not the "cause" of the undead scourge, apocalyptic events will test religious beliefs.

Nevertheless, when the dead rise, parents will face a choice: nihilism or hope. Nihilistic parents, believing that life is meaningless and nothing that they do matters, will engage in negative religious coping. In turn, this will make the traumas they endure more challenging to handle and increase the parenting stress experienced. In contrast, those choosing hope, believing that life has a purpose, may seek God and engage in positive religious coping. Finding hope in a bleak world will be difficult. But for those that do, it is likely that they will become more religiously conservative, as the Bible touts rewards for the faithful. After all, terror management theory contends that parents can achieve literal immortality in the afterlife (e.g., Heaven) and symbolic immortality by passing on their religious beliefs to their children. This viewpoint will intensify for those that believe in the sanctification of parenting and have a supportive religious community in their midst.

Box 6.2: *Sante Muerte*

Given the brutality of the Zombie Apocalypse, parents may look to religious beliefs or deities that protect others and provide absolution for their sins, be they violent or nonviolent. Santa Muerte, a female personification of death and Mexican folk saint (i.e., a holy spirit of the dead with miracle-granting powers), provides both. Worldwide, 10 to 12 million people follow her,[14] in and of itself a large number, but small in comparison to the nearly 1.1 billion Catholics.[15] Despite the depiction of Santa Muerte as a shrouded skeletal figure holding a scythe, her believers assert that she can heal the injured, protect followers from violence, harm enemies, and provide safe passage to the afterlife. Not surprisingly, Santa Muerte is particularly popular among those currently living in dangerous and violent communities. It would be no surprise to see her popularity swell during the Zombie Apocalypse.

Parents' Upbringing

Parents' upbringing plays a critical role in the caregiving they extend to their children. Psychologists refer to this phenomenon as the *intergenerational transmission of parenting*. This process can occur at both conscious (e.g., choosing to parent in a particular way) and unconscious (e.g., parenting without volition) levels of awareness. At times, caregivers know precisely why they employ their own parents' childrearing strategies (e.g., "That's how Mom raised me, and I turned out OK"). At other times, parents do not realize that their upbringing is affecting how they interact with their children, even when they disliked the parenting they experienced as a child.

Individuals' upbringing influences their parenting in different ways, as they can reject or accept the style of caregiving they received. Some imitate their parents' caregiving behaviors. An example is when parents rebuff their children's bids for comfort because of their own experiences with parental rejection while growing up. Similarly, individuals recalling a childhood where their parents met (or did not meet) their needs for attention, support, and so on interact with their children in a manner reminiscent of that care. Likewise, parents enduring physical forms of punishment as children are likely to use corporal punishment as a disciplinary technique.

In contrast, rather than imitation, adults disliking the way their parents raised them will at times treat their children in the opposite manner. For example, parents growing up in an unloving household may act warmly and affectionately toward their children. Similarly, parents raised strictly may turn into lax disciplinarians. Parents growing up as *latchkey kids* (i.e., children caring for themselves at home alone) may become hands-on in all aspects of their children's lives. While reversing course can improve caregiving, some parents go too far in the opposite direction, creating a different set of problems for their children. For example, the children of former latchkey kids experience more school-related difficulties and less psychological well-being relative to other youth. Regardless if a parent's history of care was warm and supportive, or harsh and punitive, the transmission of parenting from one generation to the next accounts for 35 percent to 45 percent of parenting-related activities and expectations.[16]

REASONS FOR THE INTERGENERATIONAL TRANSMISSION OF PARENTING. Both biological and environmental factors contribute to the intergenerational transmission of parenting. Concerning the former, stress before pregnancy can cause changes to a mother's uterine environment (e.g., blood flow) or a father's sperm (e.g., microRNA make up). In turn, these physiological changes alter the biology of the newborn (e.g., cortisol levels, brain development), adversely affecting its ability to handle stress as a child and potentially as an adult. Thus, because of biological predispositions, many stress-sensitive parents will produce stress-sensitive children who then turn into stress-sensitive parents. Keep in mind that parents without significant exposure to stress before the Zombie Apocalypse will most definitely experience stress after it has begun. As such, the pressures of the Zombie Apocalypse may adversely affect the biological functioning of parents and their children for generations to come.

Biological predispositions aside, one of the primary explanations for the intergenerational transmission of parenting involves Albert Bandura's social learning theory. *Social learning theory* posits that through direct interactions with others and by watching those around them (a phenomenon referred to as *observational learning*), children learn about the world. In the context of parenting, actions speak louder than words, and more so than admonitions, parental behaviors and their consequences capture the attention of youth. Thus, when children misbehave (or behave well, for that matter), and receive either punishments for their actions (or praise), children are not only experiencing the effects of being parented, they are also learning how to parent.

As mentioned above, some parents engage in caregiving behaviors that are the exact opposite of what they experienced growing up. Social learning theory can explain this as well. As it turns out, there are four processes involved in observational learning: attention, retention, motivation, and reproduction. For observational learning to take place, children must *pay attention* to their parents' childrearing behaviors, *retain* what they learned over a period of years, be *motivated* to perform the observed actions, and, finally, *reproduce* those behaviors as parents. The third element, motivation, is key to understanding why some parents imitate the parenting they received while others reject it.

As discussed in Chapter 5, there are many different reasons for becoming a parent, such as the desire to nurture, personal growth, economics, and societal pressure. Those reasons also affect a parent's motivation for adhering to previously observed parenting practices. When a parent's childhood experiences are consistent with her current motivation for raising children, imitation is likely to follow. In contrast, when childhood experiences and current motivations are at odds, the rejection of previously observed parenting methods will often occur. For example, individuals raising children because of a desire to nurture would likely imitate parents that historically provided them with sensitive and responsive care, but dismiss the parenting style of caregivers that were unresponsive or rejecting of their emotional needs during childhood.

During the Zombie Apocalypse, the acceptance or rejection of an earlier generation's parenting behaviors will still be dependent upon a parent's motivation for raising children. However, equally important will be the match between a parent's childhood environment and the apocalyptic surroundings in which they currently find themselves. When the two settings are dissimilar (such as when parents of the apocalypse grew up in nonviolent communities), it will be harder for adults to accept or reject the efficacy of their upbringing, for parenting that worked in times of plenty may seem efficacious in times of violence and despair.

In contrast, when the circumstances of the Zombie Apocalypse are similar to the conditions of a parent's upbringing (e.g., impoverished and violent), it will be easier to evaluate the need for a generational change in parenting behavior. After all, firsthand experience, as well as observations of family and friends, has taught parents about the dangers of the world in which they live and the utility of different caregiving behaviors. However, even if parents desire to raise their children differently than how their parents raised them, the cruel nature of the Zombie Apocalypse may prevent them from doing so.

Final Thoughts

As mentioned above, personality, biological predispositions, and a variety of other psychological components influence parenting. However, environmental pressures, trauma, and stress can alter these contributing elements. Thus, during the Zombie Apocalypse, *hardiness*—the ability to resist and cope with stress—will become a central feature of parental interactions with their children. Three components comprise hardiness: control, commitment, and challenge. *Control* is synonymous with the concept of internal locus of control, with higher levels of perceived control associated with greater hardiness. *Commitment*, much like spirituality, involves gaining purpose in life through dedication to a cause, an activity, or a belief system. However, the sphere of commitment goes well beyond faith and includes finding meaning through engagement with family, friends, the community, or even work. Finally, *challenge* refers to perceiving life's difficulties as either threats or obstacles to overcome.

Parents high in hardiness recognize that change is not only an inevitability but also an opportunity for personal growth. In the face of stressful and changing environments, hardiness results in a flexible, adaptive, and self-regulated sense of control. Such characteristics allow parents to solve problems and effectively handle parenting stress. Hardiness will be an invaluable characteristic to possess during Zombie Apocalypse. Feeling in control, having a sense of purpose, and viewing the dystopian nightmare in which parents find themselves as something that they can overcome should result in more productive parenting.

7. Characteristics of the Child

During the Zombie Apocalypse, those that live to share their adventures will have used a variety of weapons and methods to dispatch the undead, for as any survivor will most assuredly say, combat techniques that work well in one situation may be completely ineffective in another. Case in point: shooting a lumbering zombie from the vantage point of a second story window is not even a remote possibility when being attacked by the undead in a darkened and seemingly deserted alley. In reality, parenting is no different from this. Childrearing techniques that work well at one age or with one type of child may be completely ineffective at other ages or with other types of children. To illustrate, whereas parents can readily discuss survival strategies suited for specific situations with adolescents, infants and toddlers lack the requisite cognitive abilities to comprehend parental admonitions and suggestions.

There are also times when the characteristics of the child, regardless of their age, make it challenging for caregivers to parent effectively. Take Sam Anderson from *The Walking Dead*, who experiences a series of traumas after this dead rise.[1] Sam lives at home with an abusive father, who Rick later kills after the abuse is discovered. After learning that Sam is following her, Carol threatens to feed him to the undead. Later, a roving band of marauders invades Sam's home. To protect herself and her family, Sam's mother Jesse kills one of the attackers with a pair of scissors. Sam does not witness the killing, but the bloody aftermath is apparent to all in the household. After enduring all of these stressful events, Sam finds it difficult to leave his bedroom and becomes increasingly scared and withdrawn. No matter what she tries, Jessie is unable to help her traumatized child. Likewise, Sam's older teenage brother, Ron, also suffers numerous traumas during the Zombie Apocalypse, including the death of his father and witnessing his mother stab the abovementioned intruder repeatedly. However, rather than withdrawing from others as Sam does, Ron becomes increasingly angry, hostile, and violent.[2] Despite her efforts, Jesse is unable to quell Ron's ire. Two children, one parent, and zero parental effectiveness.

As discussed in the previous chapter, parental characteristics influence the caretaking of children. However, parenting does not take place solely within the confines of a parent's mind. As the process model of parenting points out, and as exemplified above, an additional factor that influences parental behavior is the characteristics of the child. Below, I discuss three child-based determinants of parenting: developmental differences, temperament, and childhood mental health disorders.

Developmental Differences

Development refers to the psychological, social, emotional, cognitive, and physical growth of humans across the lifespan. For ease of understanding, psychologists demarcate development in terms of ages, stages, or periods. Thus, *developmental differences* are variations in capabilities across those boundaries. In Chapter 3, I detailed a variety of developmental challenges that children face as they age. In this chapter, I discuss the effects of children meeting, or not meeting, several of those tasks on parents' decision-making, emotions, and behavior. In particular, I focus on age-related competencies in areas of paramount importance during the Zombie Apocalypse: behavioral self-control, emotional self-regulation, and aggression.

Behavioral Self-Control

Even in a world without zombies, impulsive behavior places children at risk for accidents. Starting at age one and lasting well into adulthood, unintentional injury is the leading cause of death in the United States.[3] Every day, three children die from drowning, two perish from poison (mostly due to household chemicals and medicines), and another two die from burns. Because of accidental falls, an additional 8,000 youth find themselves in the emergency room annually.[4] Each day, around 2,000 children and adolescents worldwide die from preventable, unintentional injuries.[5]

Moreover, children living in embattled areas of the world face the risk of dismemberment, disfigurement, and death from the remnants of old conflicts and the hazards of new ones. In the late 1990s and early 2000s, there were an estimated 450,000 active land mines in Afghanistan left over from armed conflicts more than two decades old.[6] Almost daily, unexploded ordnance in open fields and schoolyards left dozens of Afghan children severely injured or dead. Young children and illiterate youth were especially vulnerable to these hidden hazards, as they could not read signs warning of their presence.[7] As these sobering statistics imply, youth do not always recognize potential dangers and threats to their well-being, nor do they correctly judge the severity of the peril in which they have placed themselves. Depending upon a child's age and temperamental characteristics (discussed in detail below), parents may frequently find themselves in the position of having to rein in childhood impulsivity and prevent accidental harm through vigilance and preventative measures. Stated differently, a child's level of *behavioral self-control*—the ability to inhibit impulses and resist temptation—is a determinant of the parenting they receive.

INFANCY AND TODDLERHOOD. Infants are born without self-control. During an infant's first few months of life, immobility limits unsafe impulsive behavior to grasping objects within their reach and placing them in their mouths. However, once infants can locomote (by rolling, crawling, toddling, and so on), their lack of self-control becomes increasingly problematic for parents. To an infant, surprised-looking electrical outlets require exploration, as do closed cabinets filled with hazardous chemicals. Although older infants can briefly comply with the demands of their parents and stop what they are doing, without further intervention, the behavior will soon restart.

Despite their impulsivity, infants will not typically approach something that scares them, such as growling, snapping, or hissing animals. In such situations, infants will either run away from the fear stimulus or seek their parents for comfort and protection—a capability that could save their lives if predators (alive or undead) are about. However, infants do not always perceive the circumstances they are in as obviously dangerous or clearly danger-free. When unsure of what to do, infants rely on *social referencing*—paying attention to the emotional displays of others to gain information about the events, persons, or objects in their environment. Imagine an infant crawling around their backyard when they see what they believe is a ball in the bushes, only this ball has a face, and its mouth is silently opening and closing. The ambiguity of the situation gives the infant pause, and they look to their parent for more information on what they should do. In this case, the parent is looking on in horror, and the infant backs away to safety. Although social referencing demonstrates that infants have a modicum of behavioral self-control, it principally occurs when infants are anxious and unsure. Thus, if danger is present but not perceived, behaviors will go unchecked and unconstrained.

As infants become toddlers, they begin to say "No!" to their parents. Nevertheless, toddlers still have great difficulty saying "No!" to themselves. Toddlers desire independence, and when left to their own devices, they behave quite impulsively. What toddlers see, they desire, and what they desire, toddlers try to get. Still, warnings from authority figures are effective at preventing toddlers from acting on their wishes, at least for a short while. To illustrate, when told to refrain from touching a desired object (e.g., toy phone), 18-month-olds can wait about 30 seconds before they grab it. Between 24 and 36 months of age, the average toddler can wait more than a minute before succumbing to temptation. Older toddlers will even talk to themselves (saying things like "Stoppit," "No hit," and "Careful") to restrain their impulses, albeit briefly. Although self-control improves over the toddler period, ultimately the responsibility for managing a toddler's impulsive behavior lies with the parent. Of note, during toddlerhood, and virtually all other developmental periods, for that matter, it is much easier to delay the start of an activity than to stop it once it has begun.

EARLY AND MIDDLE CHILDHOOD. Although preschoolers are prone to acting impulsively, they do become better at controlling their actions. It is also during this age period that children start to develop the capacity for reflection, which allows them to compare their behavior with the expectations of others. Because of these developmental advances, two distinct systems now comprise self-control: impulsive and reflective. The *impulsive system*, which is responsible for spontaneous behavior, is reactive to objects, people, and situational cues. Case in point: when grabbed from behind, some children will quickly turn around and hit the person who startled them. In contrast, through planning, evaluations, judgments, and goal setting, the *reflective system* inhibits and overrides impulsiveness. Nevertheless, overcoming temptation, desires, and spur-of-the-moment decisions require *control resources*, which unfortunately are limited in strength and duration. Overuse can result in their quick depletion, as can multitasking, stress, and fatigue. As evidence, a night of disrupted sleep (due to hunger, noise, room temperature, or nightmares) causes children to be more impulsive the following day. Similarly, children undergoing chronic stress, due to poverty, war, or some other calamity, perform poorly on psychological tasks requiring self-control.

Although three-year-olds have more self-control than toddlers do, the reflective system is not yet strong enough to override the actions governed by the impulsive self-control system on a consistent basis. During the middle school years, impulsive and reflective systems demonstrate different developmental trajectories. Whereas reflective self-control increases between four and six years of age, and then remains flat through age 10, levels of the impulsive system stay the same from early through middle childhood. As a result, the relative difference in strength between the two systems reaches a critical threshold during middle childhood, allowing the reflective system to govern impulsive system more consistently. Nevertheless, parents will still need to monitor the behavior of their children, as impulsive actions are still prevalent.

ADOLESCENCE. Whereas impulsive self-control peaks between 16 and 17 years of age, reflective self-control is at its lowest between the ages of 13 and 18. Furthermore, the psychological, social, emotional, and biological changes accompanying adolescence deplete the control resources of most teens quickly. Having to accommodate to their rapid physical growth and maturation, sexual awakening, cognitive and socio-emotional challenges at school, and changes in relationships with their parents and peers leave few resources left to control their impulses. Environmental stressors also tax control resources, making it even more difficult for teens to rein in their impulses, no matter how dangerous. For example, stressed teens are more likely than other youth to drink excessively or take drugs. And when the source of stress is out of the adolescent's control, meaning that they can do little to combat it, drinking and drug use becomes even more prevalent.[8]

As a result of normative developmental changes, as well as the presence of environmental stressors, adolescents act in a disinhibited manner that has the potential to put their well-being and lives at risk. Statistics bear this out, as there is a heightened mortality rate associated with the adolescent years. To illustrate, in the United States, unintentional injuries of children aged five to nine cause 3.6 deaths per 100,000 children. For 15- to 19-year-olds, however, that number jumps to 20 deaths per 100,000 adolescents. Of those teenage deaths, 66 percent are the result of motor vehicle accidents, 15 percent occur as the result of poisonings or drug overdoses, and 7 percent involve drownings.[9] Similarly, as the result of sexual risk-taking behavior (e.g., unprotected sex), nearly half of all new cases of sexually transmitted diseases in the United States occur for individuals aged 15 to 24, even though they only comprise 25 percent percent of the sexually active population.[10]

Keep in mind, most teens underestimate the long-term consequences of their actions, while at the same time over-estimating the short-term gains of them. As a result, they will impulsively choose the first course of action that comes to mind rather than the best course (which a more thorough analysis could reveal). For example, on *The Walking Dead*, shortly after escaping a zombie horde, Carl and his father, Rick, hole up in a quiet little neighborhood. Injured and exhausted, Rick passes out shortly after their arrival. Upon hearing the banging of the undead at the front door, Carl rashly decides to lead the walkers away from the house. He fails to mind his environment, and an undetected walker sneaks up and nearly bites him. Two more walkers join the fray, and Carl struggles to dispatch them.[11] Although Carl survives this encounter with the dead, his reckless actions (and lack of forethought) nearly cost him his life.

THE EFFECT OF THE ZOMBIE APOCALYPSE ON BEHAVIORAL SELF-CONTROL. During the Zombie Apocalypse, oversights caused by a lack of behavioral self-control can be deadly. In addition to discarded ordnance and physically dangerous landscapes, the living dead are somewhere lying in wait, whether it be down the street, around the corner, behind the door, or just outside the window. Even a single step away from a parent could result in an unexpected zombie attack, resulting in death or worse. Thus, a child's developmental capabilities in self-control will significantly affect parenting decisions and behaviors.

A combination of limited self-control capabilities and the desire to explore makes a zombie-filled world especially dangerous for infants and toddlers. Unless confronted with an obvious danger, very young children lack the cognitive capacity to recognize perilous situations. In addition to monitoring their children's activities, parents will also need to attune to their young children's attempts at social referencing, for the world of the undead will be full of ambiguities and the difference between a familiar face and the undead version of that face may not always be readily discernable. Given toddlers' mobility, impulsivity, limited ability to resist temptation, and adverse reactions to having their behaviors curtailed (see below), parents will be especially challenged. In a world of the undead, caring for infants and toddlers will be a highly demanding task that will tax parental resources, ultimately affecting the manner in which they parent.

Although self-control improves over the course early and middle childhood, to promote survival, parents must still function as their children's reflective system to augment the control resources their children are lacking. When the undead rise, children will endure countless sleepless nights, along with chronically stressful and fatiguing circumstances. Alone, each of these factors can increase impulsive behavior in children. Collectively, they will ensure that youth will become more unconstrained in a world that demands restraint. Even though development brings improved self-control through the elementary school years, children are still prone to impulsive actions, especially when under duress. Thus, despite developmental progression, the stress of the Zombie Apocalypse will require parents to monitor and control their children's behavior vigilantly. When the dead rise, it is likely that the type of behavior exhibited by Carl (described above) will be the rule, rather than the exception, as stress-filled environments lead to disinhibited youth. As a result, parents will face the difficult task of trying to curb their teens' dangerous activities.

Emotional Self-Regulation

On *The Walking Dead*, to escape a walker horde, Rick and a few fellow survivors cover themselves with the blood and guts of zombies and head out into the amassed dead. Included in this group is Sam and his mother, Jesse. Not long after entering the sea of rotting flesh, Sam freezes, and despite her efforts, Jesse is unable to calm him. Sam whimpers, thus triggering a zombie attack and the dead quickly tear him and his mother to shreds.[12] As this example illustrates, the combination of Sam's inability to stay composed, and his mother's failure to regulate his emotions, ultimately lead to their demise.

Psychologists define *emotional self-regulation* as the use of appropriate emotions and emotional intensity in a given situation. Whereas behavioral self-control involves keeping impulses at bay, emotional self-regulation refers to holding feelings in check. Emotional self-regulation is critical for success in any environment children and adolescents find themselves in, whether it is at home, in school, or on the playground. For example, the ability to handle frustration, resolve conflicts, and cooperate with others can be the difference between completing a task or abandoning it, getting along with others or getting in a fight, being accepted or rejected by peers, or, as illustrated above, masquerading as the dead or becoming one of them. Furthermore, from infancy through adolescence, developmental differences in emotional self-regulation affect parenting behavior and stress.

INFANCY AND TODDLERHOOD. Babies cry often, and babies cry loudly. For the first two months of life, babies cry between two and three hours per day at a deafening 110 decibels. Starting in the third month, they cry significantly less, averaging around one hour per day. But it is not as if infants cry for 60 minutes straight and then remain silent for the next 23 hours. Instead, infants cry throughout the day and night: they cry when they are hungry, tired, bored, scared, or just need a cuddle. Once a fit of crying starts, infants typically require caregivers to soothe them. Thus, infants' ability to regulate their emotions is heavily dependent upon caregivers' comforting capabilities.

Throughout industrialized nations, parents regulate their infants' negative emotional states and expressions though soothing actions (such as swaddling, rocking, or cuddling), or, at times, by disregarding their fussiness completely. In contrast, through attention and joyful engagement, parents encourage the positive expressions of interest, joy, and surprise. As a result, parents teach babies to express more positive emotions than negative ones, and as the first year of life turns into the second, infants typically do just that. However, it is also possible to restrict the expression of emotions altogether, positive or negative. For example, the Aka of Central Africa prefer infants that are calm and content rather than joyful and exuberant. To accomplish this, the Aka restrict their infants' positive emotional displays (through limited face-to-face interaction) in addition to their negative ones.

As infants grow into toddlers, their overall level of emotional self-regulation improves. Because of burgeoning language development, toddlers can express their desires, wants, needs, and frustrations in words rather than actions and emotions. Nevertheless, people do not call the toddler period the "terrible twos" without cause, as tantrums and angry outbursts peak during this developmental period. *Tantrums*, which involve high-pitched screams, angry yelling, crying, flailing body parts, stomping, kicking, and throwing, can be challenging to prevent during this stage, and even more difficult to stop once started. Tantrums occur as the result of exhaustion, hunger, discomfort, frustration related to not getting what they want, and sadness. Simply put, toddlers have tantrums when they are angered or distressed. The typical tantrum can last as long as five minutes, though, for parents, any outburst can feel like an eternity, especially if being quiet is important, as it will be when the dead roam the earth.

To regulate a child's behavior, and to help them comply with parental wishes, the average parent disrupts a toddler's activities eight to 10 times per hour. Unfortunately, every intervention can lead to frustration and trigger a tantrum. However, parents of toddlers that frequently throw tantrums do the following: (1) they are overly critical and disapproving of their children's behavior; (2) they impose rigid routines based on their wants and needs, regardless of the children's activities or desires; and (3) they primarily respond to their toddlers only after they have become negatively aroused.

Although toddlers are limited in their ability to cope with negative feelings on their own, holding on to a stuffed animal, blanket, or toy can help them feel comforted. Psychologists refer to such items as *transitional objects.* Transitional objects allow children to self-soothe during times when their caregivers are not immediately available to meet their needs. The majority of toddlers utilize transitional objects on a daily basis.

EARLY AND MIDDLE CHILDHOOD. The ability to handle unpleasant emotional states, such as frustration, anger, and fear, improves during the preschool years. Newly developed cognitive skills allow children to reinterpret situations in a more positive light, divert attention away from frightening stimuli or frustrating situations, and to think about positive things rather than negative ones. Nevertheless, parental guidance is typically required for preschoolers to use these techniques in the face of negative emotional experiences such as anger and fear. Examples include telling children to take deep breaths, think positive thoughts, or look at something pleasant, such as a grove of flowers. Additionally, improvements in language allow preschoolers to more effectively communicate what they are feeling, thus reducing the frustration associated with misunderstandings. However, emotional self-regulation is far from complete. And when upset, preschoolers still cry big crocodile tears about 70 percent of the time. At this age, most instances of crying occur within the context of parent-child interactions.[13]

Despite improvements in emotional self-regulation with age, it is not until elementary school that children, on their own, can moderate the intensity of their emotions to handle the vicissitudes of life. During this developmental period, children use the following strategies to regulate their emotions: problem-solving (e.g., thinking about or engaging in behavior that allows them to resolve the distressing issue); distraction (e.g., thinking about or participating in behavior that distracts them from the distressing issue); cheering up (e.g., thinking happy thoughts); acceptance (e.g., acknowledging that, ultimately, they control their emotional states); and reappraisal (e.g., rethinking the importance of the distressing event to lessen its emotional impact).

Nevertheless, compared to preschoolers, youth in middle childhood are more likely to sulk, express sadness, and avoid interactions with people that have upset them. These behaviors occur due to the development of additional, and more undesirable, ways of handling intense emotional experiences. Such maladaptive strategies include giving up (e.g., they no longer attempt to resolve the issue); withdrawal (e.g., keeping away from others); rumination (e.g., repeatedly thinking about the distressing problem); and self-devaluation (e.g., exaggerating one's negative qualities and viewing the self as severely flawed). It is also worth noting that across middle childhood, youth increasingly blame parent-child conflicts on their parents' inadequacies and lack of time spent with them.

ADOLESCENCE. Due to the biological, psychological, and social changes that accompany adolescence, teens experience heightened emotional reactivity and an increase in the use of maladaptive strategies to regulate their emotions. Giving up, withdrawal, rumination, and self-devaluation all peak around 13 to 14 years of age, decreasing slightly after that. Still, throughout adolescence, these maladaptive strategies remain more prominent than they were during middle childhood. At the same time, several adaptive strategies reach their lowest point during this stage. For example, problem-solving, cheering up, and distraction decrease relative to their use in middle childhood, recovering only slightly after that. It is the increased use of maladaptive strategies and decreased use of adaptive ones that makes emotion regulation so challenging for teens, and, in turn, challenging for parents.

THE EFFECTS OF THE ZOMBIE APOCALYPSE ON EMOTIONAL SELF-REGULATION. During the Zombie Apocalypse, failing to control emotions will lead to behaviors that put children's lives at risk, such as yelling when silence is essential or being immobile when movement is a necessity. However, because noise draws zombies to its source, a lack of emotional self-regulation and the crying, yelling, and destructive behaviors that accompany it will place everyone near distraught children in danger as well. As indicated above, children's emotional self-regulation is heavily dependent on the quality of parent-child interactions. When the dead rise, it will be critical for everyone's survival that parents tailor their childrearing to the developmental capabilities of their children.

When living near the living dead, keeping infants calm and content will be necessary, as they make less noise than joyful or distressed babies. Furthermore, calm and content infants require less parental attention than babies that are joyful, distressed, angry or fearful. As young children age, the use of transitional objects will become essential for keeping them calm. There is, however, a downside to the use of stuffed animals and toys for comfort. Because of their importance, when they are lost or unavailable, negative emotions and tantrums will follow. Moreover, young children may inadvertently put themselves in danger when attempting to retrieve a transitional object left behind or dropped on the ground. Doing so with a zombie on their heels will be deadly.

It will be in everyone's best interest to limit tantrums as much as possible. Unfortunately, the parenting behaviors (e.g., being critical, disapproving, and rigid) that produce the most outbursts are likely to accompany the stress of the Zombie Apocalypse. For instance, to ensure the survival of their children, parents will vigilantly impose safety rules, whisking them away if a zombie should lumber too close or if another danger presents itself. Unfortunately, unless the threat is standing right in front of them (which could scare a child into a parent's arms), toddlers will become frustrated with parental interference and react accordingly.

During the preschool years, parents are supposed to help children learn strategies to control their emotions effectively. However, the stress of the Zombie Apocalypse will adversely affect parents' ability to do so. As evidence, consider the fact that Syrian parents struggling with the pressures of being a refugee find it challenging to help their children cope with their problems, including those in emotional self-regulation. Without proper guidance, children begin to rely on maladaptive strategies for regulating their emotions rather than adaptive ones. For example, Syrian refugee youth frequently become sad, fearful, and emotionally withdrawn.[14] Thus, as children of the Zombie Apocalypse progress through middle childhood and adolescence, their increasingly poor skills at emotional self-regulation will result in frequent negative interactions with their parents, peers, and others.

Across development, it is easier for children to self-regulate anger than fear, and although children have fears during infancy and toddlerhood, those fears tend to be focused on strangers and other natural cues for danger, such as loud noises. Starting in early childhood, the intensity of such fears diminish. However, other fears take their place. Those fears tend to be less tangible than before, as preschoolers now fear the dark and imaginary creatures. During middle childhood and adolescence, youth are more likely to fear real threats than imaginary ones. Thus, children's fears now center on real situations and events, especially those that are more likely to occur in their own lives. Unfortunately, the Zombie Apocalypse is rife with frightening stimuli, whether it be the undead or roaming bandits, and because fear is more challenging to self-regulate, parents will need to help assuage their children's anxiety. However, this will be a difficult task for many parents. The opening vignette, in which Jesse is unable to calm her emotionally distraught son, Sam, exemplifies this point.

In the face of *acute stress*—that is, stress associated with the demands and pressures of the current situation—emotional self-regulation can be difficult for children and adolescents. However, when stress becomes more chronic, as will be the case in the Zombie Apocalypse, emotional self-regulation becomes dysfunctional, and youth can become emotionally dysregulated. *Emotional dysregulation* occurs when youth cannot control their emotional states, and, as a result, experience more extreme, and more frequent, emotions. For some, emotional dysregulation takes the form of high levels of anxiety, depression, and social withdrawal (such as Sam). Others experience, anger, aggression, and acting out (such as Ron). Regardless, with zombies about, any emotional outburst has the potential to be deadly. After all, noise attracts the dead.

Aggression

Aggression refers to behavior intended to cause physical, psychological, emotional, or social harm to another person. Psychologists define aggression based on its purpose and the actions involved. For example, the term *instrumental aggression* denotes acts of harm done with the intention of achieving a goal, such as obtaining money or resources. Psychologists also refer to instrumental aggression as "cold" because it is planned and devoid of strong emotions (e.g., fear, jealousy). An example of instrumental aggression during the Zombie Apocalypse would be mechanically spearing the brains of zombies as they gather along a fence line to prevent its collapse.

In contrast, *reactive aggression* involves harmful acts that are impulsive and occur in response to strong emotions (such as those resulting from real or perceived threats). Psychologists refer to reactive aggression as "hot" aggression because of the intense feelings (e.g., anger, fear, jealousy) that accompany it. For example, on *The Walking Dead*, while on a mission to obtain antibiotics, a small band of walkers begins to overtake an injured Shane and an exhausted Otis as they run towards safety. Fearing for his life, Shane impulsively shoots but does not kill Otis, who then falls to the ground in agony, an agony that will soon intensify as the walkers stop to tear into him, thus ensuring Shane's escape.[15]

Three are three main types of aggressive actions: physical, verbal, and relational. *Physical aggression* describes harming others through physicality, for example, pushing, hitting, or kicking. On the other hand, *verbal aggression* involves injuring others through verbal means such as name-calling, yelling, screaming, or using profanity. Finally, *relational aggression* occurs when an individual hurts another person's relationships or group status though gossip, spreading rumors, false statements, and exclusion.

Developmentally, instrumental aggression first appears during the toddler years with reactive aggression debuting shortly after that. As children move through the preschool years and into middle childhood, physical aggression becomes less frequent, as verbal and relational forms of aggression take its place. Thus, rather than pushing, shoving, kicking, or hitting the targets of their ire, older children attempt to tease and socially isolate their peers. Overall, developmental improvements in language, emotional self-regulation, and self-control lead to a reduction in aggressive behavior during middle childhood. However, when aggression does occur during the grade-school years, it is more likely to be reactive than instrumental. Two reasons account for this fact: (1) older children are better able to identify hostile intent than younger ones and (2) school-aged children view an aggressive response to provocations (i.e., *retaliatory aggression*) as socially acceptable. An eye-for-an-eye mentality, if you will.

During adolescence, physical aggression continues to decline. Even grade-school children who frequently get into fights are unlikely to maintain high levels of aggression during adolescence. In contrast, the frequency of *violent behavior* (i.e., aggressive actions that cause significant bodily or psychological harm) increases. How is this possible? After all, most aggressive children do not become aggressive teens or adults. However, a small percentage of teens become increasingly violent across adolescence, most likely due to their more prominent physical stature and the availability, and relative ease, of obtaining weapons. Finally, relational aggression peaks during early to middle adolescence. Advanced verbal and cognitive abilities, and the fact that relative to physical aggression, peers consider relational aggression to be more socially acceptable, account for this change.

THE EFFECTS OF THE ZOMBIE APOCALYPSE ON AGGRESSION.

When the dead rise, two distinct patterns of aggression and violence will emerge across childhood and adolescence: escalating and on-setting. For *escalating* youth, the frequency and severity of their already established aggressive behavior increase over time. For example, an adolescent that rarely fights will start to do so with regularity and eventually become violent. In contrast, *on-setting* occurs when previously nonaggressive children grow noticeably more aggressive and violent.

Numerous factors contribute to both of these patterns of aggression, including changes in biological processes and parental behavior. However, being under duress is one of the most prominent causes of escalating and on-setting aggression and a staple of the Zombie Apocalypse. Furthermore, children and adolescents with emotional problems (see below) are especially likely to act aggressively when under extreme duress. Even if youth were not experiencing emotional difficulties before the Zombie Apocalypse, they most certainly would be after the dead begin to roam. As a result, on-setting and escalating aggression will become a prominent determinant of parental behavior.

Temperament

Developmental differences in behavioral self-control, emotional self-regulation, and aggression can lead to substantial differences in parenting practices during a zombie uprising. Nevertheless, similarly-aged children often respond to the same situation differently. For instance, whereas some preschoolers reliably adhere to parental directives, others readily ignore them. Psychologists refer to such age-independent variations in thoughts, feelings, and behavior as *individual differences*. As illustrated numerous times throughout this text, parenting affects the development of individual differences. However, temperament is an equally important contributor.

Temperament refers to innate patterns of behavioral and emotional reactivity to situations and stressors. In many ways, temperament is the forerunner to personality, so much so that many psychologists think of personality as the interaction between life experience and temperament. Not only is temperament foundational for personality, but it also serves as a building block for children's relationships with their parents. Thus, psychologists view temperament as a primary determinant of parenting.

Temperamental Characteristics

There many different dimensions of temperament, including regularity of sleeping and eating habits, sociability (e.g., enjoying the company of others), task persistence, attention span, ease of soothing when distressed, and sensitivity to physical discomfort. Here, I discuss four temperamental characteristics expected to affect parenting during the Zombie Apocalypse: fearfulness, negative emotionality, activity level, and executive control.

Fearfulness refers to the level of distress and wariness that children feel when faced with strangers or novel situations. Whereas children low in fearfulness will readily tackle new challenges and anxiety-provoking situations with little hesitation, children high in fearfulness shy away or withdraw from them. Levels of anger, frustration tolerance, and irritability define the *negative emotionality* temperamental characteristic. Children low on this dimension handle frustration much better and are far less likely to become angry or irritable relative to those on the other end of the continuum. For instance, during the toddler years, children high in negative emotionality quickly throw tantrums when frustrated, which, for such youth, can occur at the slightest perceived provocation.

Activity level refers to the level of children's gross motor (i.e., large muscle) activity, such as running, jumping, and climbing. Youth high on this dimension are always on the move, bouncing to and fro regardless of whether they are in a closet-sized room or a national park. On the other hand, those with low levels of activity are more likely to sit in place calmly. *Executive control* encompasses the ability to inhibit or activate behaviors as needed. Whereas youth high in executive control can focus in the face of distraction, curtail impulses, and force themselves to do unpleasant activities, children low in executive control have great difficulty doing any of these tasks. Additionally, executive control functions serve as the constitutionally based contributor to individual differences in aggression, behavioral self-control, and emotional self-regulation.

Temperamental Profiles

Temperament also influences emotional intensity, tolerance for frustration, and reaction to novelty. By clustering these characteristics together, three broad temperamental profiles become apparent: easy, difficult, and slow to warm up. Children with *easy temperaments* show a high tolerance for frustration, readily transition from one situation to another, and have a relatively sunny disposition. In contrast, those with *difficult temperaments* exhibit high levels of gross motor activity, problems in transitioning and adapting to novelty, a pervasive negative mood, and a high degree of reactivity (e.g., kicking and screaming). Finally, children with *slow-to-*

warm-up temperamental styles are relatively inactive, moody, and wary of new situations. However, they will eventually adjust to change; it just takes them a while to join others or try new things.

Goodness of Fit

Although children with difficult temperaments are generally the hardest to parent, the degree to which temperamental dimensions or profiles influence parenting is dependent upon the *goodness of fit*—that is, the compatibility between parental demands and expectations and the child's temperamental proclivities. For example, whereas some parents love nothing more than to play with, or structure activities for, highly active children, others prefer children that color quietly, read by themselves, and generally engage in more sedate activities. Even for difficult children, who are prone to behavior problems throughout development, a "good fit," in which the parent is patient and sensitive, can mitigate potential behavioral issues. However, when a "bad fit" occurs, and parents are impatient, hostile, and reactive with difficult children, behavior problems are exacerbated.

It is worth noting that in addition to temperament, the "goodness of fit" concept is also applicable to different developmental periods. Some parents are better fits with their children during specific age periods than others. For example, someone who is a sensitive and responsive caregiver to an infant (regardless of their temperament profile) may have difficulty handling the independent and combative nature of the adolescent.

Temperament and the Zombie Apocalypse

Research shows that temperamentally active youth that are low in fearfulness and executive control are prone to unintentional injuries. During the Zombie Apocalypse, children with similar temperamental profiles should fare even worse. By failing to be mindful of the hazards in their environments, active, uninhibited, and fearless youth may inadvertently place themselves within arm's reach of the undead or take unnecessary and dangerous risks in an apocalyptic wasteland. Moreover, either because the children find themselves in need of rescuing, or because their noisy behaviors attract the dead, such under-controlled behaviors will place others at risk as well. Nevertheless, when it comes to temperamental attributes, "more" is not always better, even in the Zombie Apocalypse. For example, highly fearful youth may find themselves unable to function in situations that are just slightly anxiety provoking, let alone ones that are truly scary. Just ask Sam.

When the dead roam, youth with easy temperaments will be able to adjust to the new world order better than children with either difficult or slow-to-warm-up profiles. And although slow-to-warm-up children will be more fearful than others, these children will eventually acclimate to their apocalyptic surroundings. Given their temperamental profile, and inherent problems in dealing with transitions, an undead rising will challenge children with difficult temperaments the most.

Parenting occurs in an ever-changing world, with each day bringing with it new lumps to take, pipers to pay, and pills to swallow. For many parents, the vicissitudes of life are small enough handle without affecting the status quo. The goodness-of-fit between parent and child, albeit bad or good, remains relatively unaffected. This does not mean that life is easy; just predictable. However, war, famine, natural disasters, and other long-lasting catastrophic events, such as a Zombie Apocalypse, can disrupt the fit between parent and child. To a small degree, children can modify their temperamentally-based behaviors to be more in line with the type of parenting they currently receive. However, under stressful circumstances, the onus of responsibility for maintaining a "good fit" is on the parent. And during the Zombie Apocalypse, in which parental stress will abound, patient parents will become increasingly impatient, sensitive parents will become more insensitive, and warm parents will experience greater levels of hostility. As a result, many "good fits" will become bad ones.

Childhood Mental Illness

In the previous chapter, I noted the adverse effects of parental anxiety, major depression, and PTSD on caregiving. In the current chapter, I discuss how the presence of these mental health disorders in children and adolescents function as a determinant of parenting.

Causes of Anxiety Disorders, Major Depression and PTSD During Childhood

According to the World Health Organization, worldwide, between 10 percent and 20 percent of children and adolescents have a mental illness.[16] A variety of biological and environmental conditions place youth at risk for the development of any number of different psychological disorders. Even before they are born, poor prenatal nutrition, pregnancy and birth complications, genetic factors, and maternal use of tobacco, drugs, and alcohol increase children's chances of becoming mentally ill. During childhood and adolescence, impoverished conditions, community violence, maltreatment, inconsistent or harsh discipline, and parental rejection adversely affect mental health. Moreover, the more risk exposure that children and adolescents endure, the higher the probability that anxiety, depression, or both will develop. As happens with adults, traumatic experiences during childhood and adolescence result in the onset of PTSD. In addition to witnessing or living through a highly distressing event, forced separation from parents also increases the likelihood that youth will develop PTSD.

Symptoms of Anxiety Disorders, Major Depression and PTSD During Childhood

Each mental health disorder comes with a unique set of symptoms that require parental management. Children with an anxiety disorder worry a lot. They worry during the day, which adversely affects their concentration. They worry at night, which disrupts their sleep. And for just about all other occasions, they worry. For some children, separations from parents can be quite challenging, as they worry that something terrible might happen to them or their parents while apart. Other youth are prone to panic attacks. Finally, many children and adolescents with anxiety become hypervigilant, scanning the surroundings for potential threats.

Children with major depression have profound sadness, excessive crying, the loss of pleasure in most activities, ruminating thoughts of worthlessness and guilt, fatigue, difficulty sleeping, and increases or decreases in appetite. Other symptoms include anger, irritability, and difficulty completing everyday tasks. Like adults, youth with major depression may experience suicidal ideation or attempt suicide. In fact, suicide is the second leading cause of death for children, adolescents, and young adults between the ages of 10 and 24.[17] At times, depressed teenagers will use drugs and alcohol as a form of self-medication.

Similar to adults, children with PTSD have intrusive memories, frightening dreams, flashbacks, angry outbursts, problems sleeping, avoidance behaviors, and persistent feelings of fear, anxiety, and shame. Moreover, traumatized children will often become regressive, showing marked separation distress (e.g., clinging), the loss of developed skills (e.g., toilet training) and an increase in infantile behaviors (e.g., thumb sucking).

Parenting Children with Mental Illness

Whatever psychological disorder they may have, parenting children with anxiety, depression, or PTSD is challenging. Besides managing their children's symptoms, parents must also govern their treatment regimen, assuming they have one. In the United States, only half of all eight- to 15-year-olds receive needed mental health services.[18] If their children are in or out of treatment, parenting youth with mental illness takes a toll on caregivers. For example, parents with mentally ill children report high levels of parenting stress and an overall lower quality of life. Moreover, parenting stress increases when parents feel they should be able to help their children but cannot. To make matters worse, other adults minimize the issues that children with mental health disorders face, going so far as to suggest that better parenting or firmer discipline would lead to a quick resolution of their problems. Parents also report that others expect them to be able to control their children's behavior better than they actually can. All told, the combination of self-blame and condemnation by others leads many parents of mentally ill children to feel helpless about their situation.

The Effects of the Zombie Apocalypse on Childhood Mental Illness

As the dead rise, so will the mental health problems of children and adolescence. How can they not? Not only will youth endure the same apocalyptic-related pressures as their parents (e.g., poverty, trauma, violence, and the like), but they will also have to contend with stressors unique to childhood, such as the quality of parenting. As mentioned in the previous chapter, the Zombie Apocalypse will increase parenting stress and the occurrence of mental illness in parents, both of which will adversely affect the care that children receive. Moreover, immaturities in the physical, social, emotional, and cognitive domains of development will render children more vulnerable to the adverse effect of disasters than adults, and without mental health treatment, the probability of childhood mental health disorders improving on their own is quite small.

Psychologists describe the emotional and behavioral problems of youth in terms of two broad dimensions: externalizing and internalizing. *Externalizing behaviors* refer to aggressive, oppositional, or otherwise negative behaviors directed at other people or objects. Examples include fighting, yelling, and the destruction of property. In contrast, *internalizing behaviors* occur when emotional negativity turns inward, leading to self-loathing, guilt, fearfulness, social withdrawal, loneliness, and sadness.

Both externalizing and internalizing behaviors occur when youth have difficulty coping with stressful situations. Both types of behaviors will increase during the Zombie Apocalypse. Because externalizing behaviors are loud and disruptive, parenting children exhibiting these behaviors will be especially problematic when surrounded by the dead. Noise is, after all, an attractant to zombies. Internalizing behaviors are by their very nature quiet, as they reside in the minds of children and adolescents. Nevertheless, they could prove equally deadly when the dead rise as a profound sense of hopelessness can lead to suicidal behavior. If the suicide occurs in private and does not destroy the brain, the decedent will reanimate as the living dead.

Final Thoughts

What differentiates highly aggressive and violent youth from others? Psychologists contend that the answer lies in the relative triggering of the *behavioral activation* and *behavioral inhibition systems*. The behavioral activation system promotes the use of justified, rewarded, and unpunished aggressive actions, such as using force to obtain provisions or receiving accolades from peers after pummeling an acquaintance. In contrast, by generating feelings of anxiety, the behavioral inhibition system "puts the brakes" on aggression, thereby reducing the probability of its occurrence. Highly aggressive children and adolescents function with a hypoactive behavioral inhibition system. Without feelings of anxiety or guilt, once an aggressive behavior starts, it rarely stops. As you can see, when the benefits of aggression outweigh the perceived detriments, aggression will continue unabated.

During the Zombie Apocalypse, prohibitions against violence toward the dead will be virtually non-existent. Similarly, parents, peers, and other community members will reward youth for dispatching zombies. At the same time, as youth destroy the brains of more and more walkers, the anxiety generated by the behavioral inhibition system will diminish. In other words, youth will become desensitized to the killing of zombies, which will make all forms of aggression and violence more palatable. Thus, changes to the behavioral activation and behavioral inhibition systems caused by the killing of zombies will most likely result in increased aggression towards the living. In support of this contention, consider that youth playing highly aggressive contact sports, such a football and wrestling, are more likely than other youth to get into serious fights.

Similarly, veterans returning from active combat have higher rates of aggressive and violent behavior in their civilian lives than veterans without combat exposure. Thus, parents must make sure that their children will be violent enough to survive a zombie attack, but not so violent that they injure, maim or kill humans unless necessary. Eastern philosophy, such as that found in martial arts, may prove beneficial to parents in reducing carry-over violence. In fact, despite the aggressive and combative nature of the sport, teens engaging in martial arts show a reduction in aggressive behavior over time. Proponents of the martial arts contend that its focus on fighting without aggression, the demonstration of respect for teachers and opponents, the use of meditation, and the promotion of self-restraint and non-violence accounts for this finding.

8. Contextual Sources of Stress and Support

As portrayed on *The Walking Dead*, the lives of Lizzie Samuels and Carl Grimes have many parallels. Both had a parent die in front of them. Lizzie's father succumbed to a walker bite. Carl's mother perished during childbirth. Both feel very comfortable around the undead. For Lizzie, it is to befriend them. For Carl, it is to slaughter them. Both have killed children in cold blood. Lizzie stabbed her younger sister to death. Carl shot a teenage enemy combatant as he was surrendering. Both profess reasons that make sense only to them for taking those lives. For Lizzie, the killing meant that her sister, Mika, would have eternal life as a walker.[1] For Carl, it was a justified shooting of a potential threat.[2] Finally, because of their violent actions, others expressed concerns over their psychological well-being.

Following their respective homicidal acts, there is one noteworthy difference related to the continued care of Carl and Lizzie. Rick's friends were willing to help monitor and guide Carl after the shooting. In contrast, finding themselves in isolation, Carol had only her traveling companion, Tyreese, to help watch over a decidedly dangerous (and out of touch with reality) Lizzie, along with Judith, an infant in their care. At the time, the probability of finding someone to help manage Lizzie seemed highly unlikely. In the end, Rick gives Carl a lecture and a reprieve. Carol, on the other hand, takes Lizzie into a field, tells her to look at a grove of flowers, and quietly puts a bullet into the back of her head.[3]

As these examples illustrate, during the Zombie Apocalypse, the presence of a supportive environment can be the difference between life and death. In the two previous chapters, I discussed how parent and child characteristics independently influence parenting. However, the interpersonal

136

contexts in which parents find themselves, along with the social support and stress they produce—collectively referred to as *contextual sources of stress and support*—are also critical determinants of parenting.

Contextual sources of stress and support occur in the broader social contexts in which parents find themselves. Such contexts can take place within or outside of the primary family setting. *Within the family* contextual sources include intimate partners, children, and extended family members that live together. In contrast, *outside of the family* contextual sources are friends, coworkers, neighbors, relatives, and the like that live separately from the parent. In both contexts, individuals outside of the parent-child dyad provide the parent with support, stress, or both. Regardless, parenting is affected.

Within Family Contextual Sources of Stress and Support

Within the family, parents encounter numerous sources of stress and support, including relationships with their intimate partners, children, and other family members. First, I review the indirect effects of intimate partner conflict and satisfaction on parenting. Subsequently, I discuss the influence of co-parents, alloparents, and the family system as a whole on parenting stress and behavior.

The Influence Intimate Partner Relationships on Parenting

For better or worse, intimate partners directly affect each other's self-esteem, self-confidence, emotional states, psychological well-being, and ability to cope. In turn, these characteristics influence a parent's mood while interacting with their children, the amount of parenting stress they perceive, and, ultimately, the caregiving they provide.

RELATIONSHIP CONFLICT. *Relationship conflict* refers to expressions of aggression, disagreement, and hostility between intimate partners. Conflicting couples quarrel over just about anything, including relatives, money, politics, jealousy, and alcohol consumption. Other problems are more specific to parenting, such as the use and type of discipline, educational decisions, and the performance of essential childcare. Nevertheless, psychologists do not solely measure intimate partner relationships by the amount of arguing alone, but also by the quality of it.

John Gottman forwards four distinct communications styles that when present can do irreparable harm to an intimate partner relationship. Collectively he refers to them as the "Four Horsemen of the Apocalypse." In the biblical version of the four horsemen, the appearance of Conquest, War, Famine, and Death signified the end of times. In Gottman's relationship-centered version, the presence of criticism, contempt, defensiveness, and stonewalling indicate that a potential dissolution of a relationship is imminent.

The first Gottman horseman, *criticism*, refers to nonconstructive negative statements about an intimate partner that emphasize defects in their character in absolute and extreme terms. An example is telling an intimate partner that they are always self-centered, thinking of no one but themselves. The second Gottman horseman, *contempt*, involves attempts to make one's intimate partner feel worthless through hostility, name-calling, condescension, ridicule, and disrespect. When an individual engages in contempt, they do so to assume a position of moral superiority over their intimate partner. The next Gottman horseman, *defensiveness*, is a form of self-protection. It frequently occurs in response to criticism. Defensive individuals present themselves as innocent victims and frequently employ reverse blame rather than accepting any responsibility for the couple's problems. The final Gottman horseman, *stonewalling*, often occurs in response to contempt. Individuals using this communication style stop responding to their intimate partners, tune them out and distance themselves from them both emotionally and physically. When stonewalling is present, one partner erects a metaphorical barrier between themselves and their intimate partner. Even in the best of circumstances, Gottman's four horsemen can wreak havoc on relationships. However, as life becomes increasingly stressful, criticism, contempt, defensiveness, and stonewalling become routine and intimate partner relationships suffer.

RELATIONSHIP SATISFACTION. *Relationship satisfaction* refers to the sense of gratification and contentment between intimate partners. In addition to the amount and type of relationship conflict present, other dynamics influence relationship satisfaction, including interpersonal communication, the ability to solve problems jointly, having fun, and accepting, tolerating and adjusting to each other's differences. However, one of the strongest predictors of relationship satisfaction is *affective affirmation—*

the communication of a loving and accepting attitude toward, or the unconditional approval of, an intimate partner. Couples that frequently engage in affective affirmation report higher levels of relationship satisfaction than those that do not. Finally, when something terrible happens, couples low in relationship satisfaction are likely to blame their partners, rather than placing responsibility on factors outside of their relationship, such as fate or unforeseen circumstances. And as intimate partners become less satisfied with one another, the prospects of them staying together for more than a few years drops dramatically.

PARENTING IN THE CONTEXT OF RELATIONSHIP CONFLICT AND SATISFACTION. Many people believe that having children will bring intimate partners closer together. Is this truly the case? For most couples, the answer is "No." As evidence, consider that couples without children report higher levels of relationship satisfaction than couples with children. Although most couples perceive the birth of a child to be an amazing and beautiful moment, within a year or so after the birth, 67 percent of intimate partners report a decrease in relationship satisfaction,[4] and with each successive child, relationship satisfaction continues to decline. Parents note that the restrictions of freedom associated with parenting, and disagreements over child rearing, adversely affect relationships with their intimate partners.

What about the reverse? Does the quality of an intimate partner relationship extend to parenting? To address this question, Fincham and Hall forward three potential explanatory models. First, there is the *compartmentalization model*, which contends that relationship conflict, satisfaction, and overall quality *do not* affect parenting, as parents can successfully separate (i.e., compartmentalize) romantic relationships from their caregiving responsibilities. Thus, regardless of the conflict and satisfaction existing between intimate partners, sensitive parents remain sensitive, harsh parents remain harsh, and inattentive parents remain inattentive. According to this model, romantic relationships neither improve nor detract from parenting. Under the *compensatory model*, parents convert the negative energy, frustration, and emotions generated by poor intimate partner relationships into positive parenting practices. Thus, to compensate for an unrewarding romantic relationship, parents create a fulfilling one with their children. Finally, there is the *spillover model*, wherein the emotional tone of the intimate partner relationship "spills over" into the parent-child relationship. Thus, love, affection, and sensitivity between parents turns into responsive and sensitive caregiving behaviors toward children. In contrast, conflicts between parents (and the accompanying negative feelings, such as anger, resentment, and disgust) turn into maladaptive parenting behaviors, such as yelling, hostility, ignoring, and punitive actions.

So which of the three models does empirical research support? First, there is little evidence that parents can compartmentalize their feelings and effectively separate relationship issues and emotions from their parenting or that parents can convert negative relationship energy into positive caregiving practices. So while compartmentalization and compensatory behavior are theoretically possible, it seems that they are both practical improbabilities.

However, there is support for the spillover model. For example, high levels of relationship conflict and low levels of relationship satisfaction lead to maladaptive parenting practices, such as harsh, critical, and guilt-inducing forms of discipline. Moreover, such couples tend to reject, or inconsistently respond to, their children's emotional needs. In contrast, couples high in relationships satisfaction and low in relationship conflict are warm, sensitive, and responsive to their children's needs. As you can see, as long as intimate partner relationships flourish, so does parenting, but when relationships begin to sour, caregiving suffers.

RELATIONSHIP CONFLICT AND SATISFACTION IN THE ZOMBIE APOCALYPSE. Stress negatively influences intimate partner relationships. It does so by increasing relationship conflict and decreasing relationship satisfaction. Psychologists pinpoint four significant sources of stress that can adversely affect intimate relationships and bring about Gottman's four horsemen: life changes, daily hassles, economic conditions, and catastrophes. *Life changes* refer to significant changes in a person's life, such as getting married, starting a new career, or losing a loved one to a roaming band of the undead. Most of the time, people can effectively cope with a single life change without adverse consequences to an intimate partner relationship. However, when there are a number of life changes occurring at the same time, the readjustment required to cope becomes overwhelming and intimate partner relationships deteriorate.

Although life changes can bring stress to intimate partner relationships, the "little things" in everyday life can also cause significant problems. Examples of such *daily hassles*—everyday difficulties that cause stress—include leaving dirty clothes on the floor and toothpaste remnants in the sink, failing to shut dresser drawers and toilet lids, and annoying habits such as chewing loudly. Nevertheless, there is considerable variation in the daily hassles of intimate couples, with problem behaviors in one relationship considered innocuous in another. Regardless of their source, the cumulative effect of daily hassles on stress is powerful, affecting both an individual's psychological and physical health and the couple's well-being.

Regarding stressful economic conditions, more than three billion people (which is close to half of the world's population) live in poverty, surviving on $2.50 each day or less. And in the United States, a country of more than 325 million people, close to 41 million Americans, including 13 million children under the age of 18, live in poverty.[5] One stress-inducing aspect of impoverishment is *food insecurity*, defined as a lack of consistent access to food for a healthy life. Those with high levels of food insecurity not only worry about obtaining food and having food run out, but they also experience disrupted eating patterns (e.g., cutting or skipping meals) and reduced food intake.[6] In addition to suffering from a number of physical ailments (such as malnutrition), impoverished parents and their children also experience significant psychological difficulties, such as increased levels of anxiety and depression. Moreover, couples under economic strain show reductions in warmth and support while at the same time engaging in more hostile and conflictual interactions.

Finally, social scientists define *catastrophes* as events that disrupt lives and cause death and destruction for a large number of individuals. Examples include natural disasters, pandemics, wars, and, of course, apocalyptic events involving zombies. The unpredictability of catastrophic events and the perceived lack of control they engender result in physical, emotional (e.g., anger, fear), and psychological difficulties (e.g., anxiety, depression) that adversely influence relationships. Moreover, the effects of cataclysmic events last long after the imminent danger from the disaster has passed. For example, five years after Hurricane Katrina devastated New Orleans, the city's suicide rate was still more than double of what it was before the storm.[7]

The Zombie Apocalypse brings with it all of the stressors mentioned above. The catastrophic nature of an undead rising will result in intimate partners perceiving little control over their lives. Life changes will be plenty, as all will need to adjust to their new apocalyptic way of being. Food insecurity will be the norm for most, at least until agrarian communities and trade routes can be set up. Nonetheless, finding acceptable foodstuffs for infants will be especially tricky. Infants require breast milk or formula for survival before eventually transitioning to solid foods between four to six months of age. Even then, their food has to be mashed before they can eat it safely. Thus, a significant source of stress for parents of infants will be finding food appropriate for consumption.

Zombie Apocalypse or not, there is no getting around daily hassles, but in a zombie-filled landscape, new forms of these everyday annoyances will arise, such as braining the undead gathering on the fence line, burning corpses, or cleaning rotting flesh off of the window sills. Moreover, the effect of having to combat the undead, and at times the living, will take a toll on intimate partner relationships. United States soldiers report that upon returning from combat duty, their intimate partner relationships become more conflictual and less intimate. During the Zombie Apocalypse, couples needing to kill the living and re-kill the living dead will experience similar harmful effects.

Taken together, the pressures associated with living through an undead rising will produce feelings of individual distress, which in turn will lead to conflict between intimate partners. And where there is intimate partner conflict, Gottman's Four Horsemen of the Apocalypse are sure to follow. As relationship conflict rises, and relationship satisfaction decreases, the ability to effectively parent will also diminish. Furthermore, relationship problems are extremely draining for parents, and when relationships become distressed, many parents will find it difficult to recognize when their children are in need of support. However, even if parents correctly identify their children's necessities, they may not be able to muster the resources necessary to respond to them appropriately or sensitively.

The Family System

Regardless of how many individuals are involved, parenting always takes place within a network of family members. *Family systems* may contain few members, as is the case of a single parent living with their only child, or many members, such as in a multigenerational household. According to the systems viewpoint, the lives of family members intertwine, affecting relationships both directly and indirectly. For example, following an argument between parents about burning corpses upwind of the family home, Parent #1 acts hostilely toward their oldest child, who in turn bullies a younger sibling. After witnessing the bullying behavior, Parent #2 tells Parent #1 that they are a bad role model for their children and an argument about childrearing ensues. Thus, interactions between family members can cause ripple effects throughout the entire household, with struggles or encouragement in one part of the system disrupting or benefiting other parts.

Next, I review additional systems operating with the family which affect parenting, namely, co-parenting, alloparenting, sibling relationships, and the family environment (when viewed as a unit).

CO-PARENTING. Parenting and co-parenting are not the same. *Parenting* refers to the process of caring for the psychological, social, emotional, cognitive, and physical needs of children from infancy through adulthood. In contrast, *co-parenting*—the ability of parents to work together in child-rearing—centers on the parent-parent relationship, with a focus on the presence or absence of mutual support and coordinated efforts in child care. Co-parenting occurs when two or more parents or parent figures (regardless of their biological relationship to the child or their romantic interest in each other) share the responsibilities of raising one or more children. As an example, consider the opening vignette of this chapter. Carol and Tyreese travel through a zombie-infested wasteland with three children (Lizzie, Mika, and Judith) in their care. After Lizzie kills Mika, Carol and Tyreese (functioning as de facto co-parents) agree to murder Lizzie to protect Judith. Regarding their co-parenting, Carol and Tyreese effectively work together to enact their final child care decision related to Lizzie—filicide.

Psychologists distinguish between three types of co-parenting interactions: cooperative, conflicted, and disengaged. *Cooperative co-parents*, like Carol and Tyreese, share in child care duties and view the arrangement as fair (even if one parent provides more child care than the other), appreciate and support each other's parenting decisions, and solve parenting disagreements amicably. In contrast, *conflicted co-parents* disapprove of their co-parent's childrearing, argue over the raising of their progeny, expect and enforce different rules and standards of behavior, and rarely cooperate. Take Rick and Lori, parents of seven-year-old Carl in *The Walking Dead* comic book. Against Lori's wishes, Rick provides Carl with a firearm and trains him how to use it. Rick and Lori conflict over this significant parenting issue, with Lori stating that her opinion, as a parent, no longer matters. The conversation ends when Lori walks away in disgust.[8] Finally, *disengaged co-parenting* occurs when co-parents function independently of one another, rarely discussing issues related to the care of their children. Although conflicts between co-parents are rare, so is cooperation, and, at times, contact.

A co-parent's individual ability to handle life's stressors, whether they are the result of daily hassles, significant life events, economic strain, or catastrophic events, is of paramount importance for effective co-parenting.

When stress becomes overwhelming for one parent (or both), the quality of their co-parenting suffers. This relationship dynamic occurs because parents struggling to meet the immediate demands of the situation (such as food insecurity, safety, and finding shelter) have few resources left with which to devote to co-parenting. In support of this contention, please consider the following statistic: for couples living in poverty (a source of chronic stress), cooperative co-parenting occurs less than 50 percent of the time.[9] Similarly, when a parent has a psychological disorder (such as anxiety, depression, or PTSD), they perceive parenting to be increasingly stressful. Subsequently, the quality of their co-parenting worsens, and the affected parent becomes less cooperative with, and more combative to, their partner.

ALLOPARENTING. Alloparenting refers to the feeding, care, and protection of children by their siblings and extended family members, such as grandparents, aunts and uncles, and cousins. Alloparenting is common in traditional societies, such as the foraging Toba of Formosa in Northern Argentina, where grandmothers and sisters regularly take care of infants and younger siblings. Across the Atlantic Ocean, for the Efé of the Ituri Forest in the Democratic Republic of the Congo, five-month-old infants spend more time with allomothers than with their birth mothers. Alloparenting is common in industrialized societies as well. Currently, more than 60 million Americans (comprising 20 percent of the population) live in multigenerational households,[10] resulting in many opportunities for within-family alloparenting. Alloparenting can also occur outside of the within-family context, as in the case when a parent drops their children off at a relative's house for daycare.

When parents are in need, when they have difficult decisions to make, when resources are lacking, or when something terrible happens to their family, alloparents can provide a much-needed boost in the form of *social support*—where one individual or group offers aid to another individual or group. Numerous studies show that people manage stress and trauma more successfully when they have the support of others. The same is true for parental functioning. Parenting is most effective, and perceived parenting stress is lower, in the presence of a robust social network than in its absence.

Parents benefit from four types of social support: emotional, tangible, informational, and appraisal. *Emotional social support* involves the provision of love, acceptance, concern and a listening ear. This type of support provides parents the opportunity to share painful emotions (e.g., feeling as though they are letting their children down; feeling sorry about having to re-kill their child's best friend), which if left unexpressed would become increasingly stressful. *Informational social support* involves the sharing of suggestions, advice, and information regarding the management of children. Examples include communicating disciplinary practices, strategies for getting kids to sleep, or techniques for distracting children in the face of disturbing events, such as seeing a zombie maul the neighbor. *Tangible social support* refers to direct assistance, such as changing diapers, taking kids to the park, teaching them how to brain a zombie, or just about any other parenting-related activity. Finally, *appraisal social support* imparts constructive feedback, affirmation, or judgments useful for self-evaluation. For example, family members may praise a parent for their handling of a particularly tricky situation but suggest that they monitor their children more, given the dangers of living in an apocalyptic environment.

Grandparents as Alloparents. Living in a multigenerational household has its challenges. There are more mouths to feed, fewer opportunities for privacy, the stretching of resources, blurred responsibilities, and relationship challenges with grandparents and intimate partners. Thus, rather than providing parents with social support, grandparents can add to, rather than detract from, parenting stress. Sometimes, parenting stress results from indirect processes, such as when the presence of a grandparent strains a couple's relationship satisfaction, which in turn increases parenting stress. At other times, the effect of grandparents on parenting stress is more direct. For example, the presence of an alloparenting grandparent can diminish a parent's sense of parental competence and effectiveness. Some grandparents may even undermine the parent's childrearing strategies (e.g., ignoring house rules related to braining a zombie alone), thereby introducing difficulties into the parent-child relationship.

An additional challenge to childrearing occurs when parents find themselves sandwiched between older and younger generations, providing simultaneous care for their aging parents and their growing children. Some see this arrangement as fulfilling, relishing in the fact that they can attend to a loved one that once took care of them. In fact, multigenerational caregivers that can master their dual roles successfully report high levels of life satisfaction and an overall positive sense of well-being. However, many who engage in multigenerational caregiving find the arrangement overwhelming, as they have little time for themselves, experience emotional and physical exhaustion, and struggle to meet the needs of both generations. Not surprisingly, such parents experience a great deal of stress related to caregiving.

Siblings as Alloparents. In many families, older siblings help reduce parenting stress by aiding their parents in the care of their younger brothers and sisters. Caretaking activities include meeting physiological needs (e.g., feeding, changing diapers), providing emotional support (e.g., comforting, soothing), and engaging in supervisory activities in which they keep their siblings occupied and out of harm's way. If necessary, older children can become permanent caregivers of their siblings. For example, due to the AIDS epidemic in Africa, close to 132,000 orphaned Tanzanian youth live in sibling-run households, with the average sibling-caregiver being 12 to 15 years of age.[11]

Although siblings can serve as stress-reducing alloparents, conflicts between siblings can add to parenting stress. Siblings fight with words, deeds, and fists, and they use power, tattling, deceit, and humiliation to prevail. When siblings fight, some parents intervene, whereas others let it naturally play out (within limits). Regardless, sibling conflict forces parents to decide on what to do next, thus contributing to the amount of parenting stress experienced. Parents express numerous concerns about the effects of their children's frequent squabbles. Some believe that the fighting will cause psychological damage and emotional scars in addition to the inevitable physical ones. Others are worried that their children will become bullies or fail to develop empathetic concern for others.

Nonetheless, it is normal for siblings to fight and fight often. Once the younger child enters toddlerhood, sibling squabbles occur at the rate of eight conflicts per hour. By middle childhood, siblings quarrel much less, around one to two times per day. As youth transition away from their families during adolescence, sibling relationships become more egalitarian and less intense than during childhood. However, throughout development, siblings that fight the most tend to have the most aggressive relationships, with painful physical altercations the norm.

FAMILY ENVIRONMENT. As the previous sections revealed, the presence of grandparents and siblings can either reduce or increase parenting stress. However, beyond the individual contributions of each family member, the family unit itself (composed of parents, children, and live-in relatives) is a strong determinant of parenting. Imagine a situation in which a parent gives their child a direction (e.g., "Be quiet or you'll attract the dead"), but rather than acquiescing, the child responds with belligerence. In turn, the parent becomes angry and hostile. Some parents start their discussions in a hostile and aggressive manner, and their children respond in kind. Such parent-child interactions become increasingly aversive, and, as a result, the children grow more aggressive. Over time, such interactions develop into a *coercive family environment*—defined as a home in which family members act aggressively or antisocially toward one another.

According to Gestalt psychology, the whole is greater than the sum of its parts, meaning that the way we perceive the world is more than just a simple combination of the individual components we take in. With regard to the impact of the family on parenting, this contention seems appropriate as well. To illustrate, let us examine Reuben Hill's ABC-X model of *family stress*—stress that threatens the functioning of the family.

According to Hill, stress results from the interaction of three types of variables referred to as "A" factors, "B" factors and "C" factors. "A" factors refer to stressors, events, or situations that place pressure on the family system and tax its collective resources. Examples include illness, loss of capital, destruction of the family home, or the resurrection of the dead. By comparison, "B" factors are the family's capabilities, assets, and strengths that help it cope with the stressors it encounters. As will be illustrated below, additional "B" factors come from supportive resources outside of the family, such as friends or community members. "C" factors refer to the meaning and appraisal of the stressors by the family. For example, whereas one family may view a difficult situation as manageable, another family may view it as a lost cause. Finally, the "X" factor is the likelihood that a family-based crisis will develop. Families that effectively manage the ABCs can balance the demands of the stressful situation and continue to function well as a family. However, families will become distressed when the cumulative effect of the ABCs tax family resources and capabilities, which ultimately results in tension-filled and dysfunctional behavior (such as a coercive family environment). At that point, parenting will take a backseat to the crisis the family is facing, and, as a result, the perceived level of parenting stress will increase.

The Family System in the Zombie Apocalypse. During the Zombie Apocalypse, factors that adversely affect co-parenting (such as the presence of mental illness and impoverished conditions) will be plentiful. As a result, previously cooperative co-parents will increasingly fight, and if the couple clashed before the apocalypse, there is no reason to believe that its co-parenting will improve once the dead rise; if anything, its co-parenting should get worse. Furthermore, the stress of the Zombie Apocalypse will adversely affect emotional self-regulation and aggressive tendencies for both parents and children alike. As a result, coercive family environments will increase in frequency, which will ultimately lead to the escalation or onset of aggressive behavior in children and adolescents. Indeed, youth raised in war zones that also endure high levels of family conflict act more aggressively than similarly stationed families, sans the conflict.

Potential mitigation of parenting stress will come in the form of social support offered by alloparents. The catastrophic nature of the Zombie Apocalypse means that families will need all kinds of social support, including emotional, informational, tangible, and appraisal. However, when extended family members are huddled together out of necessity rather than choice, the interactions between family members may become more stressful than supportive. Sibling relationships may fare no better. After all, the factors that increase sibling conflicts, such as hunger, fatigue, illness, overcrowding, and changes to the family constellation (e.g., a family members leaves, dies, or zombifies), will be mainstays of the Zombie Apocalypse. Although there is potential for parenting stress to decrease in the presence of supportive co-parents and family members, the likelihood of receiving such support diminishes when everyone in the family is stressed and in need of assistance as they will be when the dead rise.

It is unlikely that parents will have to endure the stress of being sandwiched between generations. The reason is simple: the elderly will have great difficulty surviving an undead wasteland. Medical conditions alone will cause a great deal of death among the aged. By way of illustration, the majority of elderly Syrian refugees in Lebanon have hypertension, nearly half have diabetes, and close to a third have heart disease. Because there are no medications readily available to manage these conditions, the risk of death increases dramatically. Regardless of age, the greatest threat to the survival of refugees is the absence of adequate medical care.[12]

The elderly's lack of mobility and stamina will lead to their demise as well. Imagine that a swarm of zombies is quickly approaching an encampment, and the people there must make a swift escape. Parents will be able to scoop up infants and young children with relative ease and whisk them away to safety. Older children and adolescents will be able to run away on their own. However, moving the elderly is a much harder feat to accomplish. As a result, family members will leave behind many of their aged relatives. Sadly, this was the case in Somalia during a period of drought and famine. To survive, Somalians needed to walk for days without food and water. Knowing beforehand that the conditions of the journey would mean certain death for the aged, adult children often had to leave their elderly parents behind.[13]

Finally, let us see how the ABC-X model explains the effects of the Zombie Apocalypse on the parenting stress experienced by two different families of four (both with two adults and with two teens). First, we have Family #1, who has been living off the grid and preparing for an apocalyptic event (of any sort) for some time. Next, we have Family #2, who shops three times a week at Wegmans, earns its living on the Internet, and has access to few tools and zero weapons. On the first day of the Zombie Apocalypse, both families wake to find their houses surrounded by the living dead (the "A" factor). For Family #1, positive "B" factors might include its physical strength and combat training, along with its abundant food stores, medical supplies, and weapons cache. On the other hand, the fact that its resident medical expert is now a member of the zombie horde, and the unfortunate loss of power due to a broken generator, comprises the negative "B" factors. Family #2 is also without power and access to medical care. However, without the Internet, and lacking any survival skills whatsoever, it has few positive "B" factors. Regarding "C" factors, the Zombie Apocalypse will validate Family #1's extensive preparations and lifestyle, engendering a positive outlook for its survival. On the other hand, Family #2, realizing that it is ill prepared for a loss of power for two days, let alone an undead rising, view the situation as dire, and the likelihood of their survival beyond a week as minuscule. Taking all of the ABCs into account, the possibility that the Zombie Apocalypse will cause Family #1 to become dysfunctional is relatively low, whereas for Family #2 it is almost a certainty. Finally, the level of parenting stress in Family #1 will be much smaller than that experienced by Family #2.

Outside Family Contextual Sources of Stress and Support

When thinking about the determinants of parenting, the old African proverb "It takes a village to raise a child" begs the question "By what method does that happen?" Earlier, I discussed how family members living in the same household serve as contextual sources of stress and support for parents. Here, I consider the influence of friends, neighbors, and extended family members (i.e., *social networks*), as well as entire communities, on child-rearing.

Social Networks and Community Support

Raising a child in social isolation makes parenting difficult and potentially dysfunctional. Without others to rely on, parenting stress can build up quickly, reducing the quality of parenting and potentially placing children at risk for maltreatment.[14] In contrast, social networks benefit parents through the various types of social support they provide. For example, through the provision of both emotional and appraisal forms of social support, social networks reduce parenting stress by improving a parent's sense of well-being and caregiving efficacy. Similarly, information and tangible assistance gathered through social networks can strengthen parenting by providing techniques for effective parenting and guidance on the appropriateness of children's behavior. Thus, social networks ease parenting stress because they allow parents to free up resources that would otherwise go to parenting-related activities. In essence, social networks provide care for caregivers. However, for a social network to be effective, the support provided needs to match the support desired. Case in point: parents in need of tangible support (e.g., babysitting) may find appraisal support unwelcomed, especially if the advice given is unrequested and critical of their parenting.

Beyond social networks, the broader community in which parents live also influences childrearing. Communities consist of an array of different people, civic groups, businesses, religious organizations, and governmental agencies. Psychologists refer to the social networks operating within and between groups in a community as *social capital*. Examples of social capital include neighbors helping neighbors, 12-step programs, food banks, libraries, and neighborhood watches. Social capital provides community members with social support in all of its forms. Parents benefit from social capital is a variety of ways, ranging from community centers that offer after-school activities and tutoring services to support groups for single parents or those that have recently lost a family member. Thus, social capital allows parents to function effectively as its helps them accomplish goals that would be difficult, if not impossible, to achieve on their own.

Social Networks and Community Support in the Zombie Apocalypse

Social networks and community resources provide parents with social support that can both reduce the harmful effects of adversity or prevent adverse situations from occurring in the first place. However, during violent and hazardous conditions of the Zombie Apocalypse, where supportive resources will be scarce and social capital lacking, many survivors will behave in a competitive, self-focused, and predatory manner. As an illustration, consider Cabrini-Green, one of the most notorious public housing projects in the United States. Residents, steeped in poverty, lived in one of eight 15-story high-rise apartment buildings designed with motel-like exterior hallways encased in steel mesh. Gang violence and drug use were rampant. Its problems were so severe and so long lasting that after decades of disrepair and hazardous living conditions the city tore it down.

Not surprisingly, living in Cabrini-Green made parenting extremely challenging. For example, parents were afraid to allow their children to play on the grounds of the complex because of concerns of potential victimization. Children living in dangerous neighborhoods do experience high levels of victimization, either by experiencing it themselves or by witnessing it firsthand. One study found that in violence-prone neighborhoods around 50 percent of children report seeing a shooting, stabbing, or killing.[15] Thus, parents living in high-risk (i.e., violent, drug infested, and impoverished) neighborhoods like Cabrini-Green face two distinct parenting-related tasks: (1) helping their children survive the hazardous environment in which they live and (2) promoting positive youth outcomes (e.g., academic success). When the dead rise, expect these parental tasks to replicate in every community. However, before children can thrive, they must stay alive.

To promote their children's survival, many parents will insulate youth from their surroundings by strictly supervising and controlling their behavior as well as painstakingly monitoring their friends, whereabouts, and activities. For example, parents in violent neighborhoods impose curfews, restrict friendships to children of their liking, and chaperone their children (or have someone they trust to do so in their stead) when they venture out of their homes and into the neighborhood. Additionally, parents will seek opportunities for their children outside of their communities to help them thrive (such as attending school and partaking in extracurricular activities miles from home). As you can see, a high level of parental vigilance and effort is required when rearing children in violent and crime-ridden neighborhoods devoid of sufficient social capital. And when the dead rise, there will be little social capital left from which parents can draw.

During the Zombie Apocalypse, both informal and formal support groups/organizations in the community will cease to exist, and their members will be either dead or experiencing life circumstances (e.g., poverty, loss of a family member) similar to those seeking help. When the challenges of providing aid become overwhelming or the emotional drain of assistance too intense, support providers become less available, withdraw their support entirely, or refuse to assist those asking for help. And when individuals in need of aid engage in bizarre or dangerous behavior, few people are willing to assist.

When the dead rise, the inherent dangers of living in an apocalyptic hell-scape, and the stretching or absence of resources, means that few survivors will be able and willing to offer their assistance to others. With social networks gone and social capital absent, parents will find themselves raising their children with little support from others and potentially in social isolation. In turn, parenting stress and the probability of child maltreatment will both increase.

Harkening back to the opening vignette, it becomes clear that Carol and Tyreese lacked social support. Because of their isolation, they were unable to obtain information on trauma-induced mental illness or its treatment. There was no one to offer them tangible support (e.g., monitoring Lizzie's behavior), and there was no one outside of their relationship to appraise their caretaking or discuss the emotional strains of watching a murderous, delusional pre-teen. Carol and Tyreese were alone, similar in circumstance and without the resources needed to be supportive of one another. Even if someone were available, the bizarre nature of Lizzie's behavior would have made it difficult to find help. As happens in highly stressful situations lacking in resources and social support, child maltreatment followed.

Final Thoughts

As demonstrated in the last three chapters, parent and child characteristics, along with contextual factors, independently influence parenting. However, because a parent's behavior is multiply determined, the interaction of the various subsystems also affects parental beliefs, attitudes, and practices. Keep in mind that each of the three determinants of parenting operates in either a supportive mode or stressful mode (Box 8.1 provides examples of each). Whereas the *supportive mode* engenders competent, growth-promoting parenting, the *stressful mode* impedes it. Thus, parenting is at its best when child, parent, and contextual determinants are all in supportive modes and least effective when they are all in stressful modes. For example, during the Zombie Apocalypse, raising a temperamentally difficult child (stressful child characteristic), without an available social network (stressful context) will be more challenging for parents with personality characterized by emotional instability (stressful parent characteristic) relative to parents whose personalities are more emotionally stable (supportive parent characteristic).

Box 8.1: *Examples of Supportive and Stressful Modes for the Primary Determinants of Parenting*

Supportive Modes

- **Parent Characteristics:** high in openness, agreeableness, extraversion, and conscientiousness, and low in emotional instability
- **Child Characteristics:** an easy-going temperament; high levels of emotional regulation
- **Contextual Sources:** a supportive close-knit family living near one another; a supportive intimate partner

Stressful Modes

- **Parent Characteristics:** high in emotional instability and perfectionism; a history of maltreatment; the presence of depression, anxiety, hostility, and anger
- **Child Characteristics:** difficult temperament; emotional dysregulation
- **Contextual Sources:** conflicts with intimate parents; coercive family environments; dangerous neighborhoods

---

Take Syria, a war-ravaged country from which nearly 5.5 people have fled since 2011. Approximately 48 percent of Syrian refugees are under 18 years of age, with 14 percent age four or younger.[16] Researcher Aala El-Khani has documented the struggles that refugee parents face as they attempt to raise their children under incredibly difficult circumstances. El-Khani's findings point to the three determinants of parenting as the primary sources of stress that parents encounter on a daily basis.

Contextual sources of stress include difficulties stemming from their camp/living conditions. For example, food insecurity, poor sanitation, lack of clothing, filth, disease, and a chaotic and dangerous environment make providing a safe and stable setting for children difficult, if not impossible. The second source of parenting stress involves characteristics of the child, such as behavioral issues (e.g., disobedience, impulsivity, aggression), emotional difficulties (e.g., increases in sadness, fear, emotional withdrawal) and communication problems (e.g., ignoring requests, disrespectful responses, shouting). Syrian parents describe their children's play as becoming more violent and their behaviors with others as increasingly rude and hostile. In fact, almost one-third of Syrian refugee youth show marked increases in aggression and behavioral problems.[17] Moreover, parent-child conflict occurs daily, as children attempt to explore (out of boredom or interest) their surroundings, only to have their parents impose limitations on their behavior. Finally, parent characteristics related to stress include feeling guilty about their increasing use of corporal punishment, their inability to meet the needs of their children, and struggling with feelings of anger, abandonment, sadness, and anxiety related to their predicament.

Remember, these difficulties occurred even though Syrian refugees received more than $5 billion worth of aid, resulting in 2.5 million people getting food support, 1.1 million people benefiting from improved water systems, 1.5 million refugees undergoing healthcare consultations, and close to one million children enrolled in educational programs.[18] Now, remove the food and water support, take away access to health care, and eliminate the educational system. Without the help of others, conditions go from catastrophic to apocalyptic. When the dead rise and civilization falls, parenting stress will skyrocket. Sources of that stress will emanate from the child, the environment, and the parents themselves. To make matters worse, contextual sources of support will diminish or disappear altogether. During the Zombie Apocalypse, all three determinants of parenting will be decidedly negative, and the world will experience the adverse circumstances currently faced by refugees all over the world.

Section Four:
Parent-Child Relationships

9. Attachment

Benny Imura—the angst-ridden teenage protagonist in Jonathan Maberry's dystopian post-apocalyptic zombie novel *Rot & Ruin*[1]—has a vivid first memory, though it is not a pleasant one. It took place on First Night—the day when the dead became the living dead. Eighteen-month-old Benny remembers his mother, dressed in a white blouse with red sleeves, screaming; there was lots of screaming. Benny recalls his mother placing him into the waiting arms of his 20-year-old brother, Tom, who carried him out of a first-story bedroom window and away from the terror inside. Benny helplessly watched as a zombie, who just happened to be his father, grabbed his mother from behind and pulled her out of view. He would never see either of his parents alive again.

Fast-forward 14 years and one thing is clear: Benny is still angry with the undead for taking the lives of his parents and even more furious with Tom for letting it happen. What is less clear is what happened in the years between First Night and the present. Tom, a zombie hunter, spent a lot of time away from the community in which Benny was raised. Who soothed Benny when he was sad? Who comforted him when he cried? When Benny woke up in the middle of a zombie-filled nightmare, who was there to drive his fears away? Equally important to the question of who cared for Benny is the issue of the quality of care that Benny received. Was it loving and kind or was it controlling and harsh?

Do these questions even require answering? Starting in middle childhood, most children have few, if any, specific memories of their lives before age three or four—a phenomenon known as *childhood amnesia*—and as children age, they possess even fewer recollections from toddlerhood. If children cannot remember their earliest interactions with others, how important can they be to their attitudes, behaviors, and overall well-being? In short, very! The long answer, which delves deeply into attachment theory, follows.

Core Elements of Attachment Theory

In the late 1950s, John Bowlby developed attachment theory to explain the nature of a child's emotional bond to its mother. Before Bowlby, the accepted belief was that because feeding was enjoyable the infant associated pleasure with the source of its food, usually the mother. As a result, the child created an emotional connection to her. However, as research in this area coalesced, it became clear to Bowlby that attachments to caregivers developed independently of feeding. Instead, Bowlby surmised that attachment was an evolutionary adaptation. In the environment of evolutionary adaptedness, infants who formed attachments to caregivers survived long enough to reproduce. In contrast, infants without attachment relationships, even if well fed by those around them, were still at significant risk for predation as well as accidental harm from the dangers in their environments. Attachment equated to protection and survival in the environment of evolutionary adaptedness, and it will continue to do so once the dead rise.

During infancy, an *attachment* refers to a long-lasting emotional bond between an infant and its caregiver (i.e., an *attachment figure*). Beyond infancy, attachment bonds can form between siblings, among friends, and in intimate partner relationships. However, given attachment's foundational importance to the developing child, this chapter will primarily focus on the attachment of children to their parents.

The Attachment Behavioral System

The *attachment behavioral system* is an organized set of behaviors designed to achieve proximity to an attachment figure. Enacted by themselves, or in combination, behaviors such as arm raising, reaching, crawling, crying, smiling, and clinging bring (or keep) the attachment figure and child together. The attachment behavioral system operates in service of the emotional bond that connects a child to its caregiver. Internal conditions, such as pain, illness, and fatigue, elicit attachment behaviors. So do environmental circumstances, such as frightening stimuli, strangers, and impending or enduring separation from an attachment figure as well as interpersonal conflicts and rebuffs from others. Regardless of the cause of their activation, the desired result is the same: proximity to the caregiver.

In infancy, the activation of the attachment behavioral system requires physical contact with, or at the very least proximity to, an attachment figure for attachment behaviors to ease. A parent's hug can soothe a crying child, calm a frightened one, or reassure a child of its parent's availability for future comfort and care (if needed). However, with increasing age, children feel comforted by the mere sight of their attachment figures or the sounds of their voices, a phenomenon known as *felt security*. Even pictures of caregivers can make children feel safe and secure. As children age, their newfound mobility allows them to crawl, toddle, walk, or run to protective attachment figures as needed. Not surprisingly, such proximity seeking behaviors are predisposed to occur in times of distress.

Attachment in the Context of Other Behavioral Systems

In addition to the attachment behavioral system, Bowlby identified four other systems that affect children's proximity to their attachment figures and thus potential protection from harm: the fear behavioral system, the exploratory behavioral system, the sociable behavioral system, and the caregiving behavioral system. I address each in turn.

The *fear behavioral system* helps children avoid, escape, and garner protection from frightening and potentially dangerous situations and stimuli. Evolution has ensured that loud noises, darkness, being alone, and sudden movements naturally activate the fear behavioral system. So can objects and events that did not exist in the environment of evolutionary adaptedness, but through experience or observation, became associated with peril. Take, for instance, the severed head of a zombie lying on the ground, which, despite its lack of a body, is still capable of biting and infecting humans. Some young children may be predisposed to investigate the head out of curiosity or a desire to play with it. However, through scolding and loud warnings, infants and toddlers will quickly become fearful of this seemingly playful, moveable "toy."

Once activated, the fear behavioral system results in three primary actions. First, infants and children can cry, scream, or otherwise signal their distress to bring attachment figures to them. Second, youth can run away from the fear stimulus and hide. Concealment behaviors typically occur when no attachment figures are available. Third, children can move toward their attachment figures. To illustrate, imagine a situation where a group of zombies attacks an encampment. Upon seeing the dead, some children scream, many run and hide, and others venture across the zombie-infested courtyard to find their parents. In such situations, children running to their caregivers will find themselves closer to jeopardy. Unfortunately, rather than finding the protective arms of their parents, some youth will inevitably run into the outstretched arms of the undead.

Nevertheless, more children are likely to survive dangerous situations by heading toward protective caregivers than away from them. Consider this: for youth attempting to run and hide, there may be other revenants lying in wait in the direction of their escape route and nobody there to protect them. Thus, proximity seeking behavior increases the probability that at least some (though not all) children will survive the threat. It is worth mentioning that the activation of the fear behavioral system also results in the activation of the attachment behavioral system. Both work in concert to protect the child from danger.

The *exploratory behavioral system* compels infants and children to investigate their surroundings. In contrast to the attachment and fear behavioral systems, the exploratory behavioral system moves children away from their attachment figures, thus increasing the distance between a child and its potential source of comfort and protection. Nevertheless, the exploratory system provides a survival advantage because it helps children learn about the social and physical intricacies of their environments. At the same time, children must balance their desire to explore with their need for protection. To achieve equilibrium between these two competing motivations, children engage in *secure-base behavior*—defined as exploring the environment, but remaining close enough to an attachment figure to receive comfort and protection, if the need should arise. Once the attachment behavioral system activates, regardless of the cause (e.g., injury, loneliness, or danger), exploration stops and will not continue until a caregiver meets the child's attachment needs.

Attachment relationships are not the only interpersonal connections that children develop. Across childhood, youth establish friendships with peers, siblings, and adults. The *sociable behavioral system* governs behaviors related to friendliness, companionship, and sociability with others. When this system is activated, youth desire to interact and play with attachment and nonattachment figures of all ages. However, there are marked differences between the attachment and sociable behavioral systems. First, situations and stimuli that activate both the fear and attachment behavioral systems (such as being alone, startled, and injured) terminate the sociable behavioral system. For instance, children scared at the sight of an approaching zombie will stop whatever games they are playing and seek the safety of caregivers. Notably, this example also illustrates the second difference between the attachment and sociable behavioral systems: children use their friends for play, but not protection. Third, much like the exploratory behavioral system, it is only after meeting attachment needs that the sociable behavioral system can activate.

Unlike the behavioral systems above, the final behavioral system operates within the attachment figure rather than the attached child. The *caregiving behavioral system* consists of behaviors that promote proximity to the child as well as providing nurturance, comfort, and support when the child is in real, perceived, or potential danger. Principal behaviors in the service of the caregiving behavioral system include retrieval, restraining, reaching, calling, and soothing.

With regard to reproductive fitness, attachment theory proposes that parents are motivated to protect their young. In turn, the infant promotes its survival by assuring proximity to a protective caregiver (whether the child goes to the caregiver or vice versa). Picture several infants sitting on the ground playing with the rocks that lay at their feet. Out from the surrounding bushes shambles a hungry zombie. Too young to crawl away, the infants howl in fear of the approaching stranger danger. Upon hearing the cries of their children, the parents rush in to protect them, either by bashing in the revenants' heads or by scooping up their babies and running away. As this example illustrates, the attachment and caregiving behavioral systems are complementary, each sharing the same goal—protection of the child.

A final note on the nature of a parent's tie to their child. Typically, parents do not emotionally connect with their children through attachment bonds. Instead, they connect through a unidirectional *caregiving bond* that goes from the parent to the child. Nevertheless, both the attachment and caregiving behavioral systems give rise to intense emotions between parents and their children. Another word for the feelings associated with both attachment and caregiving bonds is "love."

CORE ELEMENTS OF ATTACHMENT THEORY AND THE ZOMBIE APOCALYPSE. Regarding behavioral system activation, the undead will cause a dramatic increase in both the fear and attachment behavioral systems. Infants and young children are wary of strangers whether the unknown person lumbering toward them is undead or alive. Even if infants and young children cannot see the dead, the dead nevertheless create natural cues for danger. The walking dead moan, snarl, and bang their fists against walls and doors or just about anything in their way. Potential victims scream when the undead get too close. Victims scream even louder once a zombie starts to tear into their flesh—that is, until they begin to moan.

All of these sounds naturally cause fear in the young, which activates their attachment behavioral systems while simultaneously shutting down their exploratory and sociable behavioral systems. At this point, the child is in need of comfort and protection. Additionally, the combination of a child's attachment behaviors and the parent's perception of danger will cause the parent's caregiving behavioral system to activate. In attempting to protect their young, many parents, and their offspring, will most assuredly die. Nevertheless, the complementary nature of the attachment and caregiver behavioral systems, at the very least, affords infants and children a chance at survival.

During infancy and childhood, youth develop three to four attachment bonds, though for some that number may be slightly lower or higher. Because infants attach to caregivers that frequently respond to their emotional needs, parents and siblings, as well as extended family members, are the most likely candidates to serve as attachment figures. And during the Zombie Apocalypse infants and children will need the emotional support and protection of every one of them. Nevertheless, attachment figures are not of equal importance to infants; instead, they view them in a hierarchy. At the top of the hierarchy is the primary attachment figure, followed by the secondary attachment figure, the tertiary attachment figure, and so on.

To illustrate, imagine a room with an infant in the center and an attachment figure located in each corner. Now, startle the infant with a series of loud zombie snarls, growls, snaps, and moans. The frightened baby will crawl off in the direction of an attachment figure. The question is, which one? In times of stress, infants will preferentially seek their primary attachment figures. It is only when the primary attachment figure is unavailable that an infant will direct their attachment behaviors towards a secondary attachment figure and so on. Furthermore, compared to a secondary attachment figure, an infant has a harder time separating from a primary attachment figure.

Moreover, an infant experiences more grief at the loss of a primary attachment figure relative to a secondary one. As illustrated in the opening vignette, the loss of primary and secondary attachment figures will be a common occurrence during the Zombie Apocalypse, and, unfortunately, lower ranked attachment figures cannot easily replace or make up for the loss of attachment figures above them in the hierarchy. Although the attachment figures are eventually replaceable, the process is painful and requires a period of mourning before a restructuring of the attachment hierarchy can take place. Chapter 11, Parenting and Grief, discusses this process in detail.

The Making and Breaking of Attachment Bonds

To a certain extent, the attachment behavioral system is always active. Nevertheless, when infants and children feel secure, meaning there are no internal or external threats to their well-being, behaviors related to social interactions and exploration supersede those of attachment. However, once the fear behavioral system activates, anxiety replaces feelings of security, and the attachment behavioral system ramps up in intensity. Exploration and sociability cease, and proximity to caregivers becomes of paramount importance. When all is well, the attachment and caregiving behavioral systems then work in concert to quell the child's sense of dread. Love trumps fear, attachment bonds solidify, and children return to exploring the world around them. However, when all is not well, children's attachment needs go unmet. What happens to attachment bonds then?

The answer to this question is dependent on which of the following three circumstances children encounter: (1) a lack of parental sensitivity and responsivity; (2) *social neglect*, meaning the absence of adequate social and emotional care during infancy and early childhood; or (3) the loss of multiple attachment figures. Below, I detail the effects of each on these circumstances on attachment.

Parenting and the Quality of Attachment

Across development, *selective attachments* (i.e., person-specific attachment bonds) exist in two qualitatively different forms: *secure* and *insecure*. Based on a history of sensitive and responsive parental care, infants and children with secure attachments wholeheartedly believe that their caregivers will consistently meet their emotional needs. Secure infants use their parents as a secure base for exploring their physical and social worlds as well as a haven of safety if they should be frightened, hurt, or otherwise in need of comfort. In contrast, infants and children with insecure attachments believe that their emotional needs will be ignored, inconsistently responded to, rejected, or some combination thereof.

Psychologists recognize three types of insecure attachments: *insecure-avoidant, insecure-ambivalent,* and *insecure-disorganized.* Based on a history of having their emotional needs rejected, insecure-avoidant infants and children suppress feelings (e.g., anger) that could lead to further rejection and minimize the use of their caregivers for comfort and support. Doing so guarantees proximity to a caregiver (and access to care in case of dire need), while at the same time reducing the possibility of being rebuffed. Thus, when feeling stressed, insecure-avoidant infants and children do not readily go to their attachment figures; instead, they stoically carry on by themselves. On the other hand, insecure-ambivalent infants and children intensify their emotional expressions and relentlessly use their caregivers for comfort and support. This "squeaky wheel gets the grease" mentality helps insecure-ambivalent infants and children ensure that predictably unreliable caregivers will be there to meet their emotional needs. In support of this strategy, even the slightest aggravation can result in crying, tantrums, clinging, and difficulty soothing.

Because both insecure-avoidant and insecure-ambivalent infants and children utilize clear behavioral strategies with caregivers, collectively, researchers refer to them as insecure-organized. However, other infants and children fail to develop clear strategies for interacting with their caregivers, and, as a result, receive the label insecure-disorganized. Often, abuse produces disorganized attachments. In such instances, infants and children are unable to resolve the internal conflict resulting from having the source of comfort also being a source of fear. In other cases, parents respond to their children's bids for comfort and protection with fearful expressions, erratic behavior, or inappropriate emotions (e.g., laughing while comforting a crying child), which further compound their children's fears. During times of stress, disorganized infants' and children's behavior toward their caregivers vacillates between avoidance and resistance or becomes fearful and confused (e.g., rocking back and forth).

As previously mentioned, children attach to multiple caregivers. Nevertheless, the quality of an attachment bond is caregiver specific. A child can demonstrate a secure attachment to one caregiver, but an insecure attachment a different one. Ultimately, the caregiver's behavior determines the child's attachment quality. Thus, when caregiving differs between parents, so does the child's pattern of attachment. To keep track of their various attachment figures' caregiving proclivities, infants and children make use of *internal working models*—mental representations of a specific attachment figure's availability, sensitivity, and responsiveness—along with the success or failure of their attempts at eliciting care when frightened, lonely, or otherwise stressed. Internal working models allow children to predict caregiver behavior and develop strategies for interacting during times of stress.

Infants and children continually update and change their internal working models to match the current state of their caregiving experiences. Such cognitive flexibility allows children to make the most of the care they are currently receiving, even if that care is less than desirable. However, a failure to adjust cognitively to changing parental behavior will result in a strategy of interaction that no longer fits the situation. For example, a child expecting an insensitive and rejecting caregiver to be sensitive and responsive places itself at risk for both emotional and physical pain. Conversely, a child's failure to use an available caregiver will hinder its ability to thrive in its current environment.

Over time, internal working models for specific attachment figures coalesce into a more wide-ranging, global representation of attachment relationships. For example, a secure child's internal working model of a trusting caregiver turns into a general view of the world where others consistently meet their needs. The global internal working models of insecure children, by contrast, are fraught with negative relationship qualities, such as emotional rejection, inconsistent and insensitive responding, and harmful treatment.

THE QUALITY OF ATTACHMENT IN THE ZOMBIE APOCALYPSE. In middle-class populations in North America, around 62 percent of infants securely attach to their primary caregivers, 15 percent establish insecure-avoidant relationships, 9 percent become insecure-ambivalent, and the remaining 15 percent develop insecure-disorganized attachments.[2] For the most part, the quality of selective attachments remains unchanged as children grow. Secure infants transition into secure children and adolescents. Similarly, insecure infants and children remain insecure as they age, continuing to demonstrate the specific form of insecurity (e.g., avoidance, ambivalence, disorganization) first evident during infancy. Secure attachments are both commonplace and stable when parents raise their children in predictable environments with ample resources and limited amounts of stress. The Zombie Apocalypse is none of those things.

The landscape provided by living dead will be treacherous, impoverished, and war-torn. Attachment figures will be battered, bruised, and psychologically damaged, thus placing children at risk for malnourishment and maltreatment. In such circumstances, both insecure-organized and insecure-disorganized attachments will flourish. Case in point, between

40 percent and 50 percent of children born to alcohol- and drug-addicted mothers are insecure-disorganized. Similarly, rates of insecure attachments (both organized and disorganized) rise for parents with unresolved loss, trauma, or depression. For malnourished children in impoverished conditions, insecure-disorganized attachments are the norm, rather than the exception, and secure attachments occur far less frequently. In the case of child maltreatment, nearly 50 percent of children demonstrate a disorganized form of attachment, with most of the remaining children classified as insecure-organized, and few if any children identified as secure.

Ultimately, parental care determines a child's attachment security or insecurity. The pressures of living among the living dead will adversely affect parents' ability to meet their children's needs consistently, sensitively, and responsively. Insecure attachments will dramatically rise. In all likelihood, insecure-disorganized attachments will be the universal norm, as the environmental conditions of the Zombie Apocalypse lead to malnutrition and frightening parental behavior as well as trauma, loss, and depression. In the land of the dead, secure attachments will be possible. However, for those to develop, parents will somehow need to make children feel secure in a world without security.

The Outcomes of Attachment Quality

Beyond its survival function, the importance of attachment lies in the effects that it has on children's current and future well-being. Psychologists consider attachment foundational for children's sense of the self and their ability to regulate emotions as well as their current and future relationships with others. Moreover, the quality of attachment is a crucial determinant of children's functioning in these domains of development.

Not only does parenting affect how children view their attachment figures, but also how they see themselves. Having experienced sensitive and responsive care, secure children view themselves as lovable and worthy of having their needs met. Conversely, the insensitive, unresponsive, inconsistent, and emotionally rejecting parenting experienced by insecure children results in representations of the self as unlovable and undeserving of benevolent care. Thus, children's sense of self-worth is a direct reflection of the treatment they receive from their attachment figures.

Relative to insecure children and adolescents, secure children and adolescents demonstrate greater competency in handling negative emotions (e.g., anger, fear, and sadness) and even more so as those feelings intensify. When faced with stressful and emotional situations, secure children's ability to engage in emotional self-regulation allows them to stay focused on the task at hand, problem solve, and seek support from others, if needed. In contrast, insecure youth do one or more of the following: argue, berate the self, act out aggressively, or *catastrophize*—that is, make the situation seem far worse than it is.

The quality of attachment to caregivers also influences children's interactions with others. Nowhere is this more evident than in peer relationships. Secure children interact with peers in the same manner that their attachment figures interacted with them. Thus, having their attachment needs sensitively and responsively met leads secure children to interact with their peers with a similar focus on positive relationship qualities. Secure children competently interact with their peers and demonstrate positive peer relationships across childhood and adolescence.

For insecure-avoidant children, concerns of rejection permeate their social relationships. To avoid rejection, insecure-avoidant children and adolescents withdraw from social situations, limit physical contact and self-disclosure, and rarely ask others for help. The experience of chronic rejection in attachment relationships, and the corresponding belief that rejection accompanies all relationships, leaves insecure-avoidant children prone to anger, hostility, aggression, and bullying. Moreover, when interacting with their peers, insecure-avoidant children are deficient in *empathy* (i.e., feeling the emotions of others) and *empathetic responding* (i.e., helping others in emotional distress).

The hyperactivation of emotions required to obtain parental care hinders insecure-ambivalent children's ability to interact effectively with their peers. Moreover, these children frequently engage in attention-seeking behaviors from non-parental adults (such as teachers), while demonstrating both social inhibition and submissiveness toward their classmates. They are hypervigilant toward potential threats (which would require protection from attachment figures), and thus fearful and anxious around their peers. These behaviors place the insecure-ambivalent child in jeopardy of victimization. During adolescence, insecure-ambivalent teens seek closeness with others but have difficulty finding relationships satisfying. Finally, across childhood and adolescence, those classified as insecure-ambivalent report feeling lonely.

For about a third of infants, disorganized behaviors first evident during infancy continue into early and middle childhood. However, for the remaining two-thirds of children with disorganized attachments, the preschool years bring about fundamental changes to the parent-child relationship. Specifically, rather than the attachment figure parenting the child, the child parents the attachment figure. Two forms of role-reversed relationships exist: controlling-punitive and controlling-caregiving. Children with a *controlling-punitive* strategy use verbal threats as well as coercive, hostile, and harsh behaviors when interacting with their parents. In contrast, youth identified as *controlling-caregiving* maintain the attention and involvement of their caregivers by making them feel happy and helpfully guiding their behavior.

Compared to children demonstrating other patterns of attachment, insecure-disorganized youth (regardless of subtype) engage in more aggressive, disruptive, defiant, and delinquent acts (i.e., externalizing behaviors) throughout childhood and adolescence. Not surprisingly, insecure-disorganized youth are less competent with peers compared to both insecure-organized and secure children. Of note, the highest frequency of externalizing behaviors occurs for children and adolescents with a controlling-punitive form of disorganization. Additionally, because they are accustomed to being in charge, controlling-punitive youth have difficulty following rules set forth by authority figures such as teachers and community leaders.

THE OUTCOMES OF ATTACHMENT QUALITY IN THE ZOMBIE APOCALYPSE. The Zombie Apocalypse will shatter internal working models of the world as a safe place and negatively affect children's beliefs that their parents can meet their needs effectively and keep them from harm (assuming such views were in place before the apocalypse). Consequently, children's negative opinions about the world will turn into negative feelings about their selves. As the number of insecure-avoidant children rises, so will incidents of anger, hostility, aggression, and bullying. At the same time, insecure-avoidant children's inability to empathize with others will adversely affect their relationships with peers. For the increasing number of insecure-ambivalent children, feelings of loneliness, fearfulness, anxiety, submissiveness, and inhibition will follow. For children experiencing maltreatment, disruptive behavior, defiance, and emotional dysregulation and catastrophizing will soar. As disorganized youth approach adolescence, those with controlling forms of disorganization will not only be in conflict with their parents but also with those in leadership positions.

Disorders of Nonattachment

To stay alive in the face of extreme adversity, infants and young children will at times forgo the development of attachment bonds with current or future caregivers. Such a strategy promotes survival at the expense of emotional well-being. Below, I discuss two forms of *disorders of nonattachment*—long-lasting impairments in the ability to form attachment bonds—likely to accompany the Zombie Apocalypse, namely, reactive attachment disorder and disinhibited social engagement disorder.

Reactive Attachment Disorder

Reactive attachment disorder is a disorder of nonattachment characterized by the inability to initiate and respond to social interactions in a healthy manner. Children with reactive attachment disorder are characteristically unresponsive in social situations and thus present as disconnected from family members, daycare providers, and other children. They do not seek comfort when upset. They are not soothed when caregivers try to comfort them. Moreover, children with this disorder do not typically show genuine affection toward others or care about their well-being, and, as a result, they have difficulty maintaining positive relationships with family members and peers. Such youth lack empathy and can engage in disrespectful or hurtful acts without remorse. Also, they find little joy in their interactions with the world around them, rarely showing positive emotions. On the other hand, they frequently experience negative emotions, such as irritability, sadness, or tearfulness. Children with reactive attachment disorder do not trust others and feel a tremendous need to be in control of every situation, a combination that results in frequent conflicts with caregivers. Moreover, as teens, they tend to disregard parental wishes and instead follow their peers.

Adults that care for children with reactive attachment disorder experience exasperation at the ineffectiveness of standard parenting techniques, exhaustion related to the constant battles, and distress resulting from others viewing them bad, unloving parents. Moreover, they long for the reciprocated love and affection that other parents receive but they do not.

REACTIVE ATTACHMENT DISORDER AND THE ZOMBIE APOCALYPSE. In pre-apocalyptic times, reactive attachment disorder is detrimental to the psychological well-being of youth and results in large deficits in social and emotional functioning. The inability to trust others, controlling behavior, and lack of empathy prevent children from experiencing the world as a safe, joyful, and emotionally fulfilling place. During the Zombie Apocalypse, those very same characteristics may be the difference between survival and living an undead life. For instance, during an invasion of the living dead, those bit, dying, or recently deceased will need to have their brains destroyed. However, feelings of empathy and emotional distress will lead to delays and indecisions about taking the necessary precautions, and, as a result, many of the dead will rise. Furthermore, unscrupulous strangers can easily take advantage of people that are too trusting or naïve. Thus, the mistrust and lack of empathy that characterize youth with reactive attachment disorder serves as a protective factor in environments where survival is at stake, such as an undead wasteland.

Disinhibited Social Engagement Disorder

At an age when toddlers and preschoolers should be anxious around strangers, children with *disinhibited social engagement disorder* show little, if any, wariness of them. In fact, when meeting an adult for the first time, the child will act in an overly familiar way. They will fearlessly approach a stranger and raise their arms to be picked up, held or hugged or sit on the stranger's lap. When in need of comfort, children with disinhibited social engagement disorder will go to people unknown to them for soothing. They explore environments without concern for their safety, fail to check in with their caregivers, and even wander off in pursuit of, or with, people they do not know. Older children and teens with this disorder act in an overly familiar manner with their peers, resulting in awkward interactions.

Parents of disinhibited social engagement disordered youth are anxious that their children's overly familiar behavior with strangers will unwittingly place them in dangerous situations. Moreover, parents find their children's failure to demonstrate preferential attachments to them frustrating.

DISINHIBITED SOCIAL ENGAGEMENT DISORDER AND THE ZOMBIE APOCALYPSE. Raising a child with either reactive attachment disorder or disinhibited social engagement disorder is challenging for parents. However, during the Zombie Apocalypse, keeping a child with disinhibited social engagement disorder alive will be especially problematic. The ease with which children wander off and approach strangers places them in jeopardy of encountering a zombie alone and unprotected. Keep in mind that although zombies are visibly distinct from humans from the front, the undead are more challenging to identify from behind (especially if they are freshly turned and wearing clothes untouched by the elements). Unaware of strangers' negative life status, disinhibited social engagement disorder youth may unknowingly approach a zombie and attempt to grab its attention. Unfortunately, in such situations, the undead will grab them back.

Determinants of Disorders of Nonattachment

Reactive attachment disorder and disinhibited social engagement disorder both develop in response to inadequate social and emotional care and the loss of one or more attachment figures. For instance, disordered attachment occurs when infants are unable to form even a single attachment bond due to social neglect. Such is the case for infants placed into poor quality institutional care *before* they can attach to a primary caregiver. Also, disorders of nonattachment occur when infants or young children experience the loss of essential attachment figures without being able to form any replacement attachment bonds. At times, this failure is the result of social neglect perpetrated by caregivers whereas at others times it is due to a lack of opportunity.

Take, for instance, an infant with a demonstrable attachment to its primary and secondary attachment figures. Due to an unfortunate encounter with a zombie horde, both of the infant's parents die. With no family available to assume responsibility for the infant's care, community members place it into a makeshift orphanage. Although caregivers meet the infant's basic physiological requirements, a high turnover of daycare providers results in the neglect of the infant's basic social and emotional needs. Thus, with no reliable attachment figures available, the infant is unable to form any new attachment bonds and a disorder of nonattachment may follow.

Additionally, the repeated loss of attachment figures (whether due to death or permanent separation) can lead to disorders of nonattachment. Let us consider the case of an infant attached to its drug-abusing single parent. Because of neglect or maltreatment by the parent, the court places the infant in foster care. While there, the infant develops an attachment bond to its foster parent. A year later, social services reassigns the child to a different foster home, and after that, places the child with an extended family member. In each instance, the child established an attachment bond with its caregiver, and in each case, the relocation of the child into a new home disrupted an established attachment relationship. From the child's perspective, this situation is akin to enduring a series of parental deaths, for, in each instance, the child permanently lost contact with someone they loved.

Rarely do children that continue to live in the circumstances that gave rise to their disordered attachment develop normal attachment bonds. However, children with reactive attachment disorder do show marked improvements in their social and emotional relationships once they move to better environmental conditions and experience sensitive and responsive caregiving. In contrast, despite changes in rearing environments and improvements in parental care, the symptoms of disinhibited social engagement disorder tend to persist. Evolutionary psychologists posit that disinhibited social engagement disorder is an evolutionary adaptation in which mitigating the need for attachment figures turns children into opportunistic care seekers. For children enduring multiple parental deaths, the use of interchangeable caregivers reduces the emotional pain associated with losing yet another attachment figure.

DETERMINANTS OF ATTACHMENT DISORDERS AND THE ZOMBIE APOCALYPSE. Parental and caregiver death will be ever-present during the Zombie Apocalypse, resulting in the rescue of never-attached newborns and previously attached but orphaned infants and children. Unfortunately, many of these infants and children will never (again) receive the individualized care necessary for the creation of new attachment bonds, and, as a result, when the dead rise, disorders of nonattachment will occur more frequently.

Two reasons account for this prediction. First, given the difficulties of living in an apocalypse wasteland, it is likely that a cadre of people will take care of orphaned infants and children with no one person being consistently present or responsive enough for an attachment to develop. This situation alone is enough to increase the incidence of reactive attachment disorder as well as disinhibited social engagement disorder. To make matters worse, even if children can establish additional attachment bonds, many of their attachment figures will suffer premature deaths. To illustrate, let us consider Judith Grimes from *The Walking Dead*. Within the first few years of her life, Judith has experienced the loss of at least six essential caretakers (through permanent separation or death), including her father and brother (but not counting her mother, who died during childbirth).[3] If her remaining parent, Michonne, were to die, a disorder of nonattachment would likely follow. During the Zombie Apocalypse, the loss of multiple attachment figures will increase the probability that children like Judith will develop attachment disorders.

When the dead walk, it is doubtful that institutional care will be a source of attachment trauma, as large-scale institutions will cease to exist. Of course, there will be communities with orphaned children and small orphanages to care for them. However, given the expected increase in infant mortality, it seems unlikely that there will be enough babies to fill, let alone overcrowd, a communal home for children. Regardless of who is rearing an infant, finding a quiet place in which to do so will be of the utmost importance. Sound insulated locations will give parents latitude regarding the need to soothe a crying infant quickly.

Moreover, childproofing potential hazards will allow caregivers to leave children by themselves when apocalypse-related matters require their undivided attention. For example, parents will place children in protected rooms to go hunt, forage, and fight off the living dead. Some caretakers may even leave children alone for hours on end, day after day, depending on survival requirements. Upon their return from hunting, fighting, and foraging, parents may be too tired to meet the emotional needs of infants and children in their charge. As a result, many children will endure social neglect (albeit unintended) and an increased risk of developing a disorder of nonattachment.

Final Thoughts

Compared to other species, humans possess far less strength, speed, and agility. And without talons, claws, razor-sharp teeth, bone-crushing jaw strength, or venom, humans end up in the middle of the food chain, with the top spots reserved for *apex predators* (i.e., animals with no natural predators) such as polar bears, wolves, lions, and saltwater crocodiles.[4] Despite their ability to kill the living, the living dead are not apex predators either. According to the London Zoo, Komodo dragons, vultures and rats would make tasty meals out of the walking carrion.[5]

However, Tsachi Ein-Dor's *social defense theory* posits that the survival of the species necessitates more than just individuals' predatory behavior and response to danger. Instead, human survival requires the assistance of others (i.e., a social-defense response). Thus, the power of the human species lies not in its ability to detect and counter threats but in its capacity to work as a group to overcome the dangers it faces. As illustrated by the devastation wrought by a zombie horde, there is great strength in numbers. However, defeating the undead will take more than just numbers. It will take the right kind of numbers. According to Ein-Dor's social defense theory, this means a heterogeneous group of attachment orientations.

Attachment theory is first and foremost about threat detection and survival. Fear and anxiety activate attachment behaviors, which subsequently elicit protection and support. Individual differences in attachment quality reflect the child's best strategy for dealing with the vicissitudes of parental care, with internal working models providing the mechanism to generalize these strategies beyond the confines of the parent-child relationship. Starting in adolescence, the dimensions of anxiety (e.g., worries about the availability of others; fears of abandonment) and avoidance (e.g., discomfort with intimacy; distrust of others; reliance on the self) combine to determine an individual's *attachment orientation*—defined as a systematic pattern of emotions, needs, and expectations in relationships. Secure individuals are low in both anxiety and avoidance, and as such, they enjoy intimacy and are comfortable with and trusting of others. In contrast, insecure attachment orientations have a high degree of either avoidance or anxiety.

Attachment orientations also differ in regard to their fear-activated *fight-or-flight response* (i.e., fighting or fleeing from danger) and *social-defense behavior* (i.e., proximity to others, not just attachment figures). Individuals with an anxious attachment orientation possess a hyperactivated and anxiety focused attachment behavioral system. Despite the fact that they seek proximity to those around them, their dependence and over-reliance on others mutes their fight-or-flight response in fearful situations. Thus, they will be the last group of people to enter a fray (if at all) and only if there are no other options available. The survival of those high in attachment anxiety is dependent upon their ability to identify threats and dangers in their environments and notify others of their presence (who will presumably defend them). Social defense theory refers to the anxiously-attached individual's hypervigilant and continually active search for potential threats as *sentinel* behavior.

In contrast, individuals with an avoidant attachment style utilize a *rapid fight-or-flight* strategy in which they quickly engage in self-reliant, self-protective behaviors, and limited, if any, social defense responses (such as joining others). Their first course of action is to save themselves and escape the threat (if possible) without purposefully alerting others to the danger. If others die so they can live, so be it. Because others may notice their behavior (e.g., breaking a window to escape), the self-preservation tendencies of avoidant individuals may inadvertently save those around them.

Secure individuals, being neither overly anxious nor appreciably avoidant, have a balanced sense of social responsibility and individual self-preservation. Excelling at leadership, coordinating group activities, and problem-solving with others, secure people can rally those around them to save the day. However, compared to insecure orientations, secure individuals are relatively weak at threat detection, have a tendency to minimize the gravity of their situation, and are slower to use self-protective behaviors as they tend to help others before they help themselves.

Imagine a room filled with survivors of the Zombie Apocalypse enjoying a light afternoon meal. Unbeknownst to all, a small but deadly group of the undead has made its way into the room through a door left slightly ajar. Social defense theory predicts that, because of their sentinel behaviors, individuals with anxious attachments will be the first to notice the undead threat. After alerting the group to the terror that approaches via a scream, they will run toward their protectors (most likely those with secure orientations). In the meantime, those with avoidant attachments will be making their way to the quickest egress, which in this case happens to be a nailed-shut window located catty-corner to the door. To get out, they throw a chair through the window. The sound of the breaking glass will cause heads to turn, and upon seeing the avoidantly-attached crawl through the open window to safety, others will follow. At this point, the securely-attached will unite and begin to defend their position to allow for those near the window time to escape. When it looks as though they are about to be overrun, the securely-attached will retreat through the opening.

Now, let us replay the same scenario using homogeneous groups based on attachment orientation. First, because of their sentinel behavior, a room full of anxiously attached individuals would identify the zombie threat early on. However, due to their reliance on others and inability to defend themselves, they would soon join the undead army. In contrast, if only avoidantly oriented individuals were present, a zombie attack would trigger a mass attempt by all to save themselves at the expense of others. Not only would avoidant individuals fail to coordinate their defensive efforts, but in all likelihood they would end up fighting each other as they simultaneously try to use the best escape routes. Many would die because the avoidant group could not work together effectively. Lastly, a group of secure people would rally and work together. However, their relatively poor threat detection and underestimation of the danger would result in their coordinated efforts being too little, too late to save the group as a whole. As you can see, it is only through the collaborative efforts of secure, anxious, and avoidant (be it reluctantly) individuals that the group can maximize its chances of survival.

Throughout the lifespan, secure attachments produce the most beneficial social and emotional outcomes and the most rewarding interpersonal relationships. In contrast, the attachment orientation of insecure individuals reap few, if any, benefits for psychological well-being. Though potentially maladaptive at the individual level, insecure attachments are adaptive for groups. During the Zombie Apocalypse, the unique manner in which the insecurely attached detect and respond to threat will ultimately help themselves, and those around them, survive.

10. Parenting Styles

Parents laugh, cheer, and show great pride once their children start to crawl, roll sideways across a floor, or pull themselves to a stand and are even happier when they take their first steps. Once children start to move about on their own, however, the nature of parenting undergoes a significant change. No longer can parents turn their backs on their children, even for a few seconds, with the expectation that when they turn around again, they will be in the same place. Many parents find this out the hard way, but nevertheless end up with light-hearted stories of their children eating food out of the dog bowl or covering themselves with markers. Other parents get small frights as they find their children climbing over gates or using dresser drawers as makeshift ladders and some parents see their children fall down the stairs. During the Zombie Apocalypse, not all stories about young escape artists will end with cute anecdotes. With the undead lurking all around and dangerous environmental conditions ever present, one misstep, one impulsive reach, or one failure to attend to an important detail, by either the child or the parent, could end one life or several.

Zombies are not the only dangers that parents and their children will face when the dead rise, as the world will be replete with the living willing to exploit and harm others, much as they do today. For example, in Nigeria, Boko Haram militants repeatedly raid villages to kidnap young girls to become "wives" and forced sexual concubines. With zombies to the left and militants to the right, how are parents supposed to bridle the unbridled nature of youth, and raise emotionally healthy children, when no matter which way they turn potential death awaits?

During the Zombie Apocalypse, an essential component of childrearing will be sheer luck. For those that fortune favors, bullets will fly by, bites will take away fabric rather than flesh, and falling debris will land to the side of children instead of on top of them. For parents unwilling to rely on providence alone, the difference between successful (i.e., mentally fit and alive) and unsuccessful (i.e., mentally ill or dead/undead) caregiving will, in part, lie in the style of parenting employed and the type of discipline administered.

Styles of Parenting

Parenting style characterizes the strategies caregivers use when rearing their children. It is a rather broad term that encompasses a wide range of parental behaviors, emotional displays, and organization capabilities as well as the amount and quality of their responsiveness and demandingness. All the same, psychologists primarily describe parenting style in two distinct ways. The first approach emphasizes a series of unique dimensions that capture the nature of caregiving-related to specific features and qualities, such as warmth and emotional rejection. Think of each of these characteristics as being on a scale from 0 to 10, with numbers closer to 0 signifying little of that dimension and higher numbers indicating a great deal of it. For the second approach, psychologists combine these singular dimensions of parenting to create a series of discrete parenting typologies. Below I discuss each of these conceptualizations of parenting style and the likely outcomes of using them once when the dead rise.

Dimensions of Parenting

According to Ellen Skinner, Sandy Johnson, and Tatiana Snyder, there are six dimensions of parenting that affect parents' ability to socialize their children—that is, teach them the rules, standards, beliefs, and values of their culture. Those dimensions are warmth, rejection, structure, chaos, autonomy support, and coercion.

Warmth refers to the expressions of affection, kindness, and appreciation. Warm parents are emotionally available and supportive of their children. They are child-centered, loving, and caring. Warm parents act this way despite the difficulties that they may be facing. Picture the following scenario: after a fierce battle with a zombified friend (who they kill via a shiv to the brainstem), parents watch their distraught child trip over the newly undead corpse. In such situations, warm parents would sweep their children up in their arms to console and soothe them.

On the other hand, *rejection* involves harsh, hostile, irritable, aversive, and negative overreactions toward children. Moreover, rejecting parents demonstrate an active dislike of their children through disparaging, critical, and condescending words or deeds. They are parent-centered, rarely displaying warmth or sympathy. At times, rejection occurs in response to a child seeking out comfort and support. At other times, parents reject their children regardless of what they are doing and without bids for care. Using the example above, upon seeing their child trip over the undead body, a rejecting parent would make derogatory remarks to their child about their lack of coordination and common sense.

Structure refers to providing children with information as well as organizing their physical environments or social situations to achieve desired outcomes (e.g., completing homework, sharing toys equitably, or resolving conflicts with siblings). To accomplish this, parents convey clear rules and expectations to their children, which they reliably enforce. A hallmark of this parenting dimension is consistent limit setting. During the Zombie Apocalypse, a high degree of structure could mean teaching children how to scavenge a car safely in order to avoid injury or bites (e.g., knocking on the windows and checking the back seat before entering a vehicle) or placing limits on their noise-producing behavior to prevent the ensuing hullabaloo from attracting zombies.

In contrast, *chaos* refers to lax control as well as inconsistent, unpredictable, and arbitrary discipline. For example, after seeing their child rummage through a car without checking the back seat first, a parent high in chaos would threaten to prohibit any more scavenging and ground them for the day. However, not long after this pronouncement, the chaotic parent would allow their child to scavenge on their own and without consequence. Chaotic parenting is also non-contingent, meaning that parental responses are often unrelated to what their children actually did. For example, after seeing their eldest child share a toy with their younger, a parent high in chaos might comment on the child's earlier failure to scavenge correctly.

Autonomy support involves respecting children's individuality, providing them with freedom of choice, and encouraging them to explore and discover their own goals, preferences, and beliefs. Autonomy support also occurs whenever parental decisions and problem-solving takes into consideration their children's views and opinions. For example, during the Zombie Apocalypse, parents high in autonomy support would consider their children's rationale for wanting to carry a weapon and their ability to do so safely. Note, autonomy support does not mean that the parent always agrees with the child and lets them do as they please. Instead, the child is made to feel as though they are genuinely part of the decision making process.

In contrast, *coercive* parents require strict obedience to their demands, which they accomplish by being overly restrictive, intrusive, dictatorial, and punitive. They enforce rules without compromise, expecting their children to follow their many directives the first time they are given. Children have little say regarding what they can do and when they can do it. Parents engaging in coercion will undermine children's self-worth, induce anxiety, shame, and guilt, and threaten the withdrawal of love to ensure compliance. Examples of coercive parenting include telling a child that (1) they are too dumb to survive the Zombie Apocalypse on their own; (2) they would most likely shoot themselves if given a gun; and (3) they had better follow parental rules or they will most assuredly die, and it will be nobody's fault but their own.

OUTCOMES ASSOCIATED WITH DIFFERENT PARENTING DIMENSIONS. Based on self-determination theory (Chapter 1), attachment theory (Chapter 9), and expectations regarding the self's ability to produce desired outcomes and prevent undesired ones (i.e., *perceived control*), Skinner and colleagues posit a motivational model of development in which the aforementioned six dimensions of parenting influence children's feelings of relatedness, competence, and autonomy.

By way of review, autonomy refers to the child's need to feel a sense of control over their behaviors, thoughts, goals, and so on; competence involves the child's belief that they can complete tasks; and relatedness refers the child's sense of connection with others, particularly their parents. Concerning the six dimensions of parenting, warmth improves parent-child relatedness, and rejection works against it. As an example, consider the fact that parental warmth is a central component of secure attachment while rejection and insecure attachment go hand in hand, and although parental structure helps children develop a sense of *self-efficacy* (and the belief that they can accomplish anything), parental chaos makes achieving a sense of personal competence much more difficult to obtain. Finally, although autonomy support results in children feeling comfortable with independent behaviors and the expression of their ideas, coercion impedes these outcomes. Instead, children develop emotional problems (such as anxiety, depression) and behavioral problems (such as aggression, deviance) during adolescence.

To summarize, parenting that is autonomy supporting, structured, and warm leads to autonomous, competent, and related children. Moreover, these parenting dimensions also produce children that are receptive to socialization—that is, willing to adopt parental rules, standards, beliefs, and values. For example, toddlers that are receptive to socialization demonstrate *committed compliance.* They display a willingness to comply with parental requests and a sensitivity to the rightness or wrongness of their behavior based on their parents' emotional responses. An example of committed compliance would be a toddler willing to help clean up toys (after seeing their parent frown at their initial refusal) even though they are in the middle of a fun game. For children, the demonstration of committed compliance is a big step toward the *internalization* of parental values and beliefs, in which internal standards reduce or eliminate the need for parental guidance when distinguishing between right and wrong. In other words, children "do the right thing" when their parents are no longer present.

In contrast, parenting that is rejecting, chaotic, and coercive creates ill-tempered, dissatisfied, and disaffected children that are resistant to their parents' socialization ideals and more likely than others to experience emotional (e.g., anxiety, depression) and behavioral problems (e.g., aggression, deviance). When children raised by these parenting dimensions do comply with caregiver demands, more often than not it is because of their parents' power advantage rather than a desire to comply. Psychologists refer to this type of behavior as *situational compliance.* Under such circumstances, children comply because they have to, not because they want to.

DIMENSIONS OF PARENTING IN THE ZOMBIE APOCALYPSE. In the dangerous and desolate landscape of Zombie Apocalypse, youth will have plenty of chances to pillage and plunder. They will also have opportunities to aid those in need, or, if desired, turn a blind eye to them. Will teens stop and pick up a friend who has fallen or leave them by the side of the road for the dead to tear apart? During these situations and others like them, will youth show mercy, wrath, or indifference? In large part, the decisions children and adolescents make reflect the internalization (or lack of) of their parents' values and beliefs. The stressful nature of the Zombie Apocalypse, then, will put the effectiveness of parents' socialization efforts to the test.

Parents that provided their children with autonomy support, warmth, and structure before the apocalypse will find their children adhering to the norms set by parents once the dead rise. However, as the Zombie

Apocalypse progresses, nearly every child will live in impoverished and violent conditions. As discussed in previous chapters, the stress of living with the living dead in decidedly high-risk environments will cause an increase in relationship conflict and dissatisfaction between parents, family instability (e.g., dysfunction, multigenerational conflict, and stress), and a reduction in social support. Such adverse conditions will reduce the positive parenting dimensions of parental warmth, structure, and autonomy while simultaneously increasing the negative dimensions of rejection, chaos, and coercion. As a result of these changes, children once receptive to parental socialization will now become openly resistant to it. Moreover, the emotional and behavioral problems associated with negative parenting dimensions will take hold.

In support of this contention, consider the following example from the Syrian refugee crisis. Parents living in refugee camps report a reduction in the amount of warmth they direct toward their children and difficulties in structuring their children's day-to-day activities as well as greater use of corporal punishment (the effects of which are discussed in detail below). Not surprisingly, the combination of adverse living conditions and negative parenting behaviors has increased the emotional and behavioral problems of Syrian refugee children.

Parenting Typologies

In addition to the dimensional approach described above, psychologists combine parental *responsiveness* (which contains elements of warmth, rejection, and autonomy support) with parental *demandingness* (comprised of structure, chaos, and coercion) to create four discrete parenting typologies: authoritative, authoritarian, permissive, and uninvolved. Parents with an *authoritative* style are high in responsiveness and demandingness. They provide their children with considerable warmth, structure, and autonomy support while at the same time being low in rejection, chaos, and coercion. Authoritative parents monitor their children's activities, consistently enforce rules, and provide justification for the punishments they dole out. Moreover, across childhood and adolescence, authoritative parents (who are relatively strict disciplinarians) make it a point to encourage their children's independent decision-making.

On the other hand, *authoritarian* parents are high in demandingness but low in responsiveness. They demonstrate high levels of rejection, structure, and coercion while being low on the dimensions of warmth, chaos, and autonomy support. They expect strict, unquestioning obedience to parental commands, regardless of whether they provide any rationale for their decisions. With great hostility, authoritarian parents use phrases like "Because I said so" and "It's my house, my rules" to justify their commands. Almost without exception, the authoritarian parent enforces rules rigidly.

In contrast, *permissive* parents are high in responsiveness but low in demandingness. They raise children in an environment that is warm, autonomy supportive, and chaotic as well as being low on structure, coercion, and rejection. They make few demands of their children, neither competently guiding their behavior nor enforcing rules. Although loving and caring, they rarely monitor their children's behavior, allowing them the freedom to do just about whatever they want.

Finally, *uninvolved* parents provide little in the way of responsiveness or demandingness. They are high in rejection and chaos while being low in warmth, structure, autonomy support, and coercion. In general, uninvolved parents appear to care little about their children's well-being and future. They provide children with the bare necessities of life (e.g., food, clothing, shelter), but little else. Uninvolved parents are indifferent to their children's emotional, academic, and social needs. They do not meet their children's teachers, enroll them in after-school activities, set up play dates with other children, or take them to the park. In effect, children of uninvolved parents rear themselves. Another term for uninvolved parenting is neglect, the most common form of child maltreatment.

PSYCHOLOGICAL OUTCOMES ASSOCIATED WITH DIFFERENT PARENTING TYPOLOGIES. Compared to authoritarian, permissive, and uninvolved parents, authoritative parents produce children that are more sociable, helpful, emotionally expressive, academically competent, higher in self-esteem, and better able to engage in emotional self-regulation. Moreover, children of authoritative parents are less likely than other youth to take risks, use drugs, and suffer from anxiety, depression, or behavior problems.

In contrast, children of authoritarian parents tend to have difficulty interacting with their peers and making friends. They are also unhappy, withdrawn, and distrustful of others. For children of authoritarian parents, feelings of hostility are commonplace. Additionally, authoritarian parents produce children that are low in *psychological flexibility*, meaning that they find adapting to new situations, shifting perspectives, and changing or maintaining appropriate behavior difficult.

The children of permissive parents have difficulty controlling their impulses and aggressive behavior. They also engage in significant risk-taking activities, such as experimenting with drugs and alcohol. Moreover, when using dangerous equipment (such as tractors or combines), they frequently engage in unsafe practices. Like children of authoritarian parents, they are at risk for anxiety, depression, and delinquency.

By far, the worst outcomes occur for children of uninvolved parents. They have great difficulty regulating their emotions and controlling their impulses, and they exhibit high levels of aggression, hostility, and antisocial behaviors during childhood and adolescence. Moreover, uninvolved parents produce adolescents with high rates of depression, criminality, substance use, and sexual misconduct.

HEALTH OUTCOMES ASSOCIATED WITH DIFFERENT PARENTING TYPOLOGIES. In addition to influencing psychological well-being, parenting typologies also affect children and adolescents' physical health. For example, children of permissive and authoritarian parents are more likely to be obese than children of authoritative parents. Similarly, childhood exposure to adverse environmental circumstances also increases the risk of current and future health problems. Together, permissive, authoritarian, or neglecting parenting practices along with unfavorable environmental conditions lead to health-compromising behaviors in youth (e.g., over-eating, smoking, and substance use), a reduction in the immune system's ability to stave off illness, and the release of stress-related hormones (e.g., cortisol). Over time, these factors interact to cause dangerous medical conditions such as cancer, heart disease, diabetes, and high blood pressure.

PARENTING TYPOLOGIES IN THE ZOMBIE APOCALYPSE. In violent neighborhoods and active war zones around the world, parents engage in rigid control to protect their children from harm. Under such circumstances, intense parenting stress also leads to caregiving that is low in warmth and high in hostility. Thus, when the dead rise, the pressures of the apocalypse will lead to elevated levels of control and hostility, resulting in parents that are more authoritarian. As mentioned previously, overwhelmed parents are at risk of abusing and neglecting their children. Apocalyptic-related pressure and the accompanying parenting stress it causes will lead to increases in uninvolved parenting.

Risk of Injury and Death. Despite rigid levels of parental control, children are more likely to be victims of violence when raised by authoritarian parents compared to authoritative ones. This occurs in part because children internalize admonitions (such as cautions related to unsafe behavior and the dangers lurking in the environment) best when parents deliver the message in a direct and warm (i.e., authoritative) manner.

Furthermore, adolescents are more likely to listen to parents they deem high in *legitimacy*—that is, worthy of the authority they wield because their decisions are perceived to be just and appropriate. And teens are more likely to grant legitimacy to authoritative parents than authoritarian ones. Moreover, children that view their parents as legitimate are less likely than others to engage in deviant behaviors. When the dead walk the earth, the ability to follow parental instructions in their absence will be critical for the survival of youth. Children and adolescents that fail to head their parents' warnings may find themselves in altercations with the living and the dead that lead to grievous bodily harm or death.

High levels of psychological flexibility will allow children of authoritative parents to adapt effectively to the dangers of the environments in which they find themselves. For example, the ability to shift perspective will enable youth to discover ways of avoiding confrontations with the dead or the living, for that matter. In contrast, children that lack psychological flexibility (such as the offspring of authoritarian parents) will have great difficulty finding escape routes, disentangling themselves from precarious situations, and finding alternatives to physical engagements with the enemy. As with the failure to internalize parental rules, the inability to think flexibly will result in preventable injuries and death.

The vigilant monitoring of children will be an essential component of parenting during the Zombie Apocalypse. Indeed, a lack of parental supervision increases children's risk of unintentional injury from a variety of accidents, including falls, the ingestion of poisons, and dog bites. Thus, during the Zombie Apocalypse, children of permissive and uninvolved parents will be at the highest risk of injury and death from both the ruins in their environment and the surrounding dead.

Nevertheless, even when parents are nearby, tragedies still befall children. To illustrate, consider the following: dog bites often occur because parents underestimate the likelihood of an attack and overestimate their children's ability to interact safely with animals. Now, replace the word "dog" with "zombie," and you begin to see the problem parents will face as the Zombie Apocalypse progresses. Regardless of parenting typology, as parents become more comfortable with living with the dead, complacency may set in, and if it does, needless injuries and death will rise.

Psychological Well-Being. During the Zombie Apocalypse, parenting typologies will also affect the psychological well-being of children. In violent areas of the world, children and adolescents of authoritative parents exhibit the best psychosocial outcomes, such as positive peer relationships, effective emotional self-regulation, and a positive sense of well-being. For example, Israeli teens exposed to terror attacks, missile bombardments, and armed conflict exhibit fewer behavior problems and less aggression when raised by authoritative mothers compared to authoritarian ones. These benefits should remain once the dead walk the earth.

Physical Health. Regarding current and future physical health, children and adolescents of authoritative parents should fare far better than youth raised by other parenting styles. To understand why, I first need to explain a critical biological change that links adverse childhood experiences with illness during adulthood: accelerated telomere shortening. *Telomeres* are protective caps (in the form of TTAGGG nucleotide repeats that protect genomic DNA during replication) located at the tips of chromosomes. With age, telomeres shorten and thus serve as a biological marker of aging. Moreover, accelerated telomere shortening predicts the presence of current illness and the likelihood of contracting disease in the future.

Adversity early in life, such as exposure to violence, maltreatment, and poverty, leads to accelerated telomere shorting. Of course, such conditions go hand in hand with the Zombie Apocalypse. Thus, children lucky enough to survive the undead rising will undergo telomere shortening, leading to poor physical health now and in the future. However, positive parenting practices, like authoritative caregiving, can moderate telomere shortening. Specifically, in high-risk environments, children of responsive parents have longer telomeres relative to children of less sensitive parents. Thus, authoritative parenting may help prevent the negative health outcomes associated with growing up in an undead wasteland.

Transactional Influences. Parents often respond to their children's misdeeds and aggressive behavior by becoming more authoritarian and less authoritative. In turn, such changes exacerbate children's behavior problems, aggression, and deviances, which correspondingly lead to more demanding and less responsive parenting. Psychologists refer to this type of bidirectional interaction as a transactional influence. According to the *transactional model*, both the child and the parent reciprocally influence one another over time. In other words, the child's behavior affects the parent, and the parent's behavior affects the child. Thus, worsening parenting practices result in problematic child behaviors and problematic child behaviors result in worsening parenting practices. As a result, a negative cycle of interaction develops.

During childhood and adolescence, even relatively inconsequential but negative parent-child interactions can eventually lead to dysfunctional parenting. In turn, negative parenting practices will cause youth to become anxious, depressed, and aggressive during childhood as well as violent, delinquent, and substance abusing during adolescence. As previously discussed, the violent and dangerous conditions of the Zombie Apocalypse will cause significant stress for children and parents alike. In turn, the child's behavior or the parent's behaviors (or simultaneously both) will suffer, thus starting the downward spiral of transactional interactions between parent and child.

Corporal Punishment

Imagine that you are scavenging through vehicles on a clogged freeway when you spot a small horde of zombies coming your way. To avoid certain evisceration, you take cover beneath an abandoned car, knowing that if you keep silent long enough, the undead will lumber past harmlessly. A few cars over you spy your ten-year-old daughter hiding quietly, though she is clearly frightened. During the second season of *The Walking Dead*, this is the exact situation in which Carol and her daughter, Sophia, find themselves. Unfortunately, Sophia impulsively starts to move out from her hiding place before the horde has completely passed. Startled by a previously unseen walker, Sophia screeches, further attracting the attention of the nearby dead. Terrified, Sophia scampers off into the woods with the undead at her heels. Following a brief search, Rick finds Sophia, places her in a hidden alcove on the bank of a stream, and tells her to remain there until he returns. Soon after Rick leaves, Sophia abandons the safety of the hideaway.[1] Unfortunately, no one will ever see Sophia alive again.

Twice, adults wanted Sophia to stay in place. Twice, Sophia did not listen. And twice Sophia died, once as a human, and once as a walker. In raising Sophia, what could Carol have done to drive to home the message that keeping quiet and staying in place is essential to survival during the Zombie Apocalypse? In dangerous environments, many parents rely on corporal punishment to help safeguard their children's lives.

Frequency of Corporal Punishment

Corporal punishment is a form of discipline that uses intentional physical force to cause pain or discomfort. Examples include spanking, rapping on the head, using a switch or belt, and slapping. In the United States, people use the terms "spanking," "physical punishment," and "corporal punishment" interchangeably. For research purposes, however, psychologists define corporal punishment as the use of an open hand when hitting a child on the buttocks or extremities. According to a recent UNICEF global report, more than 1.1 billion parents (and other caregivers at home) believe that corporal punishment is a necessary component of child-rearing and education. Worldwide, 63 percent of caregivers use physical punishment to discipline their children.[2] The United States is no different, with between 50 percent and 70 percent of parents regularly spanking their toddler and preschool-aged children. By the time they graduate high school, 85 percent of teens report being spanked at least once. As children age, however, the likelihood of parents using corporal punishment as a disciplinary technique decreases.[3]

Reasons for Using Corporal Punishment

Most parenting experts decry corporal punishment as a disciplinary technique (the reasons for which I discuss below).[4] Why, then, do so many caregivers rely on it? Parents report using physical punishment for a variety of reasons, such as behavioral compliance, impressing upon children the importance of socially acceptable behavior, focusing their children's attention on parental messages, and reducing future acts of aggression and antisocial behavior. Here I address the outcomes of corporal punishment in relation to each of the aforementioned parental motives for its use.

The Outcomes of Corporal Punishment

Parents spank to achieve a near instantaneous behavioral change, especially when children are in dangerous environments or their safety is otherwise at risk. Indeed, spanking does lead to immediate compliance to parental demands more than other disciplinary techniques (e.g., reasoning, time out, or threats). Thus, corporal punishment appears to be an effective strategy to compel obedience when children are in immediate danger.

Nevertheless, parents will face situations in which spanking for immediate compliance is not an option. For example, in the abovementioned scene from *The Walking Dead*, Carol is too far away from Sophia to use physical punishment. But what if Carol had previously spanked her daughter for impulsive behavior? Would that have prevented Sophia from leaving her hiding spots? To answer this question, I must first address whether spanking helps or hinders children's willingness to abide by parental expectations when their parents are no longer in sight.

As a reminder, socialization is the process whereby children acquire the rules, standards, and values of a culture. Besides survival, one of the primary goals parents have is for their children to internalize socialized ideals—that is, believe in them and follow them in the absence of parental oversight. Although children enduring corporal punishment may adhere to their parents' commands when they are nearby, they do not typically follow parental directives when their parents are no longer in the immediate vicinity. Physically punished children do not internalize many of their parents' behavioral expectations. They do what they want when they want, regardless of parental warnings. To avoid detection, and the associated consequences, children disciplined with corporal punishment minimize contact with their parents and behave sneakily. A classic example is a grounded teenager slipping out of their bedroom window to attend a party. Parents are often unaware of their children's sneakiness and thus falsely believe that corporal punishment has been effective at socializing desired behaviors and instilling parental values.

Rather than behaving in socially acceptable ways, spanked children are more likely than other youth to engage in aggressive and antisocial behavior. At the same time, they feel little guilt over their misdeeds and rarely attempt to make amends for the pain they have caused others. Furthermore, when parents discipline elementary school children using corporal punishment, the adverse effects worsen over time, with many children turning into aggressive and violent adolescents. It should come as no surprise to learn that spanked children have more problems with their peers than other youth.

Although spanking does focus children's attention on parental messages, the messages parents intend to deliver may be different from the ones that children receive. For example, if a parent were to spank their child for leaving a hiding spot too soon, the message received could be "Stay hidden as long as I can still see you." Given the proximity of Carol to Sophia, it is possible that prior corporal punishment (for similar misdeeds) could have prevented Sophia from moving out from under the car. However, once alone in the woods (where her mother was out of sight), previous spankings would not have prevented Sophia from leaving the alcove by the stream.

Parents state that they spank their children to protect them from the hazards in their environments and to prevent them from engaging in dangerous activities. But how useful is corporal punishment in safeguarding children? Unfortunately, there are few statistics on corporal punishment and mortality. Nevertheless, psychologists contend that the use of corporal punishment for prevention and protection in high-risk environments is ineffective. Here is why. First, harsh parenting increases children and adolescents' risk of witnessing and becoming victims of violence. Second, corporal punishment results in aggressive and antisocial youth, thus increasing the likelihood of fights, injuries, and victimization. Finally, the act of corporal punishment itself can lead to unintentional or intentional (i.e., physical abuse) injuries. Essentially, rather than protecting children, corporal punishment places children in harm's way.

Of note, corporal punishment can occur for any parenting typology, even an authoritative style. However, the manner in which spanking occurs for authoritative parents is different from other parenting styles. Authoritative and responsive parents use *instrumental* forms of physical punishment in which they plan spankings and deliver them without intense emotions. Moreover, research suggests that parental responsiveness and warmth may buffer children against the adverse effects of spanking, such as emotional and behavioral problems. In contrast, non-authoritative parents tend to use spanking impulsively and accompanied by strong emotions, and, in particular, anger. Generally, negative parenting styles, in combination with impulsive spanking, tends to exacerbate the adverse psychosocial effects of corporal punishment. Regardless of parenting style, as the frequency and severity of corporal punishment increases, so do the adverse effects associated with its use. For example, twice a week spanking is enough to cause long-term emotional and behavioral problems.

Corporal Punishment in the Zombie Apocalypse

Several different situations increase parents' use of corporal punishment. Not surprisingly, the Zombie Apocalypse will be replete with all of them. First, parents are likely to spank when they are angry with or frustrated by their children's behavior. As discussed previously, when the dead rise, children will likely experience emotional and behavioral problems that will challenge the patience of their parents.

Second, parents tend to use corporal punishment when they are feeling angry, frustrated or otherwise upset in general. Parents in a negative mood before their children's misdeeds are inclined to use corporal punishment after them, a phenomenon which occurs because physiological arousal (e.g., heart rate, blood pressure) is slow to dissipate. Lingering arousal from previous circumstances adds to the arousal generated by a subsequent event, resulting in a heightened level of arousal. Psychologists refer to the relocation of arousal from one occasion to another as *excitation transfer*. Regarding corporal punishment, if the child's behavior typically causes the parent only a slight amount of irritation (which would not result in a spanking), the presence of leftover arousal will result in the parent feeling very angry and frustrated and thus more likely to impulsively use physical punishment.

Third, reliance on spanking as a disciplinary tool intensifies when parents are anxious or depressed. Finally, parents under extreme duress often rely on corporal punishment as a disciplinary tool. Given that negative mood states, stress, adverse conditions, and mental illness will be prevalent during the Zombie Apocalypse, the use of corporal punishment will occur more frequently and intensely.

SPANKING AND PHYSICAL ABUSE. There is a fine line between corporal punishment and physical abuse. According to Elizabeth Gershoff, the distinguishing feature between the two is the outcome resulting from the use of force. Whereas physically abusive behaviors (e.g., kicking, hitting with a closed fist, burning, whipping) cause significant injury, corporal punishment does not. However, attempts to correct children's behavior through corporal punishment can get out of hand, and, as a result, become abusive.

Furthermore, the same factors that lead parents to increase their usage of corporal punishment (such as stress and depression), also increase the probability that corporal punishment will turn into physical abuse. And the more parents use physical punishment, the higher the likelihood that they will become abusive in the future. Worldwide, nearly one in four children endure physical abuse.[5] During the Zombie Apocalypse, that percentage will rise, as parents will have to contend with all of the variables above that lead to physical abuse.

WHEN TO USE SPANKING. Spanking can lead to short-term compliance, which should be beneficial for survival during the Zombie Apocalypse, as parents will frequently need to stop their children from doing unsafe things in perilous places. However, long-term emotional and behavioral problems accompany the use of frequent spankings, and by the teenage years, harsh and punitive parenting may push youth toward dangerous situations rather than away from them. When the dead rise, the dangers will be plentiful. Rather than relying solely on corporal punishment to socialize children and promote compliance, parents should engage in more authoritative parenting, accompanied by non-punitive forms of discipline (such as timeouts and the removal of privileges) along with limited use of instrumental corporal punishment. Infrequent spankings, in combination with a warm and responsive parenting style, could be parents' best bet for protecting their children from injury and death in the short-term as well as emotional and behavioral problems in the long-term. However, for many parents, the stress of the Zombie Apocalypse will make parenting in an authoritative style a difficult, if not impossible, undertaking.

Oppositional Defiant Disorder and Conduct Disorder

From time to time, children argue with, talk back to, and disobey their parents. However, periodic tantrums, infrequent acts of aggression, and occasional bouts of uncooperativeness and deceitfulness do not meet the criteria for a psychological disorder, especially if the child is hungry, tired, or upset. Psychopathology may be present when such behaviors are (1) more frequent and severe than is typical for a child's age and (2) problematic enough to disrupt to the child's social and family life on a daily basis.

With these caveats in mind, mental health professionals define *oppositional defiant disorder* as an on-going pattern of defiant, disobedient, hostile, and vindictive behavior toward authority figures. Symptoms include arguing, refusing to follow the rules, deliberatively annoying others, an unwillingness to compromise, and being spiteful and vengeful. In contrast, *conduct disorder* refers to the continual violation of societal norms and the rights of others. During childhood, symptoms of conduct disorder include bullying, threatening, intimidation, and starting fights. In addition to these behaviors, adolescents with conduct disorder engage in theft, the destruction of property, violence involving weapons, and cruelty toward people or animals. Thus, relative to oppositional defiant disorder, the behaviors associated with conduct disorder are far more intense and severe.

The Causes and Consequences of Oppositional Defiant Disorder and Conduct Disorder

As discussed in Chapter 7, child-based characteristics, such as behavioral self-control, emotional self-regulation, and temperament, can adversely affect parenting behavior. Likewise, these characteristics also influence the onset of mental health disturbances during childhood and adolescence. For example, independent of parenting style, children with temperaments high in negative emotionality (e.g., they are easily upset and difficult to soothe) and impulsivity are at risk for developing both oppositional defiant disorder and conduct disorder.

Moreover, certain personality characteristics, and, in particular, the presence of *callous-unemotional traits*—a lack of empathy, guilt, and remorse, along with emotional insensitivity—consistently predict the most severe and violent cases of conduct disorder. Children with callous-unemotional traits lie, cheat, and steal their way through childhood, feeling neither guilt nor remorse for their anti-social behavior. Meanwhile, they present themselves to others as good-natured and apologetic. In reality, callous-unemotional children and adolescents put on such displays to fool or appease others. Across childhood and adolescence, parents low in warmth and structure but high in rejection and coercion place their children at significant risk for the development of callous-unemotional characteristics.

For both oppositional defiant disorder and conduct disorder, the earlier the disorder presents itself, the higher the probability that negative consequences will follow, including rejection by peers, difficulties in parent and sibling relationships, social isolation, academic challenges, and emotional problems such as anxiety and depression. Once developed, these disorders show little improvement through adolescence and early adulthood. Moreover, when parenting is predominantly rejecting, oppositional defiant disorder frequently turns into conduct disorder. Because of conduct-disordered adolescents' antisocial tendencies, the outcomes for them are particularly troubling, with teens showing an increased likelihood of substance abuse and death (resulting from their violent actions and risk-taking behaviors).

Oppositional Defiant Disorder and Conduct Disorder in the Zombie Apocalypse

As the Zombie Apocalypse progresses, parenting stress will intensify, drug and alcohol use will occur with more regularity, and parental depression will be widespread. Consequently, caregivers will become increasingly demanding, chaotic, coercive, and rejecting, while simultaneously displaying lower levels of warmth, autonomy support, structure, and responsiveness. Because of these parenting changes, children will increasingly develop callous-unemotional characteristics, oppositional defiant disorder, and conduct disorder, and they will develop them at earlier ages.

Moreover, due to the aforementioned changes in parenting style, the behavior of children with oppositional defiant disorder will worsen and become conduct-disordered. As behavioral disorders become widespread, more youth will be able to hurt and take advantage of others without regret. Conflicts with parents, siblings, peers and authority figures will surge. As a result, children will feel more socially isolated and at risk of developing anxiety and depression.

Interestingly, parents of conduct-disordered youth often possess anti-social tendencies themselves, suggesting a genetic component to the disorder. The *diathesis-stress model of psychopathology* can explain how genetic predispositions interact with adverse environmental conditions to influence the onset of oppositional defiant disorder and conduct disorder. According to the diathesis-stress model, genetic predispositions (i.e., diathesis) place children on a continuum of risk for the development of mental illness, ranging from low to high probability. Similarly, environmental conditions vary from relatively stress-free to extremely stressful. Even the most genetically vulnerable youth can keep psychopathology at bay when conditions are stress-free. However, as environments become more stressful, as they will when the dead rise, the likelihood of childhood mental illness will significantly increase for genetically at-risk youth. Thus, many children unlikely to develop oppositional defiant disorder or conduct disorder before the Zombie Apocalypse will now cross over a threshold of risk tolerance and become symptomatic.

Final Thoughts

As adolescents become young adults, conduct disorder frequently turns in to *antisocial personality disorder*—defined as long-standing habits of maladaptive thought and behavior that violate the rules of society. Like conduct-disordered youth, adults with antisocial personality disorder readily manipulate and take advantage of others, showing little concern for their welfare. Additionally, they feel no guilt or remorse for their exploitive actions. Although many people associate antisocial personality disorder with serial killers, only 14 percent of those with the disorder are violent.[6] During the Zombie Apocalypse, there will be another name for people with antisocial personality disorder—survivors.

The ability to acquire resources by whatever means necessary, dispatch zombies with impunity, cull the terminally injured (such as those who have suffered zombie bite), and kill the living without guilt or remorse will be a survival advantage during an undead rising. Those with an antisocial personality disorder will act quickly, with the ends justifying the bloody means. Soldiers with antisocial personality disorder are an asset on the battlefield. Not only do they kill effortlessly, but they motivate others to do so as well.[7] Although having a ruthless killer on one's side to fight the living and the dead seems like a great idea, in truth, individuals with antisocial personality disorder serve only themselves. They will readily sacrifice their fellow combatants (whether it is necessary to save themselves or solely on a whim) just as easily as they would dispatch the dead.

Some mental health professionals believe that there are two forms of antisocial personality disorder: psychopathy and sociopathy. Being a cold and calculated violent manipulator characterizes the former, whereas the later experiences impulsive violence and explosive rages. Thus, the calm nature of the psychopath makes for better soldiering than the emotionally labile sociopath. Moreover, whereas psychopaths are born (with genetics at their cause), sociopaths are raised (with the disorder resulting from an abusive or traumatic upbringing).[8] Thus, during the Zombie apocalypse, trauma (rather than genetics) will cause the majority of cases of antisocial personality disorder. The resulting sociopathy and its uncontrolled violence will not likely improve their survival. As the apocalypse progresses, psychopaths will fare better than sociopaths, as the hot-headedness of the latter will render them dead, turned, or both.

Section Five:
Moving Past the Horror

11. Parenting and Grief

Death is an inevitability that awaits us all. Globally, the average life expectancy is 72 years of age. In areas of the world devastated by war, famine, or disease, however, that number drops dramatically. For example, the average person lives to be only 50 in Sierra Leone, 55 in Nigeria, and 61 in Afghanistan.[1] In a typical year, approximately 57 million people perish.[2] It is safe to say that once the Zombie Apocalypse takes hold, billions will die, and they will die quickly. As an example, let us consider the many deaths (perceived or real) of family members on *The Walking Dead*. Judith Grimes loses her mother to childbirth, her father to separation, and her brother to the undead. Maggie Rhee suffers the death of her sister to a bullet, her father to a sword, and her husband to a bat. Neither Carol Peletier's husband nor her daughter survive their last encounter with the walking dead. The undead also take the lives of Morgan Jones' wife and son as well as Michonne's son.[3]

As you can see, when the dead walk, few families remain intact, leaving bereaved parents to deal with their *grief*—the intense emotional suffering accompanying a loss—and the sorrow endured by the surviving family members. But what purpose does grief serve? How can profound sadness and emotional devastation possibly benefit the survivors of the deceased?

The Function of Grief

Why do humans grieve? In short, because of attachment bonds. As discussed in Chapter 9, infants form attachments with caregivers because doing so helps them survive. For example, attachment behaviors such as crying, clinging, and approaching elicit protection and support from care-givers. Based on the history of care experienced, infants develop internal working models (i.e., mental representations) of their parents' childrearing proclivities and devise strategies to compliment them. Over the first year of life, these strategies formalize into secure and insecure forms of attach-ment. During adolescence, internal working models associated with each parent coalesce into an overarching attachment orientation (i.e., a sys-tematic pattern of emotions, needs, and expectations in relationships). Thus, throughout the lifespan, attachment bonds are present. However, when an individual loses an attachment figure (such as a parent or a spouse), their internal working models undergo refinement and reconfig-uration.

Internal working models are predictive representations that allow individuals to forecast what their attachment figures will do in any given situation. When a loved one dies, those models are no longer accurate. For example, internal working models of secure children predict that when they cry their parents will respond quickly and responsively. They also expect that separations will be relatively short and that their parents will soon return. However, dead parents cannot soothe their children, nor can they physically comfort them, nor do they return as expected. And before the reconfiguration of internal working models takes place, bereaved secure children will still expect their attachment figures to do all of those things. When they do not, anger, fear, and sadness will predominate their emotional states. Thus, from an attachment perspective, the function of grief is to change internal working models such that they are in line with the current caregiving situation. By relying on attachment figures that are present, rather than those that are permanently absent, the psychological well-being of children improves, as do their chances of survival.

Moreover, the loss of an attachment figure forces children to recon-figure their attachment hierarchies (i.e., the preferential ordering of care-givers). Grief starts the reorganization process, which continues throughout *bereavement*—the adjustment period following a significant loss. Ulti-mately, children reorganize their attachment figures based on the sensi-tivity and responsivity of the remaining caregivers. At some point during bereavement, the emotional pain that accompanies grief begins to dissi-pate. Nevertheless, for some, the emotional distress associated with the loss of a loved one remains for years or even decades.

It is important to note that the death of an attachment figure does not necessarily mean that a child cuts all emotional ties with that person. The attachment bond persists but in an altered form. Although children cannot consider a deceased parent a source of physical comfort and protection (as they once did), perceived emotional support is still a possibility. For example, many children feel solace in the fact that their parent is looking down from heaven, watching over them. Children also keep attachment relationships "alive" by talking about their parents with others and by talking to their parents (at the gravesite or elsewhere). Psychologists contend that the continuation of attachment bonds to departed parents helps children transition to a life without those caregivers—that is, a life with a reconfigured internal working model of attachment.

During adulthood, romantic partners serve as attachment figures and assume the same supportive and comforting roles that parents provided during childhood. Thus, the death of a spouse requires changes to internal working models as well. Moreover, attachment is just one of several different types of emotional bonds. Other bonds include affiliative bonds, such as those related to parenting (i.e., a caregiving bond) and friendship (i.e., sociable bonds). Similar to attachment bonds, affiliative bonds are powerful, and the death of a loved one (such as a child or friend) requires that the associated internal working model is refined to reflect that loss. Once again, grief starts the reconfiguration process.

The Experience of Grief

Grief, painful though it may be, ultimately serves to prepare surviving family members and friends for the future. However, to progress from the devastation of a loss to a better tomorrow requires work. Below I present two different viewpoints on the process of grief. The first perspective, by Elisabeth Kübler-Ross, focuses on accepting the loss of a loved one. The second, by John Bowlby, addresses how the reorganization of attachment bonds and internal working models takes place. For each, I consider the likelihood of successful grief in the land of the dead. Afterward, I discuss developmental differences in grieving between adults and children as well as address the influence of traumatic loss on grief during childhood. Finally, I consider the connection between mourning a *living loss* (i.e., someone who is ill, but not deceased) and grieving for the living dead.

Kübler-Ross' Five Stages of Grief

According to Elisabeth Kübler-Ross, there are five stages of grief: denial, anger, bargaining, depression, and acceptance. The first stage, *denial,* refers to not accepting (i.e., denying) the reality of a loved one's death entirely. During this stage, the individual feels shocked and numb, and the world seems meaningless and overwhelming. By denying (either consciously or unconsciously) the death, the individual slowly lets the reality of the situation set in. Denial, then, helps protect the individual from the deep emotions associated with loss, providing them time to cope.

As denial gives way to the second stage of grief, *anger*, suppressed emotions begin to surface. During this stage, those grieving become angry at the situation, themselves (for not being able to prevent death), and those who have died (for leaving the surviving family and friends in disarray). The sight of others, especially those who survived similar circumstances, can evoke feelings of envy and jealousy in addition to anger. More often than not, those experiencing grief take their anger out on those closest to them. Of note, people experience less anger at the loss of the elderly (who have lived full lives) compared to the loss of someone younger, such as a child or teenager (whose lives ended too soon). Additionally, deaths following chronic illness often produce less anger than a tragic accident or an acute medical crisis.

The third stage, *bargaining*, is about negotiating away the emotional pain of a loss. When a loved one (or even oneself) is injured or dying, a person will attempt to make deals with God, the universe, or any spiritual being that might be able to provide a cure. People promise to change their ways, devote their lives to the downtrodden, or do just about anything to prevent death. Once the death occurs, however, bargaining now focuses on ridding oneself of distressed feelings caused by the loss.

When the negotiations stop, and the finality of a loved one's death is fully realized, an individual enters the fourth stage of grief, *depression.* During this stage, both sadness and grief intensify. Individuals feel empty, hopelessly lost, and alone. The fifth and final stage is *acceptance.* Accepting the loss of a loved one does not mean that the pain goes away entirely or that the death will no longer affect the lives of the bereaved. Instead, this stage is about accepting the permanency of the situation, and looking toward (but not necessarily "looking forward to") the future and a life without their loved one. However, even after acceptance has taken place, healing and recovery from the loss may still be years away. Many psychologists view acceptance as the start of the healing process, rather than its end.

Kübler-Ross points out that grieving is a flexible process and that many people do not follow the stages in the order detailed above. For some, anger predominates their lives, whereas for others it is depression. Consequently, each person experiences the loss of a loved one uniquely because of a variety of factors (e.g., life history, personality, cultural background) and the manner in which the death they grieve took place.

John Bowlby's Four Phases of Mourning

John Bowlby contends that grief has four phases: numbness and shock; yearning and searching; disorganization and despair; and reorganization. During the first phase of mourning, *numbness and shock*, the bereaved are unable to accept the reality of the loss. They are in denial. Nevertheless, periodic outbursts of intense emotions (such as sorrow, anger, and panicked anxiety) also occur. During the second phase, *yearning and searching*, those who are grieving experience an intense desire to be with those they have lost, and they will seek them in one way or another. Some will look for signs that their loved ones are still alive. They will misinterpret a sock out of place, a dream, or even the ring of a doorbell as an indication that their loved ones are not, in fact, dead. Others will search for those they lost in the afterlife. They will employ spiritualists, psychics, and mediums, and they will conduct séances to contact the departed.

Moreover, bereaved people will search for the meaning of the loss. Some will even hallucinate, thinking they hear or see their loved ones. An example of this occurred on *The Walking Dead*. Following the traumatic death of his wife, Lori, Rick experiences *psychosis* (i.e., he loses touch with reality), during which he hallucinates talking to her on the phone and seeing her around the grounds where he was living.[4] Also, Bowlby's second phase of mourning is replete with feelings of anger. Next, those in grief enter a period of *disorganization and despair*. The bereaved begin to realize the profound effect the loss will have on their lives, which leads to feelings of apathy, hopelessness, and intense sorrow. They disengage from others and no longer participate in activities that were once pleasurable. With their futures seemingly in limbo, they begin to question how they can survive without their loved ones. The final phase, *reorganization*, occurs when survivors accept the permanency of their loss, attempt to recover from it, and in the process reconfigure their internal working models.

According to Bowlby, the quality of the attachment relationship with the deceased prior to their death dramatically affects the grieving process. Adults with a secure attachment style tend to progress through the phases of mourning successfully. In contrast, those with insecure-attachments are likely to develop one of the following disordered variants of mourning:

chronic mourning or the prolonged absence of conscious grieving. Adults with an anxious attachment style (who are hyperactivated and anxiety focused) are prone to *chronic mourning*, wherein grief is intense, drawn-out, non-abating, and preoccupied with thoughts of the deceased. Those in chronic mourning find it difficult to function as they once did. In contrast, those with an avoidant attachment style (who are aloof and emotionally distant) are likely to endure a *prolonged absence of conscious grieving*, showing little anger, distress, or sorrow over the loss, and quickly returning to their regular activities following the funeral. However, rather than grief being absent, it is bottled up. In the long run, the suppression of grief, especially when the loss is sudden or traumatic, can lead to the onset of mental health problems and difficulties in adjustment (e.g., completing daily activities).

Stages of Grief in the Zombie Apocalypse

The Zombie Apocalypse will pose a challenge to the successful completion of both Kübler-Ross' and Bowlby's stages of grief. Given the similarities between the two theories, I have combined the predicted outcomes for related concepts. The lone difference is bargaining, which is unique to Kübler-Ross' theory.

(1) *Denial/Numbness and Shock.* When the dead rise, it will become easier for surviving relatives to deny the fact that their loved one is dead. After all, the "supposed" dead will make noises, move about their environment, reach out for family members, and eat. These behaviors will reinforce the belief that their loved one is not dead, but rather sick and disoriented (albeit aggressive). Unfortunately, denial during the Zombie Apocalypse will lead to even more death, as family members will fail to take appropriate precautions against attacks from the familial dead. Instead, they will approach their zombified loved ones to help them, ending up either dead or injured.

(2) *Anger/Yearning and Searching.* As the dead overtake the world, survivors will experience a tremendous amount of anger at the sudden loss of family members, especially when the decedents are young. Yearning and searching will be particularly problematic during the Zombie Apocalypse. After all, the likelihood that an undead loved one is milling about the neighborhood will be quite high. If the bereaved were to encounter a zombified version of the lost person, they might wishfully imbue life-like characteristics to the dead. In such cases, what should be a joyful reunion will quickly turn deadly and then undeadly.

(3) *Bargaining.* Similar to pre-apocalyptic times, during the Zombie Apocalypse, family members will try to bargain with God, the universe, anyone or anything else, to save their injured or bitten relatives. As an example, let us consider Hershel Greene from *The Walking Dead.* When we first meet Hershel, he and his family members are capturing walkers that wander onto their property and storing them in their barn. They do so because they mistakenly believe walkers to be alive, sick, and in need of a cure for which they are patiently waiting.[5] In such situations, and especially where loved ones are involved, both the decidedly (and temporarily) devout will attempt to bargain with God to restore their family members' health. Given the life-like functioning of zombies, even those that realize their relatives are undead will continue to bargain on their behalf in the hopes of regaining true life. Likewise, after their relatives die or turn into the living dead, many survivors will attempt to negotiate away their emotional pain. Because zombies possess some life-like characteristics, it will be difficult for many survivors to give up on bargaining entirely.

(4) *Depression/Disorganization and Despair.* When grieving, depression is a mood state specific to the loss of an individual. Thus, it differs from major depression, a chronic form of mental illness that permeates all aspects of life (see Chapter 6). However, given the traumatic nature of loss during the Zombie Apocalypse, along with the sheer number of family members that will die, the compartmentalized, depressive mood state associated with grieving will increasingly turn into depressive psychopathology.

(5) *Acceptance/Reorganization.* The reorganization of attachment bonds and the acceptance of loss will be incredibly difficult to do when the person you are grieving appears somewhat alive. To help illustrate this point, here is another example from *The Walking Dead.* Shortly after the start of the apocalypse, a walker bites Jenny Jones and turns her into a zombie. She then lumbers about the neighborhood, periodically returning to her front yard. Despite knowing what Jenny has become, and the danger she poses to the living, her husband Morgan is unable to shoot her and end her undead life.[6] In some ways, allowing Jenny to wander about as a walker means that Morgan does not have to accept the fact that she is dead. Many survivors of the apocalypse will look at zombified family members much as Morgan did his wife and see the people they love rather than the monsters that they are. Unfortunately, doing so will make accepting their death, as well as restructuring and reorganizing internal working models, problematic.

When the dead rise, billions of unfortunate souls will meet their deaths unexpectedly. Adults and children alike will be torn apart by zombies, murdered by the living, or die accidentally. Under such circumstances, completing the grieving process will be all the more difficult. As the result of an unexpected loss, survivors will endure prolonged periods of denial (i.e., shock and disbelief), intensified feelings of anger/yearning and searching and frequent bargaining to rid oneself of immense pain as well as severe depression/disorganization and despair. These stages will be intensified for those unable to bid farewell to their loved ones. In contrast, when death is expected, as will be the case following a zombie bite, survivors can prepare for the imminent loss and its aftereffects, say goodbye to their loved ones, be with them when they pass, and begin the grieving process ahead of time. When the dead rise, opportunities such as these will facilitate the completion of the acceptance/reorganization stage, though it will still be painful and demanding.

As discussed in Chapter 9, the death and destruction of the Zombie Apocalypse will make successfully meeting the emotional needs of others an exceedingly difficult task. Moreover, an undead rising will lead to the recurrent loss of attachment figures. The resultant effect of these changes will be an upsurge in the number of insecure attachments to parents during childhood, followed by a higher proportion of insecure attachment orientations during adulthood. In turn, this will lead to an increase in the frequency of disordered variants of mourning among the bereaved.

Grief During Childhood

The death of one or more parents is one of childhood's most stressful experiences. The manner in which children suffer grief is similar to that of adults, with some notable exceptions. First, whereas children grieve in shorts spurts, adults grieve continuously. Molly Gao and Marissa Slaven use a water analogy to describe this difference. They contend that children grieve as though they are jumping through puddles. When in a puddle, children experience profound sadness, but as soon as they jump out of it, they happily go about their daily activities. In contrast, adult grief is analogous to standing in a river of sorrow, which follows the bereaved wherever they go, regardless of what they are doing. Given these differences, adults need to be careful not to assume that a happy-looking child is "doing fine" and "over" the loss of their loved one, no matter if the death occurred weeks, months, or even years ago.

The second difference between child and adult grief is that as children age and their cognitive abilities improve, they may think about or experience the death of a loved one differently. For example, in the chapter on attachment, I relayed the story of Benny Imura (from Jonathan Maberry's *Rot & Ruin* series), whose first memory is of a zombie attack, in which his mother, wearing white a dress with red sleeves, places him into the waiting arms of his 20-year-old brother, Tom. There is more to the story. For years, Benny hated Tom for his cowardice in not saving his mother, believing that with Tom's help, she could have survived. It is only during his teen years that Benny finally realizes that his mother's sleeves were not, in fact, red. They were white and covered in blood. Benny's zombified father had bitten her. Rather than trying to save herself, Benny's mother last act was to get him out of harm's way. This realization helped Benny rethink his mother's death and the role that his brother played in it, thus helping Benny progress through the stages of grief. As you can see, when a child loses a parent, bereavement becomes a life-long process, with the nature of grief changing as the child develops.

GRIEF, CHILDHOOD, AND THE ZOMBIE APOCALYPSE. For children and adolescents, even under the best of circumstances, grieving the loss of a parent is a painful and challenging process. However, when the parental loss is violent, as most will be during the Zombie Apocalypse, trauma-related symptoms disrupt the typical course of mourning, a phenomenon known as *childhood traumatic grief.* Children with this disorder experience intrusive and distressing trauma-related thoughts, such as thinking they may die like their parents or believing that they could have prevented the deaths. They also face upsetting memories surrounding the traumatic losses. Examples include reliving their parents' demise or recalling a fight with their parents right before they died. Finally, disturbing images (e.g., visualizing a loved one's lifeless and bloodied body) frequently invade their minds.

Although trauma-related thoughts, memories, and images can occur without warning, there are three types of situations likely to trigger them. The first trigger, *trauma reminders,* refer to circumstances (e.g., being alone or in the dark), places (e.g., a farmhouse or shopping mall), and sensory stimuli (e.g., sight, sounds, smells) reminiscent of the location and manner in which the traumatic death occurred. The second trigger, *loss reminders,* relate to anything (e.g., a Cherokee rose) or anyone that reminds the child of their deceased parent. The final trigger, *change reminders,* consist of small or significant modifications in the child's living conditions resulting from a parent's death. A missing plate at the dinner table, someone new tucking them into bed at night, and living in a different house exemplify this type of trigger

Once activated, trauma-related thoughts, memories, and images cause increases in uncomfortable physiological states (e.g., shaking, dizziness, headaches) and emotional distress (e.g., helplessness, terror). To minimize such unpleasantness, children learn to avoid such triggers and become numb to them. Children with traumatic grief cannot even find respite in their slumber, as their dreams are often nightmares in which some grizzly horror befalls them. Not surprisingly, youth with this disorder have difficulty falling and staying asleep. All told, trauma-related symptoms make it difficult for children to accept the loss of their parents and reorganize their internal working models of attachment relationships.

During the Zombie Apocalypse, children and adolescents will likely experience the loss of loved ones repeatedly. Although a child might stave off traumatic grief following the first loss (most children do), that death will increase the likelihood of the disorder developing following a second loss. And with each successive loss, the possibility of childhood traumatic grief rises. Given that billions will die when the dead rise, expect childhood traumatic grief to be the norm.

Living Loss and Chronic Sorrow

Although most think of grief in the context of death, individuals can also grieve for the living, and when they do, psychologists refer to it a *living loss*. For example, parents of children with lifelong disabilities grieve the living loss of the "healthy child that could have been." Similarly, the elderly will grieve the living loss of a spouse, who is very much alive, but undergoing memory deficiencies and personality changes due to Alzheimer's disease. Experiencing a living loss places individuals at risk for the development of *chronic sorrow*, which is characterized by grief and profound sadness that does not abate over time. Many parents with chronic sorrow believe that they contributed to or caused their children's disability through genetics, poor choices (medical and otherwise), or a perceived lack of vigilance. Hence, parents with such beliefs endure intense feelings of guilt.

Over time, parents caring for disabled children may become angry, frustrated, and concerned about the long-term effects of the disability will have on their lives going forward. Moreover, parents with a living loss find that their sorrow, guilt, anger, and frustration intensify when other children meet developmental milestones (e.g., walking, talking, becoming potty-trained), but theirs fail to do so. For parents with chronic sorrow, the following circumstances deepen their grief: (1) they are unable to find a successful treatment; (2) they experience a sense of social isolation or stigma; 3) day-to-day activities primarily revolve around child care, leaving time for little else; and (4) when it becomes difficult to meet the needs of other family members.

LIVING LOSS, CHRONIC SORROW, AND THE ZOMBIE APOCA-
LYPSE. During the Zombie Apocalypse (and especially at the start of it), many parents will consider their zombified children to be sick and in need of care, not to mention a cure. Others will see their ghoulish wards as something other than dead, though not quite alive. On *The Walking Dead*, "The Governor" treats his zombified daughter Penny in this way. He feeds her flesh, combs her hair, and attempts to reason with her.[7] Rather than perceiving their children as dead or undead, some parents will grieve for their zombified children as a living loss, rendering themselves vulnerable to chronic sorrow and the guilt, anger, sadness, and frustration that accompany it.

In fact, most (if not all) of the factors that lead to chronic sorrow will be prevalent during the Zombie Apocalypse. First, there is no cure for zombiism. Second, others will stigmatize those caring for the living dead as mentally unfit. Third, because parents must imprison their undead children (lest they break out and start eating the neighbors), daily activities will involve checking the security of holding cells as well as making sure that others do not break in to dispatch the dead. To avoid such concerns, many parents will choose to isolate their families from the surrounding community. Fourth, caring for the living dead means that there will be less time available to spend with healthy family members (if any exist). Finally, many parents will view the zombified state of their children as a result of poor parenting, such a lack of oversight or a failure to socialize proper safety precautions. When the dead rise, the factors leading to chronic sorrow will be plentiful. And once chronic sorrow sets in, parents may never be able to accept that their zombified children are indeed dead. As a result, there will be no end in sight to their grief.

The Loss of a Parent

Globally, nearly 125 million children under 18 years of age have lost at least one parent, including 15 million who have lost both.[8] Although the pre-apocalyptic likelihood of parental death in Western countries is relatively low (3 percent to 4 percent of children will experience the death of a parent by the time they are 18),[9] living in parts of the world ravaged by disease, famine, or war dramatically increases the chances that a child will lose one or more parents. For example, in Guinea, Liberia and Sierra Leone, Ebola killed nearly 16,000 parents.[10] Similarly, six years of war turned 100,000 Syrian youth into orphans.[11] The exceedingly high mortality rate of the Zombie Apocalypse will mean that most children will experience parental loss.

Death and Parentification

Following the loss of a loved one, some children act parent-like, forgoing their own expressions of their grief out of concern that their sadness may exacerbate the sorrow experienced by other family members. Psychologists refer to the process of children taking on a significant caregiving role as *parentification*. In actuality, there are two types of parentification: instrumental and emotional. *Instrumental parentification* occurs when children assist their parents by taking on non-emotional parental responsibilities such as cooking meals or doing laundry.

In contrast, *emotional parentification* involves meeting the emotional and psychological needs of others, for example, reassuring a crying parent or comforting a younger sibling. Concerning mourning, parentified children spend a great deal of time consoling others rather than grieving themselves. Children engage in both forms parentification to provide stability to an unstable family and reduce the family's overall level of anxiety. Of the two, emotional parentification is more deleterious, often resulting in dysfunctional patterns of grief as well as anxiety disorders, depression, and other forms of mental illness.

Death, Parentification and the Zombie Apocalypse. When the dead rise, children and adolescents will take on parenting responsibilities out of necessity. In addition to caretaking and household duties, acts of instrumental parentification will include dispatching the dead, removing carcasses, and foraging for supplies. For some parents, the loss of one or more family members will cause mental health issues (see below), resulting in children having to engage in emotional parentification. As mentioned above, on *The Walking Dead*, Rick suffers a psychotic break following the death of his wife during childbirth. As a result of his father's fragile state, Carl withholds his own expressions of grief.

Even without the presence of severe mental illness, parents of the apocalypse will rely on their older children for emotional support. Such practices are commonplace in military families during periods of deployment. Unfortunately, the deployed parent's homecoming does not always lead to better outcomes for parentified children and adolescents. The boundary ambiguities created by parentification, and the feelings of role confusion that accompany it, result in frequent conflicts between the child and the returning parent. Given the scavenging required to survive the Zombie Apocalypse and the potential for skirmishes between communities, older children and adolescents will be needed to meet the emotional needs of family members left behind while their parents go off to war or search for provisions. Such burdens will place youth at risk for emotional problems when their parents return as well as disordered grief and mental illness if they do not.

Children's Understanding of Death

The death of a loved one, be it a parent, friend, or family member, is incredibly painful for children and adults alike. To an adult, death is the cessation of life, as indicated by the absence of a heartbeat, the failure to breathe, and the lack of brainwave activity. However, across childhood and adolescence, age-related differences in the concept of death can affect the course of mourning as well as the parents' ability to help their children grieve. To comprehend death, children need to understand its five primary subcomponents: (1) irreversibility (i.e., following death, living things cannot become alive again); (2) non-functionality (i.e., biological processes cease upon death); (3) universality (i.e., all living things die); (4) inevitability (i.e., the living cannot avoid death); and (5) causality (i.e., the breakdown of bodily processes cause death). Here is what to expect as children age.

Children under three do not comprehend the concept of death or its subcomponents. Nevertheless, toddlers notice the absence of deceased family members, but trust that they will eventually return. As such, the very young engage in active search behaviors, such as looking around the house for the departed and calling out their name. Following the death of a parent, grandparent, or sibling it is common for very young children to ask where the person is and when they are coming home.

Between three and five years of age, children misunderstand many of the biological aspects of death, believing it to be a functional, temporary state in which the dead can see, hear, and feel. They even believe that the deceased still needs to breathe, eat, and drink. They are very concerned about their loved one's suffering upon seeing them buried in a casket. Many preschoolers fail to understand the causal aspect of death and may imagine that they triggered the death of a loved one because of something they said, did, or thought. This type of *magical thinking*—defined as the belief that one's desires, wishes, and thoughts can influence the world around them—can also lead preschoolers to assume that by wishing hard enough they can bring their loved ones back to life. Religious and spiritual teachings related to death (such as heaven and the afterlife) can confuse preschool-aged children, leading them to believe that the dead go to a location from which they can return. Not surprisingly, they are devastated when they do not. Similarly, telling children that the loved one has "gone away" can lead to feelings of abandonment (when they do not return) and unrealistic hope that they will come home. Moreover, euphemisms for death, such as "eternal rest" and "resting in peace," can lead young children to equate slumber with death, resulting in sleep difficulties.

Around age six, most children understand that death is inevitable, non-functional, and irreversible. At the start of the elementary school years, magical thinking begins to wane, though it will not disappear entirely until early adolescence. However, younger elementary school-aged children find it difficult to comprehend how the deceased can be both in heaven and buried in the cemetery at the same time. By the time they are 10, children's understanding of death dramatically improves, with children fully grasping the concepts of inevitability, irreversibility, universality, non-functionality, and causality. Finally, during adolescence, teens begin to think about death as it relates to the meaning of life.

CHILDREN'S UNDERSTANDING OF DEATH IN THE ZOMBIE APOCALYPSE. When the dead walk, developmental differences in children's understanding of death will place preschool-aged children and younger in tremendous danger and elementary school-aged children at an increased risk of death. Here is why. For very young children, the inability to understand the concept of death means that zombies, especially those sustaining few injuries, will look mostly alive. Thus, from a toddler's perspective, the zombified parent staggering toward them is merely an absent parent returning home. The very young will greet their "returning" parents as they usually would following a brief (e.g., coming back from work) or prolonged separation (e.g., returning from a tour in the military). Typically, these happy greetings include running toward their loved ones excitedly, the loved ones happily meeting them with their arms wide open. However, this situation will be especially problematic when their loved ones are undead, and their open arms are searching for flesh to tear, rather than a hug to give.

When magical thinking is at its zenith during early childhood, upon seeing zombified loved ones, young children may gleefully believe that their wishes and desires had come true and steadfastly approach those they lovingly miss. It is not until middle childhood that children will no longer be highly vulnerable to magical thinking. Even as children begin to internalize the subcomponents of death during the elementary school years and magical thinking diminishes, there is still the possibility that older children will believe that their loved ones have returned to them, as per their desires. Older children will be most vulnerable to magical thinking when they are in the yearning and searching phase of grief. Unfortunately, during an undead uprising, even a momentary lapse of reason involving the undead can prove deadly.

The Effects of Parental Loss on Psychological Well-Being and Physical Health

As previously discussed, throughout the bereavement process, children and adolescents go through a variety of negative emotional states such as anger, fear, and sorrow. Beyond the experience of grief, the death of a parent affects other aspects of children's psychological well-being and physical health. For example, from early childhood through adolescence, sleeping and eating disturbances are commonplace. Moreover, relative to their non-bereaved counterparts, children experiencing the loss of both parents are more likely to become physically ill during the first two years of bereavement. Parental death also places children and adolescents at risk for psychological disorders such as PTSD (especially if the death is traumatic), anxiety disorders, depression, and substance abuse. Such deleterious effects can last for years or even decades. For example, seven years after the Bosnian war, children orphaned by one or both parents were at increased risk for psychopathology, including depression and PTSD. Additional research on Jewish holocaust survivors indicates that parental loss during World War II was predictive of deficits in well-being, greater social isolation, significant depression, and severe PTSD 60 years later.

Of note, the loss of a parent also manifests itself differently across development. During the preschool years, grieving children's play frequently turns aggressive. When frustrated, previously docile children may now find it difficult to control their impulses, responding with hitting, pushing, yelling, and the grabbing of toys. Children 10 and under often experience *regression*, whereby they engage in behaviors that were appropriate at earlier stages of development but no longer are. An example is a potty-trained child starting to wet their bed at night. Elementary school-aged children, as well as adolescents, may begin to have difficulties in school (e.g., concentration problems, inability to complete tasks), act out, behave aggressively, and withdraw from friends. Finally, in contrast to their younger counterparts, many adolescents encounter role confusion following the death of a parent. In particular, they have a hard time figuring out their place in the modified family constellation.

Between the ages of five and 11, children may be the most vulnerable to the effects of traumatic loss. According to Maja Lis-Turlejska and colleagues, *threat awareness* (e.g., recognition of potential injury or death) is a crucial determinant of PTSD. Due to cognitive limitations, preschool-aged children do not experience an increase in threat awareness following a parental loss. In contrast, threat awareness goes up for both elementary school-aged children and adolescents. However, only adolescents are developmentally advanced enough to comprehend the threat component of parental loss and cope with it effectively. Thus, an awareness of threat accompanied by a lack of coping skills places children in middle childhood at significant risk for PTSD.

THE EFFECTS OF PARENTAL LOSS ON PSYCHOLOGICAL WELL-BEING AND PHYSICAL HEALTH DURING THE ZOMBIE APOCALYPSE.

When all goes well, child and adolescent bereavement proceeds without significant complications, emotionally painful though it may be. Youth will successfully move through the stages of grief with minimal effects on their short-term or long-term psychological well-being and physical health. Even when a parental death is traumatic, most children and adolescents still able to complete the grieving process *without* deviating from the norms of wellness. Nevertheless, when environmental stressors and personal liabilities compound, psychological well-being and physical health are bound to suffer. The following affect children and adolescents' mental and physical health deleteriously: (1) an insecure attachment to the deceased prior to their death; (2) an insecure attachment to the surviving parent or caregiver; (3) minimal social support for the surviving child or parent; (4) instability in the family environment; (5) experiencing multiple deaths (or traumatic experiences); and (6) being in middle childhood.

As previously stated, the Zombie Apocalypse will likely cause an increase in insecure attachments; reduce social support for children and adults alike; cause continuous family instability; and expose children to multiple traumatic deaths and experiences. The death of a parent is by no means the sole cause of short-term or long-term psychological disturbances and health issues in children and adolescents. However, parental death does increase children and adolescents' susceptibility to physical and psychological problems. Thus, the death of a parent, in combination with developmental and individual vulnerabilities, along with the harsh, dangerous, and traumatic conditions of the Zombie Apocalypse, will mean a dramatic rise in the number of physically and mentally ill children and adolescents.

When a Parent Loses a Child

Globally, seven million infants, children, and adolescents predecease their parents each year, with the majority of these deaths being preventable.[12] Most parents perceive the death of a child as more tragic, profound, intense, and painful than the loss of either a spouse or an aging parent. Regardless of how the death occurred, be it the result of a sudden medical emergency, prolonged illness, unforeseeable accident, or homicide, parents find it difficult to find meaning in the loss. Many parents lose faith in the Almighty, as God failed to act when their child desperately needed divine intervention. Other parents struggle with the fact that their view of the world as a relatively predictable, safe, just, and fair place no longer applies. Similarly, the death of a child challenges parental beliefs about the "natural order of things," specifically the principle that children should outlive their parents.

In addition to the universal emotions accompanying grief, such as sorrow and anger, parents often experience other negative feelings. For example, many parents feel shame or guilt at not being able to protect their children from harm, creating many "If only I had done that differently my child would still be alive" scenarios in their minds. Such thoughts and emotions occur more frequently when the loss is sudden rather than prolonged due to illness. In contrast, with a terminal illness, a sense of release often accompanies the end to their child's pain and suffering. Consequently, such feelings mortify many parents. At other times, parents are subjected to feelings of guilt because they are alive while their child is dead. Psychologists refer to this type of self-reproach as *survivor guilt*.

Survivor guilt can occur for any cause of death (e.g., disease or accident), for any number of dead (e.g., few or many), and regardless of whether the parent was present or absent at the time of death. However, it is most likely to occur following traumatic incidents involving multiple deaths in the presence of the parent. In such situations, parents will question why they lived and their child died. Many parents begin to idealize their children while simultaneously perceiving themselves as undeserving of life.

Additionally, disconcerting ruminations frequently enter the minds of bereaved parents. They wonder what their child was thinking or feeling just before death: Were they scared? Were they lonely? Were they calling out for them? As time progresses, a parent's wish to "move on" from the death often conflicts with their desire to "not forget" their child's uniqueness. Parents create memorials, hold on to remembrances, put up pictures, and do other things in an attempt to retain the memories of the lost child in as much detail as possible. Despite these efforts, many parents realize that their efforts to memorialize the child cannot fill the void left by death.

The Effects of Child Loss on Psychological Well-Being and Physical Health

As when a child loses a parent, a variety of adverse physical and psychological outcomes occur when a parent loses a child. Minor aches and pains (e.g., headaches, stomach upset, and other somatic ailments) become frequent, as do more severe health maladies, such as cardiovascular problems and cancer. Bereaved parents even have a higher mortality rate than parents who have not lost a child. In part, these deaths result from poor coping choices, such as smoking, drinking, and drug use, as well as a weakened immune system due to the stress of prolonged grieving. Such adverse health consequences can last for decades.

Following the death of a child, *global self-esteem* (i.e., the overall sense of self-worth), *parental self-esteem* (i.e., perceived worthiness as a parent), perceived quality of life, and sense of well-being all diminish. Many parents struggle with a new, and unwanted, identity: that of a "bereaved parent." Parents that lose their only child (or their last remaining child) even wonder if they can still call themselves a "parent." At least five years post-death, bereaved parents are at an increased risk of developing psychiatric problems so severe that they require hospitalization. After this period has elapsed, parents will still be at significant risk for anxiety, depression, and PTSD for years to come, and even more so if the death was sudden or violent. Moreover, the death of a child increases a parent's risk of *suicidal ideation* (i.e., thinking about or planning suicide) and attempted suicide.

Worldwide, around 800,000 people die by means of suicide each year, a number that translates into one death every 40 seconds.[13] Although depression is at the root of most suicides, individuals with other psychological disorders, such as PTSD and substance abuse, also take their own lives. From interviews with people who attempted suicide but survived, and from messages left by those who completed suicide, psychologists have identified multiple motivations for taking one's life. Here are a few: ending physical pain, eliminating psychological suffering and feelings of hopelessness, punishing others by making them feel guilty, the belief that their death will ease the burden of others, and impulsive behavior during times of desperation. Those that attempt suicide often think that the *only* solution to the problems they are currently facing is death.

THE EFFECTS OF CHILD LOSS ON PSYCHOLOGICAL WELL-BEING AND PHYSICAL HEALTH DURING THE ZOMBIE APOCALYPSE.

When the dead rise and children fall, the stressors of apocalyptic living among the dead will increase the adverse psychological and physical outcomes associated with child loss. How can they not? Even if a parent does not lose a child, the Zombie Apocalypse is replete with uncertainty, unpredictability, deprivation, loss, and traumatic stress. Alone, each of these factors can lead to mental and physical problems. Now, combine them and add profound grief to the mix, and you can see how stress will quickly overwhelm the physical health and psychological well-being of bereaved parents.

During the Zombie Apocalypse, those grieving the loss of a child will experience many of the emotions, thoughts, and situations previously mentioned to justify suicide attempts. There will be suffering, emotional pain, hopelessness, attempts at social isolation, and desperation. Additionally, with the dead all around, it will be impossible to avoid a preoccupation with death, a key component of suicidal ideation. Hotlines and support services for those thinking about suicide (such as the National Suicide Prevention Lifeline [1-800-273-8255]) will no longer be functional. With few family and friends about, social support will be difficult to find. Whether related or not, others will likely be traumatized as well, thus hindering their ability to provide adequate aid. Although not all parents will attempt to take their own lives following the loss of a child, the factors increasing the likelihood of suicide will be plentiful.

Final Thoughts

For some parents, the tragic loss of a child means an end to parenting, at least until another child is born, adopted, or fostered. For other parents, childrearing duties continue, as one or more siblings survive the deceased. In such cases, parents must grieve an unimaginable loss while simultaneously parenting a grieving child. Even with support from family and friends, many parents find themselves overwhelmed, neither grieving nor parenting effectively.

A typical response to the loss of a child is for parents to become overly protective of their surviving children. Not surprisingly, the cause of this behavior is the fear that their other children will die as well. In the same vein, bereaved parents tend to become stricter disciplinarians. The combination of these two changes tends to an increase in parent-child conflict, adding an unneeded additional stressor to the family system. Nevertheless, not all interactions between parents and children become negative. Parents report cherishing their surviving children's developmental milestones, both big (e.g., walking, reading) and small (e.g., losing a tooth). Parents also end up spending more time with their surviving children as well as becoming closer to them and more sensitive to their needs. These positive outcomes beg the question: Do parents ever "fully recover" from the loss of a child? According to psychologists Jennifer Buckle and Stephen Fleming, the answer is "No." However, when both parents and children successfully grieve, the family system can regenerate and move forward with the hope of a brighter future.

For many parents, especially those living in non-violent areas of the world, becoming overprotective and strict following the death of a child is more about the parents' mental state than it is about surviving children's actual safety. However, when the dead rise, safety concerns will be justified, and the changes in parental behavior mentioned may save lives. Nevertheless, for a family to regenerate following a tragic loss, parents will need to grieve normally and without significant complications. Given the frequency of loss and traumatic experiences, limited resources, lack of social support, and day-to-day struggles for survival during the Zombie Apocalypse, the likelihood of that happening is extremely low.

12. Post-Apocalyptic Resilience

It is Christmas Eve and in front of the fireplace is a desiccated body with an ax blade protruding from its skull. You decide to spend the night in a different home. Money in hand, you find a tooth under your child's makeshift pillow of old rags. Gently, you replace it with a meaningless tattered dollar bill, a remnant of a financial system no longer in use. On Valentine's Day, you see a bodiless human heart with an arrow through it. You wonder if there is any chocolate left in the world, as it has been years since you have seen any. Nowadays, Halloween happens once a year, but children no longer go trick or treating, for neighbors often greet unexpected knocks at the door with the barrel of a shotgun. At night, you read fairytales with happy endings to your children and assure them that there are *no longer* any monsters under the bed, in the closet, behind the door, or surrounding the house. Welcome to the post-apocalypse!

The Zombie Apocalypse is finally over. Although there are still tens of thousands of undead roaming the planet, the threat of extinction by zombie no longer exists. Humanity has effectively contained the zombie plague, even though a cure has not been found for it. The world has stopped falling apart, and the survivors have started to rebuild. Now, all that parents have to do is cope with the aftereffects of the undead rising and raise their families in a post-apocalyptic wasteland.

Risk Factors, Protective Factors and Resilience

For the majority of the book, I have taken a "deficit" orientation, in which I hypothesized that *during* the Zombie Apocalypse parenting would worsen and, for many, become completely ineffective. I further conjectured that specific parenting deficits would lead to undesirable child and adolescent outcomes. However, parenting is now taking place after the apocalypse, so I take a different approach, focusing on how parents can mitigate the harmful effects of previously experienced childhood adversity. To psychologists, *adversity* refers to events or circumstances that pose a threat to psychological well-being and physical health such as uncertain, dangerous, and harsh environments as well as traumatic and stressful experiences. In contrast, *psychological resilience*—positive adaptation and competence following exposure to significant stress—is the ability to "bounce back" from adversity. And what could be more adverse to parents and their children than a Zombie Apocalypse?

To understand psychological resilience I first need to present the concepts of risk and protective factors. Psychologists define *risk* as an increase in vulnerability to negative consequences. Thus, *risk factors* are features of the person, family, and community along with traumatic and stressful experiences that increase the likelihood of deleterious psychological and physical outcomes. In contrast, *protective factors* are personal, family-based, and community-based characteristics and experiences that either reduce the impact of, or make individuals less vulnerable to, the harmful effects of risk factors. Also, protective factors promote positive outcomes such as increasing self-esteem or self-efficacy. See Box 12.1 for examples of risk and protective factors.

The Hasbro game *Don't Spill the Beans* can help illustrate the significance of risk and protective factors for resilience. The rules of the game are simple. In front of the players sits a covered kettle that is precariously balancing on a pair of hands. The game requires players to alternate turns placing a single bean onto the pot's lid, with the goal being to keep the vessel upright. The player causing the container to spill its contents loses. Now, think of each bean placed onto the lid as a risk factor, any bean coming off of it as a protective factor, and the pot tipping over as a dysfunctional outcome. At some point during the game, a player will place a bean onto the lid which "causes" the kettle to overturn. In actuality, it is the accumulation of beans that exceeded the tipping point, not the placement of any single bean by itself. In fact, if the last bean placed onto the lid magically became the first, the kettle would remain righted (as there would be no other beans on the pot). No single bean causes the pot to spill its contents, and no one risk factor produces adverse psychological outcomes. By itself, even the vilest, goriest, and most violent experience imaginable, such as an encounter with the undead, may not necessarily cause long-term dysfunction. However, that experience, in combination with other risk

---

Box 12.1: *Examples of Risk and Protective Factors at the Level of the Child, Adult, Parent, Family and Community*

Risk Factors

- **Child:** insecure attachment; behavioral and emotional problems; aggression
- **Adult:** emotional instability; mental illness; inflexibility
- **Parent:** insensitive, punitive, and inconsistent caregiving; neglect; traumatic upbringing
- **Family:** coercive family environment; disorganization; a lack of family identity
- **Community:** dangerous and violent neighborhood; few support systems; poverty

Protective Factors

- **Child:** secure attachment; easy temperament; high levels of emotional regulation
- **Adult:** positive self-concept; available social support; adaptability
- **Parent:** authoritative parenting style; warmth; rational discipline
- **Family:** organization; cohesion; ample resources
- **Community:** effective support systems; safe neighborhoods; a sense of shared responsibility

---

factors, most assuredly will. Nevertheless, the accumulation of protective factors can mitigate the presence of any number of risk factors. Thus, psychological resilience occurs when protective factors keep risk factors from causing harm. In *Don't Spill the Beans* parlance, the kettle remains upright.

As detailed in previous chapters, the totality of risk exposure during the Zombie Apocalypse will likely overwhelm available protective factors, leading to a host of problems for parents and their children. Although the post-apocalypse will be far from a zombie-free walk in the park, fewer risk factors and an increasing number of protective factors will allow parents to handle the overall level of accumulated risk more effectively.

Trajectories of Risk and Resiliency

Psychologists contend that both risk-related dysfunction and psychological resilience occur in identifiable patterns over time, which they refer to as trajectories. Below I describe trajectories of risk and resilience likely to occur during the post-apocalypse.

Trajectories of Risk

George Bonanno and colleagues posit two common forms of risk-related dysfunction, continuous and chronic, as well as a third, less frequently observed type, delayed symptom elevation. The *continuous dysfunction* trajectory refers to the presence of pre-traumatic impairment that persists after experiencing a new trauma. For example, an individual suffering from depression before a physical assault would continue to be depressed afterward. In contrast, with *chronic dysfunction*, there is no pre-existing impairment. Instead, dysfunction begins soon after a traumatic experience, lasting for at least several years and showing few signs of improvement. Case in point: close to 43 percent of children entrenched in a Lebanese warzone, and exposed to many of the horrors of war (e.g., separated from parents, targeted by bombs and bullets, victimized, witnesses to death and injury, extreme deprivation), showed symptoms of PTSD years after the conflict ended.[1] Finally, with *delayed symptom elevation*, the initial response to a traumatic event is a relatively low level of dysfunction, however, over time trauma-related impairment increases in severity. Delayed symptom elevation is frequently associated with the grieving process. In such instances, what initially appears to be the normal progression of grief later turns into a disordered variant of mourning.

POST-APOCALYPTIC TRAJECTORIES OF RISK. Those with psychological disorders before the Zombie Apocalypse will continue to endure them throughout the undead rising and well into the post-apocalypse. If anything, the adverse conditions of the Zombie Apocalypse will intensify pre-existing mental health issues, increasing their level of severity. As discussed in the previous chapter, disordered variants of mourning are likely to occur during the Zombie Apocalypse. Given that grieving can take place over decades, delayed symptom elevation will occur post-apocalyptically for those unable to successfully progress through the stages of mourning. For children and adolescents living through the Zombie Apocalypse, chronic dysfunction will be commonplace, and the long-term consequences of the traumas they endured (such as emotional and behavioral problems) will be present well into their post-apocalyptic adulthood.

Exposure to Adversity and Chronic Dysfunction. It is important to note that significant *exposure to adversity*—the frequency, intensity, and proximity to adverse conditions and experiences—affects the likelihood of chronic dysfunction. For both parents and children, as the level of exposure to adversity increases, so does the risk of developing psychological, emotional, and behavioral problems. Conversely, less exposure to adversity improves the chances of experiencing resiliency, but by no means guarantees it. For some, the presence of a person-based risk factor (e.g., genetic vulnerability) means that the slightest perturbation in the environment results in dysfunction. For example, individuals with a genetic vulnerability for mood disorders are more likely to develop depression when raised in chaotic home environments (which will be commonplace when the dead rise) relative to stable ones.

Factors influencing exposure level include nearness to the source of the trauma (e.g., seeing bombs in the distance vs. having one's home shelled), experiencing or witnessing a life-threatening event (e.g., being shot vs. watching others get shot), the threat of danger (e.g., likelihood that one's life will be in jeopardy), and secondary losses (e.g., the destruction of the family home). In each instance, the more impactful the peril, the greater the level of exposure to adversity encountered.

To exemplify this concept, let us consider day-to-day life in two disparate communities on *The Walking Dead*: Woodbury and the Prison.[2] The residents of Woodbury live in a walled community with armed guards stationed around the perimeter and entrances. During the day, townsfolk can walk around the grounds with little concern of walkers attacking them. Any culling of the dead takes place outside of the walls and unseen to those inside them. It appears to be a little slice of heaven while living in a big slice of hell. Those living as members of the community (and not guardians of it) experience the dead from a distance and with little concern for their welfare. Thus, their daily exposure to adversity is relatively low.

In contrast, those living at the nearby prison encounter adverse conditions more directly. The prison yard is fenced, not walled. Far from sturdy, the fence is relatively weak and susceptible to collapsing under the weight of even a small group of the undead. As a result, community members must pith the dead themselves, or, at the very least, observe others doing so anytime they venture onto the prison grounds. Moreover, the prison itself is not a safe haven, as the dead occupy various cellblocks within. Those living within the prison directly encounter the dead, ensuring a relatively high level of exposure to adversity.

Everyone that survives the Zombie Apocalypse will endure a tremendous amount of exposure to adversity, thus placing them at significant risk for chronic dysfunction. During the post-apocalypse, the threat of dying at the hands and teeth of a zombie will wane, as will the probability of witnessing zombie-related carnage and having to dispatch the undead personally. However, the human-threat will remain, as will many of the social (e.g., prejudices, biases) and environmental conditions (e.g., limited resources, food insecurity) that lead to interpersonal and intergroup conflict. Thus, post-apocalyptic exposure to adversity and its associated level of chronic dysfunction will be highly variable and along the lines of the differences experienced in society today. For instance, those living in economically disadvantaged areas of the United States experience a higher level of exposure to adversity (e.g., interpersonal and community violence) than middle-class Americans.[3]

Intergenerational Transmission of Trauma. The Zombie Apocalypse will affect children that never lived through it. Psychologists refer to disturbing events occurring in one generation (e.g., parents or grandparents) influencing individuals in another (e.g., children or grandchildren) as the *intergenerational transmission of trauma.* For instance, the shock of the Zombie Apocalypse will turn emotionally stable children and adolescents into psychologically damaged adults and parents. Subsequently, during the post-apocalypse, parental instability will lead to caregiving practices that adversely affect the well-being of their children born after the apocalypse. Interestingly, the intergenerational transmission of trauma does not always require the presence of harmful parenting practices for disturbances to cross generations. For many children and adolescents, simply hearing stories about their parents' traumatic experiences during the Zombie Apocalypse, and then imagining them, will be enough to create a vicariously experienced trauma, resulting in psychological difficulties during the post-apocalypse.

Trajectories of Resilience

In addition to risk-related dysfunction, Bonanno and colleagues forward four primary patterns of resilience: distress improvement trajectory, minimal-impact resilience, recovery, and emergent resilience. *Distress improvement trajectory* is a unique form of psychological resilience in which a traumatic event leads to the immediate reduction of stress-related symptoms. In other words, trauma leads to improved psychological well-being. However, for a distress improvement trajectory to happen, individuals must be under considerable duress before the traumatic event. This type of resiliency frequently occurs when caring for terminally ill relatives.

In the United States, close to 35 million adults tend to the needs of disabled or sick family members over the age of 50 each year. The majority of caregivers spend an average of 24 hours per week caring for their loved ones and an additional 35 hours per work at paying jobs.[4] Nonetheless, caregivers often find that their expenses exceed their incomes, and, as a result, dip into their life savings for needed money. For long-term caregivers, the emotional and financial strain of caregiving leads to high levels of stress, depression, poor eating habits, and hostility. Thus, upon the death of the loved one under their supervision, some caregivers report improvements in their overall welfare, returning them to their precaregiver levels of well-being.

In response to an *acute stressor*—an isolated stressful event (e.g., car accident, physical assault, house fire) in an otherwise low-stress environment—some individuals experience minimal dysfunction and quick recovery (typically taking a month or so), a phenomenon known as *minimal-impact resilience*. Thus, in the face of single-serving-sized adversity, and despite a small deviation in functioning, the minimal-impact resilient individual can maintain healthy functioning in the long term. Surprisingly, following terrorist attacks, mass shootings, natural disasters, and epidemics, more people display minimal-impact resilience than any other type of trajectory.

However, for some, the dysfunction following an acute stressor is so intense that the time required to return to a state of well-being takes longer. Such is the case for the *recovery trajectory*, during which acute stressors cause moderate to severe dysfunctions that necessitate one to two years of graduated healing. Finally, *emergent psychological resilience* refers to favorable adjustment following exposure to a chronically stressful environment, such as living in extreme poverty or growing up in a longstanding combat zone. Examples of emergent resilience include improvements in psychological well-being and a reduction in emotional and behavioral problems. Of note, emergent psychological resilience primarily occurs after the chronic stressor abates or the individual leaves the aversive environmental conditions. Once exposure to adversity ceases, resiliency slowly develops.

POST-APOCALYPTIC TRAJECTORIES OF RESILIENCE. During the Zombie Apocalypse, the monitoring of the sick and injured will be of the utmost importance, as the newly dead can become undead in an instant. The same will hold for the post-apocalypse, as zombiism will still be a possibility. Thus, upon the death of a loved one (and the destruction of the brain to prevent reanimation), a distress improvement trajectory seems plausible, especially if the death was protracted. However, it is unlikely that this type of trajectory will occur when a loved one dies, reanimates, and wanders away, for there can be no feelings of relief following a death that becomes an undeath that can lead to even more death.

The Zombie Apocalypse occurs over an extended period and therefore does not fit the criterion for an acute stressor, thus ruling out the possibilities of minimal-impact psychological resilience and recovery trajectories. However, given the chronic stress associated with living in an undead wasteland, survivors will be able to experience emergent psychological resilience. Thus, during the post-apocalypse both emotional and behavioral problems should improve. For example, as society rebuilds, aggressive behavior will lessen, depressive feelings will lift, and symptoms of anxiety will occur less frequently and at lower levels of intensity.

Levels of Resilience

In the post-apocalyptic world, psychological resilience will be evident at the level of the individual, parent, family, and community. Although occurring in different contexts, each category of resiliency shares common characteristics. First, each has a pre-apocalyptic level of functioning. Exemplars at the individual level include a sense of well-being and self-esteem, an ability to regulate emotions, and the presence or absence of mental illness. For parents, examples include baseline levels of emotional sensitivity and responsivity and use of rational discipline. For the family, the reference point encompasses positive emotional interactions, togetherness, an open exchange of ideas, expectations regarding conformity, and the presence and nature of family-based roles, routines, and rituals. At the community level, psychologists assess functioning in terms of systems, such as access to social groups, the interconnections between individuals, groups, and organizations, and available resources for social support. Second, at each level, resiliency follows dysfunction resulting from aversive circumstances, in this case, the Zombie Apocalypse. Finally, from the individual to the community, numerous factors predict the likelihood of resilient outcomes following adversity (see below).

Individual Resilience

Individual resiliency has multiple determinants, with protective factors emanating from the individual, family, non-familial relationships, and community. Regarding child determinants, higher levels of intelligence, problem-solving abilities, adaptability to changing circumstances, self-regulation, self-efficacy, and religiosity as well as with lower levels of negative emotionality characterize resilient youth. Moreover, resilient youth are better able than others to find hope or meaning during adversity—that is, they demonstrate optimism and make sense of their experience. Authoritative caregiving and parenting that promotes secure attachment (i.e., warmth, sensitivity, and responsivity) protect children from the hardships they face. Families that communicate well and are high in cohesion and organization produce resilient children. Resilient children tend to have relationships with supportive, prosocial, and competent peers and adults outside of the immediate family as well. Finally, children that live in communities where members look out for one another and make use of available resources are most likely to demonstrate resiliency.

Many of the characteristics that lead to childhood resiliency also result in resiliency in adulthood. For example, both resilient children and adults have features (e.g., positive self-concept, adaptability) that help them steer through and ultimately overcome adversity. As with childhood resilience, quality social relationships are vital components of adult resiliency. Similar to resilient children, resilient adults respond to positive events with more joy than less resilient individuals. Moreover, resilient adults tend to avoid feelings, thoughts, and actions not beneficial to their well-being, such as comparing themselves to others, engaging in self-blame, viewing failure as an end-point, thinking negative thoughts, using drugs and alcohol to cope with problems, rejecting help from others, and isolating themselves.

POST-APOCALYPTIC INDIVIDUAL RESILIENCE. Psychological resilience is not a trait-like characteristic of the individual that once developed remains intact regardless of what happens. Instead, psychological resilience is a dynamic process that can be present at one point in life but absent during another. For example, preschool-age children that have ostensibly "recovered" from the traumas of the Zombie Apocalypse may begin to experience emotional difficulties during adolescence, at which point traumatic memories come flooding back and behavioral problems emerge. Moreover, psychological resilience is not a global state in which the individual experiences positive outcomes in all aspects of life. Instead, individuals can be resilient in one context (e.g., zombie protection), but uncontrolled and irrational in another (e.g., peer relationships). During the post-apocalypse, understanding the fluid and context-dependent nature of resilience will allow parents to better adapt to their children's changing needs. The same will hold for adult relationships as well.

An additional influence on post-apocalyptic resilience will be the nature of early-life traumatic experiences. Previous adversity can produce one of three outcomes: stress sensitization, stress amplification, or stress inoculation. The *sensitization effect* contends that early exposure to adversity creates a vulnerability in the child that reduces resiliency and increases the risk of undesirable outcomes (e.g., anxiety, depression, PTSD) following later trauma. For example, adolescents with a history of emotional abuse will be more likely than teens without an abusive upbringing to suffer from depression when faced with the violent and impoverished conditions of the Zombie Apocalypse. Moreover, post-apocalyptic resiliency will be harder to come by for sensitized youth.

The *stress amplification effect* posits that adverse experiences early in life result in very intense reactions to later stressors. For example, adolescents with a history of being abused during childhood will be more likely to become severely depressed (e.g., suicidal, unable to function) once the dead walk and less likely to improve in the post-apocalypse. In contrast, non-abused teens will still likely develop depression during the Zombie Apocalypse, but at a more moderate intensity (e.g., reduced productivity, feelings of worthlessness) and with a better long-term prognosis during the post-apocalypse.

According to the *inoculation effect*, exposure to stress early in life functions much like a vaccine, protecting youth against later trauma. Thus, during the post-apocalypse, inoculated youth will resiliently handle the challenges they face better than most. As an example, let us consider events that happen to Carl Grimes on *The Walking Dead*. When Carl is in middle childhood, he witnesses his mother die during childbirth and shoots her in the head to prevent zombification.[5] This event constitutes an "early life" stressor. During adolescence, Carl experiences a "later life" trauma when he watches helplessly as the villainous Negan uses a bat covered in barbed wire to pulverize the heads of two of his companions.[6] Carl's reaction to these gruesome deaths is one of steely resolve. It appears as though witnessing the death of his mother during childhood may have protected Carl from becoming emotionally distraught following the murders of his compatriots, thus demonstrating an inoculation effect.

The probability of experiencing an inoculation, a sensitization, or an amplification effect is dependent upon the severity of the conditions encountered early in life. Inoculation effects are most likely to happen when early life stressors are moderate in severity, for instance, non-abusive relationship difficulties with parents or peers. Such events allow youth to create (and later utilize) positive coping strategies (e.g., creative expression, cognitive reframing, support seeking behavior). In contrast, at either low or high levels of adversity, positive coping skills rarely form. At low levels of hardship, events are not stressful enough to warrant the creation of new coping strategies, and when early life events are incredibly severe (e.g., abusive conditions), the stress generated may be too intense for positive coping skills to develop. Instead, negative coping strategies, such as avoidance, acting out, and substance use, are set in place. In either situation, youth will not develop the requisite skill set needed to handle stressful events later in life, placing them at risk for sensitization and amplification effects. Given that the Zombie Apocalypse will cause severe trauma to most youth, it is unlikely that the return of the living dead will serve as a "moderate" early-life stressor. Thus, it is more probable that living through the Zombie Apocalypse will produce sensitization and amplification effects during the post-apocalypse.

Parental Resilience

Parental resilience refers to the ability to parent competently in the face of adversity. When confronted with limited resources, impoverished conditions, behavioral problems, or sick children, resilient parents utilize child-rearing techniques that promote family cohesion (i.e., emotional connectedness) and their children's well-being. Examples include authoritative parenting, use of rational discipline, tolerating frustration, and sensitively and responsively meeting their children's emotional needs. Additionally, resilient parents effectively use available support social and community resources no matter how limited in scope. Resilient parents are keenly aware of their children's limitations and take the appropriate precautions, such as closely monitoring the behavior of impulsive children. Moreover, resilient parents adapt their caregiving to meet new challenges as they arise, whether they are the result of development (e.g., puberty), or changes in relationships, family constellation, and environmental circumstances. A variety of parental factors increase the likelihood of parental resilience, including higher levels of self-esteem, optimism, spirituality, and marital support as well as a history of positive relationships with their own parents.

POST-APOCALYPTIC PARENT RESILIENCE. It is important to note that resilient adults caring for children are not necessarily resilient parents—that is, while the resilient adult may have bounced back from hardship, their parenting style can still place their children at risk for adverse outcomes. Image a situation where a clinically depressed parent has survived the Zombie Apocalypse and become part of a prosperous post-apocalyptic community. As time marches forward, the frequency and intensity of their depressive symptoms wane and eventually disappear altogether. However, the punitive and authoritarian parenting style used during the Zombie Apocalypse has carried over into the post-apocalypse. As this example illustrates, the emergence of adult resilience did not lead to effective parenting.

Characteristics of the parent that lead to successful caregiving during the Zombie Apocalypse (e.g., openness, agreeableness, self-regulation, hardiness) will also promote resilient parenting throughout the post-apocalypse. In addition, four fundamental constructs will contribute to the development of parental resilience: parental self-efficacy, parental well-being, family functioning, and social connectedness. The first construct, *parental self-efficacy*, refers to parental beliefs regarding the ability to raise children effectively. During the post-apocalypse, efficacious parents will believe that they can successfully rear their children, no matter the adversity they face, whether it is food insecurity, roving bandits, or the occasional cluster of zombies. In turn, confident parents will parent confidently.

Next, *parental well-being* refers to parents' perception of their quality of life, including general feelings of happiness, life satisfaction, vitality, a sense of purpose and so on. During the post-apocalypse, parents high in well-being will perceive themselves to have a positive quality of life even when living conditions are lacking in resources. In general, happy and satisfied parents will be better able to handle adversity, leading to lower levels of perceived stress and more thoughtful and warm parenting. Furthermore, parental well-being will lead to parenting with a purpose and the belief that positive caregiving behaviors will benefit their children now and in the future. In contrast, when parenting for survival, and when the future is uncertain, such beliefs are hard to come by and parenting suffers.

Researchers characterize *family functioning* in terms of family cohesion (e.g., positive emotional interactions, togetherness), communication processes (e.g., open exchange of ideas, expectations regarding conformity), and organization (e.g., roles, routines, rituals). During the post-apocalypse, high levels of family functioning will allow parents to raise their children in stable, emotionally warm, and non-coercive environments, thus reducing many of the family-based stressors that often impede successful parenting.

The final factor promoting parenting resilience, *social connectedness* refers to the availability of emotional (e.g., acceptance, positive regard), tangible (e.g., resources), informational (e.g., suggestions, advice), and appraisal (e.g., feedback) forms of social support both within and outside of the immediate family. As with family functioning, during the post-apocalypse, socially connected families will be able to provide for themselves better than families without such connections. With social support in hand, parents can focus on the quality of their parenting, rather than on basic survival needs.

Family Resilience

Family resilience refers to a family's favorable adjustment and adaptation in response to adversity. Unlike the abovementioned forms of resilience, family resilience does not operate at the level of the individual. Instead, it reflects the effectiveness of family functioning (as a unit) in meeting the family's psychological, emotional, physical, educational, social, and safety needs. For example, resilient families communicate effectively, clearly, and directly, and they use their words and body language to nurture, love, and support one another.

According to Joan Patterson, family resilience (or the lack thereof) results from the interplay of family demands, family capabilities, and family meanings. Stressful conditions, events, and situations that either change, or have the potential to change, family functioning comprise *family demands*. Both discrete events, such as the appearance of bandits, and *strains* (i.e., the pressures associated with needing or desiring to change something), such as living in impoverished, post-apocalyptic conditions, place demands on the family. Some family demands come from within the family system, such as the birth of a child, the onset of puberty, or the death of a parent. Others come from outside of it, such as the need to find water, food, and shelter or monitor the environment for potential threats. In contrast, *family capabilities* refer to resources the family currently has in place (e.g., a well-stocked bunker) as well as those that it can reliably obtain via social connectedness (e.g., trading food for ammo). Included in this concept are the behaviors used by the family (e.g., praying, humor, working together) to cope with the stressors it faces.

Whereas family demands put family functioning at risk, family capabilities protect it. Within the family exists another component that influences, and is affected by, both family demands and family capabilities: *family meanings* (i.e., the meaning a family gives to a stressful event). Patterson identifies three specific types of family meanings: situational, identity, and worldview. *Situational meanings* refer to the family's appraisal of the demands placed on it relative to its capabilities. For example, during the post-apocalypse, families living on a farming collective in a gated community will most likely perceive that their family capabilities can handle the family demands imposed on them. In contrast, nomadic families exploring a marauder patrolled desolate area of the world may perceive that family demands overpower family capabilities.

The next type of family meaning, *family identity*, signifies the family's view of itself (e.g., religion, organization, role assignments). For example, whereas some families may perceive themselves to be nonviolent farmers, others may view themselves as warriors. Finally, the *family worldview* reflects the family's appraisal of itself in relationship to the world around it and its collective sense of a shared purpose. During the Zombie Apocalypse, a family of warriors will most likely see themselves fitting in with their violent surroundings. However, during the post-apocalypse, the reduction in violence and an increase in the perceived complacency of survivors may result in warrior families feeling out of place.

In stable environments, families that (1) know what they can and can't do (situational meaning); (2) have a shared understanding of rules, roles, and responsibilities (family identity); and (3) realize how they fit into the world around them (family worldview) should have little difficulty in maintaining a balanced level of functioning. In such circumstances, family capabilities can mitigate the potentially harmful effects of family demands. However, when family demands pile up, the cumulative impact of stressors and strains exceed family capabilities, resulting in a crisis. When in a *crisis*, family functioning becomes disorganized, distressed, and disrupted. Nevertheless, resilient families can weather the crisis and return to positive family functioning by restoring the balance between family demands and family capabilities. To accomplish this, families will reduce demands (e.g., avoid stressful situations), increase capabilities (e.g., learn new coping techniques) or change their worldviews (e.g., finding a new purpose in life).

Post-Apocalyptic Family Resilience. When in the middle of a crisis, say, a Zombie Apocalypse, family resiliency will be a difficult task to accomplish. After all, surviving among the dead in a chaotic and catastrophic environment will increase family demands while simultaneously stretching family capabilities. Not only that, but an undead rising will shatter the worldviews of most families. It is only during the post-apocalypse when family capabilities improve and family demands decrease (though many will still exist) that family resilience will be likely. After a period of adjustment to the new world order, resilient families will ascribe purpose and meaning to events that previously seemed purposeless and meaningless.

Not all families will be able to demonstrate resilience during the post-apocalypse. However, those that can have several features in common. First, resilient families will effectively balance their members' needs for separateness (e.g., establishing a unique identity, acting independently) with their desires to feel part of an emotionally connected family (i.e., cohesiveness). For example, resilient post-apocalyptic families will forage for food together and work as a team when defending themselves against undead intruders. In support of separateness, however, they will also allow individual family members to scavenge on their own (with appropriate safety precautions in place) and use their weapon of choice for culling the dead. Second, families that successfully adapt to the post-apocalypse will show a high degree of flexibility. They will accommodate their routines, rituals, and expectations to match their current living circumstances. For example, "family game night" might turn into "family check the fence line for the undead night." During the post-apocalypse the resilient family will be hopeful for the future, believe that adversity is manageable, and understand that it can solve its problems together as a family. However, it will also recognize that to overcome adversity it will be necessary to obtain resources from the broader community in which it lives.

Community Resilience

Community resilience refers to a community's ability to achieve community-based goals, such as restoring order and stability, as well as to support the various needs of its members following adversity. According to Jay Mancini and Gary Bowen, the key to community resilience is *social organization*, defined as the collective values, rules, social norms, and behaviors that affect the way community members interact. Socially organized communities contain informal (e.g., friends, neighbors, coworkers) and formal (e.g., social service organizations, hospitals, schools) networks of individuals in which effective communication occurs within and between networks types. Although both formal and informal networks support social connectedness, in healthy communities, formal networks enhance the functioning of informal networks—that is, they provide a diverse array of programs and resources that facilitate social support (in all of its varied forms) among community members. Collectively, the available resources resulting from relationships within formal and informal networks comprise a community's social capital. In resilient communities, social capital fosters collective action and the achievement of community-wide goals. Typically, social capital develops when there is trust within community networks and reciprocity between members.

In addition to social capital, collective competence and shared responsibility also influence community resilience. *Collective competence* refers to the community's ability to meet the needs of its members and address threats to their safety and well-being. Communities high in collective competence use available social capital effectively and actively seek opportunities for communal improvement whereas communities low in this characteristic do neither of these activities. In contrast, *shared responsibility* is the degree to which community members are accountable for the community's general welfare. Communities high in shared responsibility demonstrate that it takes a village to keep a village thriving. Together, a community's collective competence and shared responsibility comprise its *community capacity*.

To understand the impact of community capacity on community resilience, Mancini and Brown cross collective competence with shared responsibility, revealing four types of community capacities: synergetic, disengaged, relational, and able. The *synergetic community* is high on both collective competence and shared responsibility. The community takes care of its members, and its members take care of the community. On the flipside of functioning, the *disengaged community* is low on both of these characteristics. Neither the community nor its members work well together or take care of each other. The remaining two communities are high on one community characteristic but low on the other. The *relational community* is high on shared responsibility but low on collective competence. Despite showing great vision for the well-being of its members, such communities are unable to turn their ideas into realities, resulting in the underutilization of available social capital. In such instances, there is often a lack of high-quality leadership. Finally, the *able community* is low on shared responsibility but high in collective competence. Although such communities can successfully come together in a crisis, in less challenging times, they have difficulty handling the day-to-day issues members face. For example, the able community might come together following a devastating encounter with a zombie horde, but once the town has structurally recovered, the community reverts to its pre-crisis lack of communal togetherness.

Based on community capacity, Mancini and Bowen contend that community resilience is most likely to occur in synergetic communities and least likely to happen in disengaged ones. In synergetic communities, all of the necessary pieces (e.g., leadership and togetherness) are in place to tap social capital and foster recovery during difficult circumstances. In contrast, in disengaged communities, the lack of shared responsibility and community competence means that the will of the people and the will of the community are equally lacking. Thus, disengaged communities cannot overcome adversity. In relational communities, community resilience is possible, though it requires the emergences of strong leaders capable of mobilizing its members. Finally, for resilience to manifest in able communities, leaders capable of building a sense of togetherness and shared responsibility must emerge.

POST-APOCALYPTIC COMMUNITY RESILIENCE. *The Walking Dead* comic provides a clear example of community resilience. Let me set the stage. It has been two years since the combined forces of three nearby communities, Alexandria, the Hilltop, and the Kingdom, defeated their joint enemy, the Saviors. With the war behind them, strong leadership in place, and the dead seemingly manageable, the rebuilding of civilization has begun. Across the collective group of synergetic communities, crops flourish, animal husbandry and coastal fishing take place, trade occurs, housing is plentiful, and members work in a variety of vocations. There is even time for a cross-communal festival.[7] As you can see, these communities exhibit formal and informal networking, copious social capital, and a high degree of community capacity.

Across the globe, hurricanes, tornadoes, fires, floods, and acts of war devastate communities, turning homes, schools, and government offices into nothing but rubble. In such instances, community resilience (e.g., reconnecting networks, improving social capital, and facilitating community capacity) rarely occurs without the help of governmental or international aid. After all, without food, water, medicine and supplies, no community (not even a previously synergetic one) can be functionally resilient. During the Zombie Apocalypse, external aid will be virtually nonexistent, formal and informal networks will unravel, social capital will disappear, and organized communities will become disorganized. It is also entirely possible that everyone in a community will die, leaving no one to rebuild it. The likelihood of community death during the Zombie Apocalypse is so high that during the post-apocalypse, rather than rebuilding resilient communities (for few will exist), the focus will be on creating new ones. Regardless, the characteristics of that foster community resilience (i.e., networking, community capacity, social capital) will also lead to the successful creation of new ones.

Interacting Levels of Resilience

As the previous review revealed, resilience occurs at the level of the individual, parent, family, and community. Although presented as independent determinants, each type of resilience has the potential to influence the others. For example, individually resilient parents, embedded in resilient families and living in resilient communities, are more likely to demonstrate resilient parenting when under duress, relative to other parents. In general, the more levels of resilience present, the greater the likelihood that parents and their children will become resilient as well. Also, each level of resilience influences, and is influenced by, the other levels. For example, resilient parenting helps create resilient families, and resilient families help maintain resilient parenting.

Psychologists refer to such cross-level connections as *developmental cascades*. In essence, developmental cascades are like bifurcating lines of dominoes on a multi-level playing field. Think of the bifurcating lines as different domains of development (such as emotional and social processes) where vulnerabilities or competencies in one domain influence connected domains. For example, during the post-apocalypse children better able to regulate their emotions (domain #1) will be more likely to make and keep friends (domain #2). In contrast, the multi-level playing field refers to the different contexts in which risk and resiliency occur, such as at the level of individual, parent, family, and community. When a developmental cascade occurs, the toppling of one domino can set off a chain reaction of events along the bifurcating lines of development (located at a particular level) that also travel up and down levels of resilience.

POST-APOCALYPTIC INTERACTING LEVELS OF RESILIENCE.
As demonstrated throughout the book, a multitude of risk factors will predominate during the Zombie Apocalypse, and, as a result, perturbations in various domains of development and levels of functioning will be the norm. As the tide turns and the post-apocalypse takes hold, protective factors will start asserting their influence. Developmental cascades will aid in this process as well, for positive developments in just one domain of development, or at only one level of functioning, can propagate between connected domains and levels, increasing positive out-

comes throughout the system. In other words, competence can beget competence.

In fairytales, resilient folks live "happily ever after." In the real world, however, resilient functioning does not necessarily signify a satisfying conclusion to a dramatic story. Rather, resiliency only places children, parents, families, and communities on the pathway to success. It by no means guarantees the destination, for, as noted philosopher George Santayana famously wrote, "those who do not remember the past are condemned to repeat it." Bear in mind, the times we currently live in will be in the past for the survivors of the Zombie Apocalypse, and in today's world, children, parents, and families often find themselves living in dangerous circumstances.

In the United States, stray bullets take the lives of children as they play. Strangers attempt to kidnap young children from convenience stores. Coaches, doctors, and clergy physically, sexually, and emotionally abuse those in their charge. Parents watch their family members die in floods, hurricanes, fires, and earthquakes or overdose on drugs. School shootings occur on a regular basis, more than 200 since 2012.[8] Millions live in poverty and experience food insecurity.

Across the world, dangers persist as well. Militants shoot teenage girls for trying to get an education or kidnap them to become their "wives." They conscript children into war, forcing them to become soldiers, suicide bombers, and human shields. To escape war, persecution, or extreme poverty, families travel thousands of miles to seek asylum in foreign lands, but upon reaching the border are unceremoniously sent back to combat zones, impoverished conditions, and oppressors.

Notwithstanding Santayana's sentiments, remembering the past does not always prevent adversity or atrocity, and sometimes, memories turn into remembrances that encourage them. According to the Southern Poverty Law Center,[9] there are more than 950 *hate groups* (i.e., groups with beliefs and practices that denigrate an entire class of people) operating within the United States. Many of these groups, such as white supremacists and neo–Nazis, have historical ties to hate groups of old.

Post-apocalyptic survivors that forget the past may inadvertently repeat the injustices performed by those that came before them, and those that remember the past may enact them purposefully. Regardless of whether the post-apocalypse ushers in a utopia, dystopia, or something in between, there will be challenging times ahead for parents, with the potential for either adversity or resiliency in their future.

Final Thoughts

Imagine parenting in a post-apocalyptic environment littered with the corpses of the dead and the remnants of a society long gone. All of the pain, be it physical or psychological, and all of the slaughter, be it of the living or the dead, will exact a heavy toll on parents and those they love. The future of children, however, will now seem bright, or, at the very least, better lit than during the Zombie Apocalypse. People will wonder how parents were able to survive the undead while simultaneously raising children when others were not so lucky on either account. Living alongside the living dead, however, affected parents, changed their parenting, and transformed their children. Life as it once was will never again be. In order to claim a final victory over the dead parents will need to look to the future with hope. Piece by piece, parents, families, and communities will then be able to puzzle the world back together.

Chapter Notes

Preface

1. *Night of the Living Dead*, Directed by George A. Romero, Image 10, 1968.
2. *Dawn of the Dead*, Directed by George A. Romero, Laurel Group, Inc., 1978.
3. *Day of the Dead*, Directed by Directed by George A. Romero, Dead Films, Inc., 1985.

Introduction

1. "Days Gone Bye," *The Walking Dead*, Directed by Frank Darabont, American Movie Classics, October 31, 2010.
2. Stephanie Pappas, "Zombies Would Wipe Out Humans in Less Than 100 Days," *LiveScience*, last modified January 6, 2017, http://www.livescience.com/57407-zombie-apocalypse-would-take-100-days.html.
3. João Paulo Almeida de Mençonça, Lohan Rodrigues Narcizo Ferreira, Leonardo da Motta de Vasconcellos Teixeira, and Fernando Sato, "Modeling Our Survival in a Zombie Apocalypse," *arXiv.org*, last modified February 19, 2018, https://arxiv.org/abs/1802.10443.

Chapter 1

1. Joe Otterson, "Walking Dead Season 8 Finale Ratings Lowest Since Season 1," *Variety*, last modified April 17, 2018, https://variety.com/2018/tv/news/walking-dead-season-8-finale-ratings-1202754602/.

2. Todd Allen, "Sales Charts: Stranger Things Laps Walking Dead on the Down Low—Image and the Independent Publishers Sales Distribution Charts for September 2018," *The Beat*, last modified October 18, 2018, http://www.comicsbeat.com/sales-charts-stranger-things-laps-walking-dead-on-the-down-low-image-and-the-independent-publishers-sales-distribution-charts-for-september-2018/.
3. "Brooks's 'World War Z' Hits Sales Milestone," *Publishers Weekly*, last modified November 10, 2011, http://www.publishersweekly.com/pw/by-topic/industry-news/publisher-news/article/49456-brooks-s-world-war-z-hits-sales-milestone.html.
4. Mark Hughes, "Top 10 Best Cult Classic Horror Movies of All Time," *Forbes*, last modified October 17, 2012, http://www.forbes.com/sites/markhughes/2012/10/17/top-10-best-cult-classic-horror-movies-of-all-time/#6725bec76872.
5. "World War Z," *Box Office Mojo*, accessed July 12, 2018, http://www.boxofficemojo.com/movies/?id=worldwarz.htm.
6. "Game Series Sales," *Capcom Investor Relations*, last modified June 30, 2018, http://www.capcom.co.jp/ir/english/finance/salesdata.html.
7. "We're Alive Reaches 50 Million Downloads," *We're Alive*, last modified October 5, 2016, http://www.werealive.com/news/were-alive-reaches-50-million-downloads/.
8. Ali S. Khan, "Preparedness 101: Zom-

bie Apocalypse," *Centers for Disease Control and Prevention*, last modified May 16, 2011, https://blogs.cdc.gov/publichealthmatters/2011/05/preparedness-101-zombie-apocalypse/.

9. "Humans vs. Zombies," *Human vs. Zombies*, accessed October 31, 2018, https://humansvszombies.org/.

10. Julio Ojeda-Zapata, "Minneapolis Zombie Pub Crawl sets a Guinness World Record," *Twin Cities*, last modified October 28, 2015, http://www.twincities.com/2014/10/12/minneapolis-zombie-pubcrawl-sets-a-guinness-world-record/.

11. "Zombies Worth Over $5 Billion to Economy," *247wallst*, last modified October 25, 2011, http://247wallst.com/investing/2011/10/25/zombies-worth-over-5-billion-to-economy/2/.

12. "Top 10 Causes of Death," *World Health Organization*, last modified May 24, 2018, http://www.who.int/mediacentre/factsheets/fs310/en/.

13. "Vector-Borne Diseases," *World Health Organization*, last modified October 31, 2017, http://www.who.int/mediacentre/factsheets/fs387/en/.

14. Stephen King, *The Shining* (Garden City, NY: Doubleday, 1997).

15. Gerard Jones, *Killing Monsters: Why Children Need Fantasy, Super Heroes, and Make-Believe Violence* (New York: Basic Books, 2002), 101–102.

16. *Natural Born Killers*, Directed by Oliver Stone, Regency Enterprises, 1994.

17. "r/Zombies," *Reddit*, accessed October 26, 2018, https://www.reddit.com/r/zombies.

18. Saba Hamedy, "'The Walking Dead' Premiere Broke a 2016 Twitter Record," *Mashable*, last modified October 24, 2016, http://mashable.com/2016/10/24/the-walking-dead-season-7-premiere-twitter-record/#dF1equ4IviqC.

19. "amcthewalkingdead," *Instagram*, accessed October 24, 2018, https://www.instagram.com/amcthewalkingdead/?hl=en.

20. "H1Z1," *Steam Charts*, last modified October 24, 2018, http://steamcharts.com/app/433850.

21. Deirdre D. Johnston, "Adolescents' Motivations for Viewing Graphic Horror," *Human Communication Research* 21 (1995): 522–552.

22. Mark Butler, "Why People Play Horror Games," *iNews*, last modified October 24, 2018, https://inews.co.uk/essentials/culture/gaming/people-play-horror-games/.

23. *Dead Snow*, Directed by Tommy Wirkola, Miho Film, 2009.

24. *Zombi 2*, Directed by Lucio Fulci, Variety Film, 1979.

25. *The Walking Dead, Seasons 1–9*, developed by Frank Darabont, based on the comic books by Robert Kirkman, Tony Moore, and Charlie Adlard, American Movie Classics, 2010–present, television series.

26. *Shaun of the Dead*, Directed by Edgar Wright, Universal Pictures, 2004.

27. *Night of the Living Dead*, Directed by George A. Romero, Image 10, 1968.

28. *Zombieland*, Directed by Ruben Fleischer, Columbia Pictures, 2009.

29. *28 Weeks Later*, Directed by Juan Carlos Fresnadillo, Figment, 2007.

30. *Dead Alive*, Directed by Peter Jackson, Trimark Pictures, 1992.

31. *Diary of the Dead*, Directed by George A. Romero, Artfire Films, 2007.

32. "Rock in the Road," *The Walking Dead, Season 7*, Directed by Greg Nicotero, American Movie Classics, February 12, 2017.

33. *Body Counters*, accessed June 18, 2018, http://www.bodycounters.com/bodycounts.php.

34. *Scream 2*, Directed by Wes Craven, Konrad Pictures, 1997.

35. Mira Grant, *Feed* (New York: Orbit, 2010).

36. Fran Michel, "Life and Death and Something in Between: Reviewing Recent Horror Cinema," *Psychoanalysis, Culture and Society* 12 (2007): 393.

37. Greg Garrett, *Living with the Living Dead: The Wisdom of the Zombie Apocalypse* (New York: Oxford University Press, 2017), 50.

38. Mathias Clasen, "The Anatomy of the Zombie: A Bio-Psychological Look at the Undead Other," *Otherness: Essays and Studies* 1 (2010): 19.

Chapter 2

1. Mira Grant, *Feed* (New York: Orbit, 2010).

2. Diana Rowland, *My Life as a White Trash Zombie* (New York: Daw Books, 2011).

3. *Left for Dead* (video game), Valve, 2008.

4. Jonathan Maberry, *Patient Zero: A Joe Ledger Novel* (New York: St. Martin's Griffin, 2009).

5. *Resident Evil*, Directed by Paul W. S. Anderson, Constantin Film, 2002.

6. *The Return of the Living Dead*, Directed by Dan O'Bannon, Hemdale Film Corporation, 1985.

7. *The Walking Dead, Seasons 1–9*, developed by Frank Darabont, based on the comic books by Robert Kirkman, Tony Moore, and Charlie Adlard, American Movie Classics, 2010–2019, television series.

8. Max Brooks, *The Zombie Survival Guide: Complete Protection from the Living Dead* (New York: Broadway Books, 2003).

9. *The Walking Dead, Seasons 1–9*.

10. *World War Z*, Directed by Marc Forster, Skydance Productions, 2013.

11. *iZombie, Seasons 1–4*, developed by Rob Thomas and Diane Ruggiero-Wright, based on the comic books by Chris Roberson and Michael Allred, 2015–2018, television series.

12. *Land of the Dead*, Directed by George A. Romero, Atmosphere Entertainment MM, 2005.

13. *Shaun of the Dead*, Directed by Edgar Wright, Universal Pictures, 2004.

14. Mira Grant, *Feedback: A Newsflesh Novel* (New York: Orbit, 2016).

15. "Too Far Gone," *The Walking Dead*, Directed by Ernest Dickerson, American Movie Classics, December 1 2013.

16. Rowland.

17. *iZombie*.

18. *28 Days Later*, Directed by Danny Boyle, DNA Films, 2002.

19. *28 Weeks Later*, Directed by Juan Carlos Fresnadillo, Figment, 2007.

20. Stephen King, *Cell: A Novel* (New York: Scribner, 2006).

21. Helen Thompson, "Mindscapes: First Interview with a Dead Man," *New Scientist*, last modified May 23, 2013, https://www.newscientist.com/article/dn23583-mindscapes-first-interview-with-a-dead-man/.

22. Timothy Verstynen and Bradley Voytek, *Do Zombies Dream of Undead Sheep? Neuroscientific View of the Zombie Brain* (Princeton: Princeton University Press, 2014), 203.

23. *Left for Dead.*

24. *Shaun of the Dead.*

25. *Zombieland*, Directed by Ruben Fleischer, Sony Pictures Home Entertainment, 2009.

26. "Whispers into Screams," *The Walking Dead, Vol. 23*, Image-Skybound, April 29, 2015.

27. Katherine A. Fowler, Linda L. Dahlberg, Tadesse Haileyesus, Carmen Gutierrez, and Sarah Bacon, "Childhood Firearm Injuries in the United States," *Pediatrics* 140, no. 1 (2017): e20163486.

28. Gabriel B. Eber, Joseph L. Annest, James A. Mercy, George W. Ryan, "Nonfatal and Fatal Firearm Related Injuries Among Children Aged 14 Years and Younger: United States, 1993–2000," *Pediatrics* 113, no. 6 (2004): 1686–1692.

29. "Does Your Child Know What to Do If He or She Finds a Gun?" *NRA*, Accessed October 25, 2018, https://eddieeagle.nra.org/.

30. "Days Gone Bye," *The Walking Dead, Vol. 1*, Image-Skybound, May 4, 2004.

31. Brandy Zadrozny, "Where Kids as Young as 5 Learn to Shoot Automatic Weapons," *The Daily Beast*, last modified September 10, 2014, http://www.thedailybeast.com/where-kids-as-young-as-5-learn-to-shoot-automatic-weapons.

32. "When Should You Start Teaching Kids to Shoot?" *AEGIS Academy*, accessed August 20, 2017, http://aegisacademy.com/teaching-kids-to-shoot/.

33. "NRA Gun Safety Rules," *NRA*, accessed June 19, 2018, https://gunsafetyrules.nra.org/.

34. Matt Simon, "Absurd Creature of the Week: The Parasitic Worm That Turns Snails into Disco Zombies," last modified September 19, 2014, https://www.wired.com/2014/09/absurd-creature-of-the-week-disco-worm/.

35. "Human Rabies: 2016 Updates and Call for Data," *World Health Organization*, last modified February 17, 2017, http://www.who.int/rabies/resources/who_wer9207/en/.

36. Crimesider Staff, "Surprising Drug Test Results in Fla. Face-Biting Attack Case," *CBS News*, last modified November 23, 2016, http://www.cbsnews.com/news/florida-face-biting-attack-austin-harrouff-drug-test-results/.

37. "Medical Examiner Rules Out Bath Salts in Miami Face-Chewing Attack," *Fox News*, last modified November 20, 2015, http://www.foxnews.com/us/2012/06/27/medical-examiner-finds-only-marijuana-in-miami-face-chewer-system.html#ixzz1z2Ne6RED.

38. "Fact Sheet: Synthetic Cathinones," *Drug Policy*, last modified June 2016, http://www.drugpolicy.org/sites/default/files/DPA_Fact_Sheet_Synthetic_Cathinones_%28June%202016%29.pdf.

39. Greg Miller, "9 Things to Know About Reviving the Recently Dead," *Wired*, last modified July 30, 2014, https://www.wired.com/2014/07/revive-the-dead/.

40. *The Princess Bride*, Directed by Rob Reiner, 20th Century Fox, 1987.

41. Robert M. Sade, "Brain Death, Cardiac Death, and the Dead Donor Rule," *Journal of The South Carolina Medical Association* 107, no. 4 (2011): 146–149.

42. *Jurassic Park*, Directed by Steven Spielberg, Universal Pictures Studio, 1993.

Chapter 3

1. "Days Gone Bye," *The Walking Dead, Vol. 1*, Image-Skybound, May 4, 2004.

2. "Safety Behind Bars," *The Walking Dead, Vol. 3*, Image-Skybound, April 18, 2007.

3. "Fear the Hunters," *The Walking Dead, Vol. 11*, Image-Skybound, January 6, 2010.

4. "What Comes After," *The Walking Dead Vol. 18*, Image-Skybound, June 5, 2013.

5. Jonathan Maberry, *Rot and Ruin* (New York: Simon & Schuster, 2010).

6. "United States Age of Consent Map," *AgeOfConsent.net*, accessed October 20, 2018, https://www.ageofconsent.net/states.

7. "Marriage Age Laws," *National Conference of State Legislatures*, last modified May 2017, https://comm.ncsl.org/productfiles/94723912/NCSL-Marriage-Age-Requirements.pdf.

8. Jacqueline D. Woolley, "Thinking About Fantasy: Are Children Fundamentally Different Thinkers and Believers from Adults?" *Child Development* 68 (1997): 1007.

9. *Here Alone*, Directed by Rod Blackhurst, Gentile Entertainment Group, 2017.

10. Secil E. Ertorer, "Managing Identity in the Face of Resettlement," *Identity: An International Journal of Theory and Research* 14, no. 4 (2014): 268–285.

11. "A New Beginning," *The Walking Dead, Vol. 22*, Image-Skybound, November 5, 2014.

12. "Stolen Childhoods: End of Childhood Report 2017," *Save the Children*, accessed September 1, 2018, https://www.savethechildren.org/content/dam/usa/reports/emergency-response/end-of-childhood-report.PDF.

13. "A," *The Walking Dead*, Directed by Michelle MacLaren, American Movie Classics, March 30, 2014.

14. "Stolen Childhoods: End of Childhood Report 2017."

Chapter 4

1. "Killer Within," *The Walking Dead*, Directed by Guy Ferland, American Movie Classics, November 4, 2012.

2. "Maternal Mortality Ratio (Modeled Estimate, Per 100,000 Live Births)," *The World Bank*" accessed April 16, 2018, http://data.worldbank.org/indicator/SH.STA.MMRT?year_high_desc=true.

3. *Ibid.* http://data.worldbank.org/indicator/SH.STA.MMRT?year_high_desc=true.

4. Robert E. Black, Linday H. Allen, Zulfiqar A. Bhutta, ... Maternal and Child Nutrition Study Group, "Maternal and Child Undernutrition: Global and Regional Exposures and Health Consequences," *Lancet* 371, no. 9608 (2008): 243–260.

5. "Preventing Unsafe Abortion," *World Health Organization*, last modified February 19, 2018, http://www.who.int/mediacentre/factsheets/fs388/en/.

6. "Intimate Partner Violence During Pregnancy: Information Sheet," last modified 2011, http://apps.who.int/iris/bitstream/10665/70764/1/WHO_RHR_11.35_eng.pdf.

7. "Intimate Partner Violence: Risk and Protective Factors," *Centers for Disease Control and Prevention*, last modified August 22, 2017, https://www.cdc.gov/violenceprevention/intimatepartnerviolence/riskprotectivefactors.html.

8. J. Gupta, K. Falb, D. Kpebo, and J. Annan, "Abuse from In-Laws and Associations with Attempts to Control Reproductive Decisions Among Rural Women in Cote d'Ivoire: A Cross-Sectional Study," *BJOG: An International Journal of Obstetrics and Gynaecology* 119, no. 9 (2012): 1058–1066.

9. "30 Days Without an Accident," *The Walking Dead*, Directed by Greg Nicotero, American Movie Classics, October 13, 2013.

10. "Infected," *The Walking Dead*, Directed by Guy Ferland, American Movie Classics, October 20, 2013.

11. "Secrets," *The Walking Dead*, Directed by David Boyd, American Movie Classics, November 20, 2011.

12. "How It Works," *plan B*, accessed September 27, 2018, http://planb.ca/how-it-works.html.

13. "Infant Health," *Centers for Disease Control and Prevention*, last modified March 31, 2017, https://www.cdc.gov/nchs/fastats/infant-health.htm.

14. "Child Mortality Estimates," *Child-Mortality.Org*, accessed August 1, 2017, http://www.childmortality.org/.

15. "Under-Five Mortality," *World Health Organization*, accessed July, 29, 2017, http://www.who.int/gho/child_health/mortality/mortality_under_five_text/en/.

16. "Malnutrition," *UNICEF*, last modified May 2018, https://data.unicef.org/topic/nutrition/malnutrition/.

17. "2018 End of Childhood Report, *Save the Children*, accessed October 27, 2018, https://www.savethechildren.org/content/dam/global/reports/2018-end-of-childhood-report.pdf.

18. Kenneth D. Kochanek, Sherry L. Murphy, Jiaquan Xu, and Betzaida Tejada-Vera, "Deaths: Final Data for 2014," *National Vital Statistics Report* 65, no. 4, last updated April 3, 2017, https://www.cdc.gov/nchs/data/nvsr/nvsr65/nvsr65_04.pdf.

19. "Global Status Report on Violence Prevention 2014," *World Health Organization*, accessed January 13, 2018, http://www.who.int/violence_injury_prevention/violence/status_report/2014/en/.

20. "Infant Mortality: Situation and Trends," *World Health Organization*, accessed September 29, 2018, http://www.who.int/gho/child_health/mortality/neonatal_infant_text/en/.

21. "Child Abuse and Neglect Fatalities 2016: Statistics and Interventions," *ChildWelfare.gov*, last modified July 2018, https://www.childwelfare.gov/pubPDFs/fatality.pdf.

22. "Common Environmental Noise Levels," *Center for Hearing and Communication*, accessed May 24, 2018, http://chchearing.org/noise/common-environmental-noise-levels/.

23. "What Would Happen If We Stopped Vaccinations," *Centers for Disease Control and Prevention*, last modified March 10, 2017, https://www.cdc.gov/vaccines/vacgen/whatifstop.htm.

24. "Polio Elimination in the United States," *Centers for Disease Control and Prevention*, last modified November 28, 2017, https://www.cdc.gov/polio/us/index.html.

25. "Measles Vaccination," *Centers for Disease Control and Prevention*, last modified November 22, 2016, https://www.cdc.gov/measles/vaccination.html.

26. "Pertussis Frequently Asked Questions," *Centers for Disease Control and Prevention*, last modified August 7, 2017, https://www.cdc.gov/pertussis/about/faqs.html.

27. *Star Trek II: The Wrath of Khan*, Directed by Nicholas Meyer, Paramount Pictures, 1982.

28. "What Is the Period of PURPLE Crying Program?" *National Center on Shaken Baby Syndrome*, accessed December 27, 2017, https://www.dontshake.org/purple-crying.

29. "Made to Suffer," *The Walking Dead, Vol. 8*, Image-Skybound, June 25, 2008.

30. Carol Kopp, "The Bridge to Gretna," *CBS News*, last modified December 15, 2005, https://www.cbsnews.com/news/the-bridge-to-gretna/.

Chapter 5

1. "Annual U.S. Sales Data," *The Toy Association*, accessed October 25, 2018, https://www.toyassociation.org/ta/research/data/u-s-sales-data/toys/research-and-data/data/us-sales-data.aspx.

2. Karla A. Mueller and Janice D. Yoder, "Gendered Norms for Family Size, Employment, and Occupation: Are There Personal Costs for Violating Them?" *Sex Roles* 36 (1997): 207–220.

3. Sui-Lee Wee, "After One-Child Policy, Outrage at China's Offer to Remove IUDs," *The New York Times*, last modified January 7, 2017, https://www.nytimes.com/2017/01/07/world/asia/after-one-child-policy-outrage-at-chinas-offer-to-remove-iuds.html.

4. "China's Two-Child Policy," *Bloomberg News*, last modified June 6, 2018, https://www.bloomberg.com/quicktake/china-s-two-child-policy.

5. David F. Bjorklund, Jennifer L. Yunger, and Anthondy D. Pellegrini, "The Evolution of Parenting and Evolutionary Approaches to Childrearing," in M. H. Bornstein, ed., *Handbook of Parenting: Biology and Ecology Of Parenting* (Mahwah, NJ: Lawrence Erlbaum Associates, 2002), 7.

6. *Cinderella*, Directed by Clyde Geronimi, Hamilton Luske, and Wilfred Jackson. Walt Disney Productions, 1950.

7. Jo Jones and Paul Placek, "Adoption by the Numbers," *National Council for Adoption*, last modified, February 15, 2017, https://www.adoptioncouncil.org/publications/2017/02/adoption-by-the-numbers.

8. "The Best Defense," *The Walking Dead, Vol. 5*, Image-Skybound, September 27, 2006.

9. "Infected," *The Walking Dead*, Directed by Guy Ferland, American Movie Classics, October 20, 2013.

10. *The Walking Dead: The Game*, Telltale Games, October 24, 2012.

11. *Resident Evil*, Directed by Paul W. S. Anderson, Constantin Film, 2002.

12. *Shaun of the Dead*, Directed by Edgar Wright, Universal Pictures, 2004.

13. *Land of the Dead*, Directed by George A. Romero, Atmosphere Entertainment MM, 2005.

14. Max Brooks, *World War Z: An Oral History of the Zombie War* (New York: Crown, 2006).

15. "Whispers into Screams," *The Walking Dead, Vol. 23*, Image-Skybound, April 29, 2015.

16. David J. Buller, "Four Fallacies of Pop Evolutionary Psychology," *Scientific American*, last modified November 1, 2012, https://www.scientificamerican.com/article/four-fallacies-of-pop-evolutionary-2012-12-07/.

17. Natalia Bonilla, "Guatemala's Civil War Has Created a Legacy of Rape and Teen Pregnancy," *Women's Media Center*, last modified July 5, 2017, http://www.womensmediacenter.com/women-under-siege/guatemalas-civil-war-has-created-a-legacy-of-rape-and-teen-pregnancy.

18. Adam Nossiter, "Boko Haram Militants Raped Hundreds of Female Captives in Nigeria," *The New York Times*, last modified May 18, 2015, https://www.nytimes.com/2015/05/19/world/africa/boko-haram-militants-raped-hundreds-of-female-captives-in-nigeria.html.

19. Lindsey Hilsum, "Rwanda 20 Years On: The Tragic Testimony of the Children of Rape," *The Guardian*, last modified June 7, 2014, https://www.theguardian.com/world/2014/jun/08/rwanda-20-years-genocide-rape-children.

20. Sue Turton, "Bosnian War Rape Survivors Speak of Their Suffering 25 Years on," *Independent*, last modified July 21, 2017, http://www.independent.co.uk/news/long_reads/bosnia-war-rape-survivors-speak-serbian-soldiers-balkans-women-justice-suffering-a7846546.html.

21. "Sexual Violence: Consequences," *Centers for Disease Control and Prevention*, last modified April 10, 2018, https://www.cdc.gov/violenceprevention/sexualviolence/consequences.html.

22. "Perpetrators of Sexual Violence: Statistics," *RAINN*, accessed February 12, 2018, https://www.rainn.org/statistics/perpetrators-sexual-violence.

23. Larisa Epatko, "Surviving Boko Haram: Kidnapped Girls Tell Their Stories," *PBS News Hours*, last modified October 19, 2016, http://www.pbs.org/news

hour/updates/surviving-boko-haram-kidnapped-girls-tell-stories/.

24. Andrew Solomon, *Far from the Tree: Parents, Children and the Search for Identity* (New York: Scribner/Simon & Schuster, 2002), 503.

Chapter 6

1. "Infected," *The Walking Dead*, Directed by Guy Ferland, American Movie Classics, October 20, 2013.
2. "Whispers into Screams," *The Walking Dead, Vol. 23*, Image-Skybound, April 29, 2015.
3. "Days Gone Bye," *The Walking Dead*, Directed by Frank Darabont, American Movie Classics, October 31, 2010.
4. "Clear," *The Walking Dead*, Directed by Tricia Brock, American Movie Classics, March 3, 2013.
5. "Conquer," *The Walking Dead*, Directed by Greg Nicotero, American Movie Classics, March 29, 2015.
6. "Bury Me Here," *The Walking Dead*, Directed by Alrick Riley, American Movie Classics, March 12, 2017.
7. Jon Hamilton, "Why Brain Scientists Are Still Obsessed with the Curious Case of Phineas Gage," *NPR*, last modified May 21, 2017, https://www.npr.org/sections/health-shots/2017/05/21/528966102/why-brain-scientists-are-still-obsessed-with-the-curious-case-of-phineas-gage.
8. "What Is a Concussion?" *Centers for Disease Control and Prevention*, last modified January 31, 2–17, https://www.cdc.gov/headsup/basics/concussion_whatis.html.
9. "DoD Worldwide Numbers for TBI," *Defense and Veterans Brain Injury Center*, last modified October 24, 2018, http://dvbic.dcoe.mil/dod-worldwide-numbers-tbi.
10. "TBI: Get the Facts," *Centers for Disease Control and Prevention*, last modified April 27, 2017 https://www.cdc.gov/traumaticbraininjury/get_the_facts.html.
11. "Mental Health by the Numbers," *National Alliance on Mental Illness*, accessed August 1, 2018, https://www.nami.org/learn-more/mental-health-by-the-numbers.
12. Hannah Ritchie and Max Roser, "Mental Health," *Ourworldindata.org*, last

modified April 2018, https://ourworldindata.org/mental-health.
13. "Exodus 21:24," *Bible Study Tools*, accessed March 1, 2018, https://www.biblestudytools.com/asv/exodus/21-24.html.
14. Duncan Tucker, "Santa Muerte: The Rise of Mexico's Death 'Saint,'" *BBC News*, last modified November 1, 2018, http://www.bbc.com/news/world-latin-america-41804243.
15. Ross Toro, "The World's Catholic Population (Infographic)," *Live Science*, last updated February 19, 2013, https://www.livescience.com/27244-the-world-s-catholic-population-infographic.html.
16. Vaishavee Madden, Jill Domoney, Katie Aumayer, et al., "Intergenerational Transmission of Parenting: Findings from a UK Longitudinal Study," *The European Journal of Public Health* 25, no. 6 (2015): 1030–1035.

Chapter 7

1. *The Walking Dead, Seasons 5–6*, Showrunner Scott Gimple, October 12, 2014–April 3, 2016.
2. *Ibid.*
3. "Mental Health by the Numbers," *National Alliance on Mental Illness*, accessed August 1, 2018, https://www.nami.org/learn-more/mental-health-by-the-numbers.
4. "What Causes Pediatric Injury?" *U.S. Department of Health and Human Services*, last modified December 1, 2016, https://www.nichd.nih.gov/health/topics/pediatric/conditioninfo/pages/causes.aspx.
5. "Preventable Injuries Kill 2000 Children Every Day," *World Health Organization*, last modified December 10, 2008, https://www.who.int/mediacentre/news/releases/2008/pr46/en/.
6. Charles Recknagel, "Afghanistan: Land Mines from Afghan-Soviet War Leave Bitter Legacy (Part 2)," *Radio Free Europe Radio Liberty*, last modified February 13, 2004, https://www.rferl.org/a/1051546.html.
7. James Dunn, "Pictured: The Harrowing Plight of Children Maimed in Afghanistan by the Thousands of Landmines Scattered Across the Country After Decades

of War," *MailOnline*, last modified August 21, 2015, http://www.dailymail.co.uk/news/article-3205978/Pictured-harrowing-plight-children-maimed-Afghanistan-thousands-landmines-scattered-country-decades-war.html.

8. "Talking to Teens About Stress," *American Psychological Association*, accessed April 13, 2017, http://www.apa.org/helpcenter/stress-talk.aspx.

9. "Unintentional Injuries," *Child Trends Databank*, last modified October 2014, https://www.childtrends.org/indicators/unintentional-injuries.

10. "STDs in Adolescents and Young Adults," *Centers for Disease Control and Prevention*, last modified September 26, 2017, https://www.cdc.gov/std/stats16/adolescents.htm.

11. "After," *The Walking Dead*, Directed by Greg Nicotero, American Movie Classics, February 9, 2014.

12. "No Way Out," *The Walking Dead*, Directed by Greg Nicotero. American Movie Classics, February 14, 2016.

13. William Roberts, and Janet Strayer, "Parents' Responses to the Emotional Distress of Their Children: Relations with Children's Competence," *Developmental Psychology* 23 (1987): 415–422.

14. Aala El-Khani, Fiona Ulph, Sarah Peters, and Rachel Calam, "Syria: The Challenges of Parenting in Refugee Situations of Immediate Displacement." *Intervention* 14, no. 2 (2016): 99–113.

15. "Save the Last One," *The Walking Dead*, Directed by Phil Abraham, American Movie Classics, October 30, 2011.

16. "Child and Adolescent Mental Health," *World Health Organization*, accessed September 22, 2018, http://www.who.int/mental_health/maternal-child/child_adolescent/en/.

17. "10 Leading Causes of Death By Age Group," *Centers for Disease Prevention and Control*, accessed June 12, 2018, https://www.cdc.gov/injury/images/lc-charts/leading_causes_of_death_age_group_2016_1056w814h.gif.

18. "Mental Health By the Numbers."

Chapter 8

1. "The Grove," *The Walking Dead*, Directed by Michael Satrazemis, American Movie Classics, March 16, 2014.

2. "Welcome to the Tombs," *The Walking Dead*, Directed by Ernest Dickerson, American Movie Classics, March 31, 2013.

3. "The Grove."

4. Sadie Dingfelder, "Must Babies Always Breed Marital Discontent?" *Monitor on Psychology* 11, no. 9 (2011): 51.

5. Jessica L. Semega, Kayla R. Fontenot, and Melissa A. Kollar, "Income and Poverty in the United States: 2016," *U.S. Census Bureau*, last modified September 12, 2017, https://www.census.gov/library/publications/2017/demo/p60-259.html.

6. "Definitions of Food Security," *U.S. Department of Agriculture*, last modified September 5, 2018, https://www.ers.usda.gov/topics/food-nutrition-assistance/food-security-in-the-us/definitions-of-food-security.aspx.

7. Alix Spiegel, "Traces of Katrina: New Orleans Suicide Rate Still Up," *NPR*, last modified August 30, 2010, https://www.npr.org/templates/story/story.php?storyId=129482180.

8. "Days Gone Bye," *The Walking Dead*, Vol. 1, Image-Skybound, May 4, 2004.

9. Tyler Jamison, Lawrence Ganong, and Christine Proulx, "Unmarried Coparenting in the Context of Poverty: Understanding the Relationship Between Stress, Family Resource Management, and Resilience," *Journal of Family and Economic Issues* 38, no. 3 (2017): 439–452.

10. D'vera Cohn and Jeffrey S. Passel, "A Record 64 Million Americans Live in Multigenerational Households," *Pew Research Center*, last modified April 5, 2018, http://www.pewresearch.org/fact-tank/2018/04/05/a-record-64-million-americans-live-in-multigenerational-households/.

11. Ruth Evans, "Sibling Caringscapes: Time-Space Practices of Caring Within Youth-Headed Households In Tanzania and Uganda," *Geoforum* 43, no. 4 (2012): 824–835.

12. Stephanie Perrin, "The Greatest Threat to Survival in Refugee Camps," *Premptivelove.org*, last modified May 2, 2017, https://preemptivelove.org/blog/greatest_threat_to_survival_refugee_camps/.

13. "Sharp Rise in Mortality Seen at

Refugee Camp in Southeast Ethiopia," *UNHCR: The United Nations Refugee Agency*, last modified August 16, 2011, http://www.unhcr.org/en-us/news/briefing/2011/8/4e4a4fd19/sharp-rise-mortality-refugee-camp-southeast-ethiopia.html.

14. "Child Abuse and Neglect: Risk and Protective Factors," *Centers for Disease Control and Prevention*, last modified April 10, 2018, https://www.cdc.gov/violence prevention/childabuseandneglect/risk protectivefactors.html.

15. Ester J. Jenkins and Carl C. Bell, "Violence Exposure, Psychological Distress, and High Risk Behaviors Among Inner-City High School Students," in S. Friedman, ed., *Anxiety Disorders in African Americans* (New York: Springer, 1994), 76–88.

16. "Syria Emergency," *UNHCR: The United Nations Refugee Agency*, accessed October 25, 2018, http://www.unhcr.org/en-us/syria-emergency.html.

17. Aala El-Khani, Fiona Ulph, Sarah Peters, and Rachel Calam, "Syria: Coping Mechanisms Utilised by Displaced Refugee Parents Caring for Their Children in Pre-Resettlement Contexts," *Intervention* 14, no. 3 (2016): 1–17.

18. "Regional Refugee and Resilience Plan 2017–2018: 2017 Progress Report," *3RP*, last modified October 2017, http://www.3rpsyriacrisis.org/wp-content/uploads/2017/10/3RP-Progress-Report-17102017-final.pdf.

Chapter 9

1. Jonathan Maberry, *Rot and Ruin* (New York: Simon & Schuster, 2010).

2. "40% of Children Miss Out on the Parenting Needed to Succeed in Life," *The Sutton Trust*, last modified March 21, 2014, https://www.suttontrust.com/newsarchive/40-children-miss-parenting-needed-succeed-life-sutton-trust/.

3. *The Walking Dead, Seasons 3–9*, developed by Frank Darabont, based on the comic books by Robert Kirkman, Tony Moore, and Charlie Adlard, American Movie Classics, 2010–present, television series.

4. Sylvain Bonhommeau, Laurent Du-

broca, Olivier Le Pape, Julien Barde, David M. Kaplan, Emmanuel Chassot, and Anne-Elise Nieblas, "Eating Up the World's Food Web and the Human Trophic Level," *Proceedings of the National Academy of Sciences of the United States of America* 110, no. 51 (2013): 20617–20620.

5. Heather Shaw, "5 Animals That Will Save You in a Zombie Apocalypse," *ZSL London Zoo*, last modified October 21, 2014, https://www.zsl.org/blogs/zsl-london-zoo/5-animals-that-will-save-you-in-a-zombie-apocalypse.

Chapter 10

1. "What Lies Ahead," *The Walking Dead*, Directed by Ernest Dickerson, American Movie Classics, October 16, 2011.

2. "A Familiar Face: Violence in the Lives of Children and Adolescents," *UNICEF*, accessed January 13, 2018, https://www.unicefusa.org/sites/default/files/EVAClong.UN0139859.pdf.

3. Elizabeth T. Gershoff, "More Harm Than Good: A Summary of Scientific Research on the Intended and Unintended Effects of Corporal Punishment on Children," *Law and Contemporary Problems* 73 (2010) 33–58.

4. Denise Foley, "The Discipline Wars," *Time*, accessed July 29, 2018, http://time.com/the-discipline-wars-2/.

5. "Child Maltreatment," *World Health Organization*, accessed September 22, 2018, http://www.who.int/violence_injury_pre vention/violence/child/Child_maltreat ment_infographic_EN.pdf?ua=1.

6. Rongqin Yu, John Geddes, and Seena Fazel, "Personality Disorders, Violence, and Antisocial Behavior: A Systematic Review and Meta-Regression Analysis," *Journal of Personality Disorders* 26, no. 5 (2012): 775–792.

7. Sulome Anderson, "Do Sociopaths Make Better Soldiers?" *Vice*, last modified July 21, 2015, https://www.vice.com/en_us/article/ppxae7/the-unique-challenge-of-being-a-psychopath-in-the-military-721.

8. John M. Grohol, "Differences Between a Psychopath vs. Sociopath," *Psych Central*, accessed August 15, 2018, https://psychcentral.com/blog/differences-between-a-psychopath-vs-sociopath/.

Chapter 11

1. "World Health Rankings," *WorldLife Expectancy*, accessed September 1, 2018, http://www.worldlifeexpectancy.com/world-rankings-total-deaths.

2. "The Top Ten Causes of Death," *World Health Organization*, last modified May 24, 2018, http://www.who.int/newsroom/fact-sheets/detail/the-top-10-causes-of-death.

3. *The Walking Dead, Seasons 1–9*, developed by Frank Darabont, based on the comic books by Robert Kirkman, Tony Moore, and Charlie Adlard, American Movie Classics, 2010–present, television series.

4. *The Walking Dead, Season 3*, Showrunner Glen Mazzara, American Movie Classics, October 14, 2012–March 31, 2013.

5. "Secrets," *The Walking Dead*, Directed by David Boyd, American Movie Classics, November 20, 2011.

6. "Days Gone Bye," *The Walking Dead*, Directed by Frank Darabont, American Movie Classics, October 31, 2010.

7. "Say the Word," *The Walking Dead*, Directed by Greg Nicotero, American Movie Classics, November 11, 2012.

8. "Orphans," *UNICEF*, last modified June 16, 2017, https://www.unicef.org/media/media_45279.html.

9. "Statistical Abstracts of the U.S. 1990," *U.S. Bureau of the Census*, Washington, D.C., U.S. Government Printing Office.

10. "More Than 16,000 Children Lost Parents or Caregivers to Ebola—Many Are Taken In by the Communities: UNICEF," *UNICEF*, last modified February 6, 2015, https://www.unicef.org/infobycountry/media_79742.html.

11. Scott Pelley, "Saving the Orphans of War," *CBS News*, last modified May 6, 2018, https://www.cbsnews.com/news/saving-the-orphans-of-syria-civil-war/.

12. "New Quality of Care Standards to Save Lives and Improve the Health of Children and Young Adolescents," *World Health Organization*, accessed July 31, 2018, http://www.who.int/maternal_child_adolescent/topics/quality-of-care/quality-standards-child/en/.

13. "Suicide Data," *World Health Organization*, accessed September 13, 2018, http://www.who.int/mental_health/prevention/suicide/suicideprevent/en/.

Chapter 12

1. Mona Macksoud, and J. Lawrence Aber, "The War Experiences and Psychosocial Development of Children in Lebanon," *Child Development* 67 (1996): 70–88.

2. *The Walking Dead, Season 3*, Showrunner Glen Mazzara, American Movie Classics, October 14, 2012—March 31, 2013.

3. "Violence and Socioeconomic Status," *American Psychological Association*, accessed November 6, 2018, https://www.apa.org/pi/ses/resources/publications/violence.aspx.

4. "Caregiving in the U.S.: AARP 2015 Report," *Caregiving.org*, accessed July 10, 2018, https://www.caregiving.org/wp-content/uploads/2015/05/2015_Caregiving intheUS_Final-Report-June-4_WEB.pdf.

5. "Killer Within," *The Walking Dead*, Directed by Guy Ferland, American Movie Classics, November 4, 2012.

6. "The Day Will Come When You Won't Be," *The Walking Dead*, Directed by Greg Nicotero, American Movie Classics, October 23, 2016.

7. "A New Beginning," *The Walking Dead, Vol. 22*, Image-Skybound, November 5, 2014.

8. Jugal K. Patel, "After Sandy Hook, More Than 400 People Have Been Shot in Over 200 School Shootings," *The New York Times*, last modified February 13, 2018, https://www.nytimes.com/interactive/2018/02/15/us/school-shootings-sandy-hook-parkland.html.

9. "Hate Map," *Southern Poverty Law Center*, accessed October 20, 2018, https://www.splcenter.org/hate-map.

Bibliography

Abugov, Jeff. *Zombies Versus Aliens Versus Vampires Versus Dinosaurs.* Los Angeles: J-Stroke Productions, 2015.

Alhusen, Jeanne L., Ellen Ray, Phyllis Sharps, and Linda Bullock. "Intimate Partner Violence During Pregnancy: Maternal and Neonatal Outcomes." *Journal of Women's Health* 24, no. 1 (2015): 100–106.

American Psychiatric Association. *Diagnostic and Statistical Manual of Mental Disorders: DSM-5.* Washington, D.C.: American Psychiatric Association, 2013.

Anderson, Keven D., and Sam Stall. *Night of the Living Trekkies.* Philadelphia: Quirk Books, 2010.

Arhant, Christine, Ricarda Landenberger, Andrea Beetz, and Josef Troxler. "Attitudes of Caregivers to Supervision of Child-Family Dog Interactions in Children Up to 6 Years—An Exploratory Study." *Journal of Veterinary Behavior: Clinical Applications and Research* 14 (2016): 10–16.

Ashburn-Nardo, Leslie. "Parenthood as a Moral Imperative? Moral Outrage and the Stigmatization of Voluntarily Childfree Women and Men." *Sex Roles* 76, no. 5–6 (2017): 393–401.

Aslam, Usman, Muhammad Ilyas, Muhammad Kashif Imran, and Ubaid-Ur Rahman. "Detrimental Effects of Cynicism on Organizational Change: An Interactive Model of Organizational Cynicism (A Study of Employees in Public Sector Organizations)." *Journal of Organizational Change Management* 29, no. 4 (2016): 580–598.

Asok, Arun, Kristin Bernard, T. L. Roth, J. B. Rosen, and Mary Dozier. "Parental Responsiveness Moderates the Association Between Early-Life Stress and Reduced Telomere Length." *Development and Psychopathology* 25, no. 3 (2013): 577–585.

Balbernie, Robin. "Reactive Attachment Disorder as an Evolutionary Adaptation." *Attachment & Human Development* 12, no. 3 (2010): 265–281.

Bandura, Albert. *Social Learning Theory.* Englewood Cliffs, NJ: Prentice Hall, 1977.

Belsky, Jay. "The Determinants of Parenting: A Process Model." *Child Development* 55 (1984): 83–96.

Berry, Jack W., and David C. Schwebel. "Configural Approaches to Temperament Assessment: Implications for Predicting Risk of Unintentional Injury in Children." *Journal of Personality* 77, no. 5 (2009): 1381–1410.

Bettelheim, Bruno. *The Uses of Enchantment: The Meaning and Importance of Fairy Tales.* New York: Random House, 1967.

Bjorklund, David F., Jennifer L. Yunger, and Anthony D. Pellegrini. "The Evolution of Parenting and Evolutionary Approaches to Childrearing." *Handbook of Parenting* 2 (2002): 3–30.

Black, Robert E., Lindsay H. Allen, Zulfiqar A. Bhutta, Laura E. Caulfield, Mercedes

De Onis, Majid Ezzati, Colin Mathers, Juan Rivera, and Maternal and Child Undernutrition Study Group. "Maternal and Child Undernutrition: Global and Regional Exposures and Health Consequences." *The Lancet* 371, no. 9608 (2008): 243–260.

Boals, Adriel, Shana Southard-Dobbs, and Heidemarie Blumenthal. "Adverse Events in Emerging Adulthood Are Associated with Increases in Neuroticism." *Journal of Personality* 83, no. 2 (2015): 202–211.

Bonanno, George A., and Erica D. Diminich. "Annual Research Review: Positive Adjustment to Adversity-Trajectories of Minimal-Impact Resilience and Emergent Resilience." *Journal of Child Psychology and Psychiatry* 54, no. 4 (2013): 378–401.

Bonanno, George A., Sara A. Romero, and Sarah I. Klein. "The Temporal Elements of Psychological Resilience: An Integrative Framework for the Study of Individuals, Families, and Communities." *Psychological Inquiry* 26, no. 2 (2015): 139–169.

Bourne, Jason L. *Day by Day Armageddon.* New York: Pocket Books, 2009.

Bowers, Mallory E., and Rachel Yehuda. "Intergenerational Transmission of Stress in Humans." *Neuropsychopharmacology* 41, no. 1 (2016): 232–244.

Boyczuk, Alana M., and Paula C. Fletcher. "The Ebbs and Flows: Stresses of Sandwich Generation Caregivers." *Journal of Adult Development* 23, no. 1 (2016): 51–61.

Bridgott, David J., Nicole M. Burt, Erin S. Edwards, and Kirby Deater-Deckard. "Intergenerational Transmission of Self-Regulation: A Multidisciplinary Review and Integrative Conceptual Framework." *Psychological Bulletin* 141, no. 3 (2015): 602–654.

Bronfenbrenner, Urie. *The Ecology of Human Development: Experiments by Nature and Design.* Cambridge: Harvard University Press, 1979.

Brooks, Jane B. *The Process of Parenting,* 8th ed. New York: McGraw-Hill, 2011.

Brooks, Max. *World War Z: An Oral History of the Zombie War.* New York: Crown, 2006.

Brooks, Max. *The Zombie Survival Guide: Complete Protection From the Living Dead.* New York: Broadway Books, 2003.

Browne, S. G. *Breathers: A Zombies Lament.* New York: Broadway Books, 2009.

Browne, S. G. *I Saw Zombies Eating Santa Claus: A Breathers Christmas Carol.* New York: Gallery Books, 2012.

Buckle, Jennifer L., and Stephen Fleming. *Parenting After the Death of a Child: A Practitioner's Guide.* New York: Routledge, 2011.

Burke, Jeffrey D., Richard Rowe, and Khrista Boylan. "Functional Outcomes of Child and Adolescent Oppositional Defiant Disorder Symptoms in Young Adult Men." *Journal of Child Psychology and Psychiatry* 55, no. 3 (2014): 264–272.

Bushman, Brad J., and Jodi L. Whitaker. "Like a Magnet: Catharsis Beliefs Attract Angry People to Violent Video Games." *Psychological Science* 21, no. 6 (2010): 790–792.

Campbell, Susan B., Susan Spieker, Nathan Vandergrift, Jay Belsky, Margaret Burchinal, and NICHD Early Child Care Research Network. "Predictors and Sequelae of Trajectories of Physical Aggression in School-Age Boys and Girls." *Development and Psychopathology* 22, no. 1 (2010): 133–150.

Carpiano, Richard M., and Rachel T. Kimbro. "Neighborhood Social Capital, Parenting Strain, and Personal Mastery Among Female Primary Caregivers of Children." *Journal of Health and Social Behavior* 53, no. 2 (2012): 232–247.

Cassidy, Jude, and Phillip R. Shaver. *Handbook of Attachment: Theory, Research, and Clinical Applications,* 3d ed. New York: Guilford Press, 2017.

Ceballo, Rosario, and Vonnie C. McLoyd. "Social Support and Parenting in Poor, Dangerous Neighborhoods." *Child Development* 73, no. 4 (2002): 1310–1321.

Chang, Iris. *The Rape of Nanking: The Forgotten Holocaust of World War II.* New York: Basic Books, 1997.

Charmandari, Evangelia, Constantine Tsigos, and George Chrousos. "Endocrinology of the Stress Response." *Annual Review of Physiology* 67 (2005): 259–284.

Chesnut, R. Andrew. *Devoted to Death: Santa Muerte, The Skeleton Saint.* New York: Oxford University, 2012.

Clasen, Mathias. "The Anatomy of the Zombie: A Bio-Psychological Look at the Undead Other." *Otherness: Essays and Studies* 1, no. 1 (2010): 1–23.

Clifford, Edward. "Discipline in the Home: A Controlled Observational Study of Parental Practices." *The Journal of Genetic Psychology* 95, no. 1 (1959): 45–82.

Clines, Peter. *Ex-Heroes: A Novel*. New York: Broadway Paperbacks, 2010.

Coccaro, Emil F., Royce Lee, Maureen W. Groer, Adem Can, Mary Coussons-Read, and Teodor T. Postolache. "Toxoplasma Gondii Infection: Relationship with Aggression in Psychiatric Subjects." *The Journal of Clinical Psychiatry* 77, no. 3 (2016): 334–341.

Cohen, Jonathan. "Defining Identification: A Theoretical Look at the Identification of Audiences with Media Characters." *Mass Communication & Society* 4, no. 3 (2001): 245–264.

Cohen, Judith A., Anthony P. Mannarino, Tamra Greenberg, Susan Padlo, and Carrie Shipley. "Childhood Traumatic Grief: Concepts and Controversies." *Trauma, Violence, & Abuse* 3, no. 4 (2002): 307–327.

Cracco, Emiel, Lien Goossens, and Caroline Braet. "Emotion Regulation Across Childhood and Adolescence: Evidence for a Maladaptive Shift in Adolescence." *European Child & Adolescent Psychiatry* 26, no. 8 (2017): 909–921.

Craig, Michael. "Perinatal Risk Factors for Neonaticide and Infant Homicide: Can We Identify Those at Risk?" *Journal of the Royal Society of Medicine* 97, no. 2 (2004): 57–61.

Cross, Dorthie L., Alexander Vance, Ye Ji Kim, Andrew L. Ruchard, Nathan Fox, Tanja Jovanovic, and Bekh Bradley. "Trauma Exposure, PTSD, and Parenting in a Community Sample of Low-Income, Predominantly African American Mothers and Children." *Psychological Trauma: Theory, Research, Practice, and Policy* 10, no. 3 (2017): 327–335.

Curtis, Valerie, and Adam Biran. "Dirt, Disgust, and Disease: Is Hygiene in Our Genes?" *Perspectives in Biology and Medicine* 44, no. 1 (2001): 17–31.

Daly, Martin, and Margo Wilson. "Discriminative Parental Solicitude: A Bio-logical Perspective." *Journal of Marriage and the Family* (1980): 277–288.

De Bellis, Michael D., and Thomas Van Dillen. "Childhood Post-Traumatic Stress Disorder: An Overview." *Child and Adolescent Psychiatric Clinics* 14, no. 4 (2005): 745–772.

Deci, Edward L., and Richard M. Ryan. "Self-Determination Theory: A Macrotheory of Human Motivation, Development, and Health." *Canadian Psychology/Psychologie Canadienne* 49, no. 3 (2008): 182–185.

Del Giudice, Marco, Romina Angeleri, and Valeria Manera. "The Juvenile Transition: A Developmental Switch Point in Human Life History." *Developmental Review* 29, no. 1 (2009): 1–31.

Demaree, Heath A., Jennifer L. Robinson, D. Erik Everhart, and Eric A. Youngstrom. "Behavioral Inhibition System (BIS) Strength and Trait Dominance Are Associated with Affective Response and Perspective Taking When Viewing Dyadic Interactions." *International Journal of Neuroscience* 115, no. 11 (2005): 1579–1593.

DeSilva, Mary Bachman, Anne Skalicky, Jennifer Beard, Mandisa Cakwe, Tom Zhuwau, Tim Quinlan, and Jonathon Simon. "Early Impacts of Orphaning: Health, Nutrition, and Food Insecurity in a Cohort of School-Going Adolescents in South Africa." *Vulnerable Children and Youth Studies* 7, no. 1 (2012): 75–87.

Dossa, Nissou Ines, Marie Hatem, Maria Victoria Zunzunegui, and William Fraser. "Social Consequences of Conflict-Related Rape: The Case of Survivors in the Eastern Democratic Republic of Congo." *Peace and Conflict: Journal of Peace Psychology* 20, no. 3 (2014): 241–255.

Dubey, J. P. *Toxoplasmosis of Animals and Humans*. Boca Raton: CRC Press, 2010.

Duncan, Catherine, and Joanne Cacciatore. "A Systematic Review of the Peer-Reviewed Literature on Self-Blame, Guilt, and Shame." *OMEGA—Journal of Death and Dying* 71, no. 4 (2015): 312–342.

Dunn, Judy, and Penny Munn. "Becoming a Family Member: Family Conflict and the Development of Social Understanding in the Second Year." *Child Development* 56 (1985): 480–492.

Eber, Gabriel B., Joseph L. Annest, James A. Mercy, and George W. Ryan. "Nonfatal and Fatal Firearm-Related Injuries Among Children Aged 14 Years and Younger: United States, 1993–2000." *Pediatrics* 113, no. 6 (2004): 1686–1692.

Ein-Dor, Tsachi, and Gilad Hirschberger. "Rethinking Attachment Theory: From a Theory of Relationships to a Theory of Individual and Group Survival." *Current Directions in Psychological Science* 25, no. 4 (2016): 223–227.

El-Khani, Aala, Fiona Ulph, Sarah Peters, and Rachel Calam. "Syria: The Challenges of Parenting in Refugee Situations of Immediate Displacement." *Intervention* 14, no. 2 (2016): 99–113.

Elbogen, Eric B., Sally C. Johnson, H. Ryan Wagner, Virginia M. Newton, Christine Timko, Jennifer J. Vasterling, and Jean C. Beckham. "Protective Factors and Risk Modification of Violence in Iraq and Afghanistan War Veterans." *The Journal of Clinical Psychiatry* 73, no. 6 (2012): e767–e773.

Ellonen, Noora, Juha Kääriäinen, Martti Lehti, and Mikko Aaltonen. "Comparing Trends in Infanticides in 28 Countries, 1960–2009." *Journal of Scandinavian Studies in Criminology and Crime Prevention* 16, no. 2 (2015): 175–193.

Erikson, Erik H. *Childhood and Society*, 2d ed. New York: W. W. Norton, 1964.

Ertorer, Secil Erdogan. "Managing Identity in the Face of Resettlement." *Identity* 14, no. 4 (2014): 268–285.

Eyal, Keren, and Jonathan Cohen. "When Good Friends Say Goodbye: A Parasocial Breakup Study." *Journal of Broadcasting & Electronic Media* 50, no. 3 (2006): 502–523.

Falconier, Mariana K., Fridtjof Nussbeck, Guy Bodenmann, Hulka Schneider, and Thomas Bradbury. "Stress from Daily Hassles in Couples: Its Effects on Intradyadic Stress, Relationship Satisfaction, and Physical and Psychological Well-Being." *Journal of Marital and Family Therapy* 41, no. 2 (2015): 221–235.

Fein, Robert A. *Threat Assessment in Schools: A Guide to Managing Threatening Situations and to Creating Safe School Climates*. DIANE Publishing, 2002.

Feinstein, Brian A., Rachel Hershenberg, Vickie Bhatia, Jessica A. Latack, Nathalie Meuwly, and Joanne Davila. "Negative Social Comparison on Facebook and Depressive Symptoms: Rumination as a Mechanism." *Psychology of Popular Media Culture* 2, no. 3 (2013): 161–170.

Feldman, Robert S. *Child Development*, 7th ed. Boston: Pearson, 2016.

Fincham, Frank D., and Julie H. Hall. "Parenting and the Marital Relationship." *Parenting: An Ecological Perspective* 2 (2005): 205–234.

Fisher, Celia B., and Barbara Lisa Johnson. "Getting Mad at Mom and Dad: Children's Changing Views of Family Conflict." *International Journal of Behavioral Development* 13, no. 1 (1990): 31–48.

Fowler, Katherine A., Linda L. Dahlberg, Tadesse Haileyesus, Carmen Gutierrez, and Sarah Bacon. "Childhood Firearm Injuries in the United States." *Pediatrics* (2017): e20163486.

Franklin, Joseph C., Jessica D. Ribeiro, Kathryn R. Fox, Kate H. Bentley, Evan M. Kleiman, Xieyining Huang, Katherine M. Musacchio, Adam C. Jaroszewski, Bernard P. Chang, and Matthew K. Nock. "Risk Factors for Suicidal Thoughts and Behaviors: A Meta-Analysis of 50 Years of Research." *Psychological Bulletin* 143, no. 2 (2017): 187–132.

Fredman, Steffany J., Yunying Le, Amy D. Marshall, Timothy R. Brick, and Mark E. Feinberg. "A Dyadic Perspective On PTSD Symptoms' Associations with Couple Functioning and Parenting Stress in First-Time Parents." *Couple and Family Psychology: Research and Practice* 6, no. 2 (2017): 117.

Freud, Sigmund. *The Standard Edition of the Complete Psychological Works of Sigmund Freud.* James Strachey, ed. Oxford: Macmillan, 1964.

Friedman, Susan Hatters, and Phillip J. Resnick. "Neonaticide: Phenomenology and Considerations for Prevention." *International Journal of Law and Psychiatry* 32, no. 1 (2009): 43–47.

Frontini, Roberta, Helena Moreira, and Maria Cristina Canavarro. "Parenting Stress and Quality of Life in Pediatric

Obesity: The Mediating Role of Parenting Styles." *Journal of Child and Family Studies* 25, no. 3 (2016): 1011–1023.

Furstenberg, Frank F., Alisa Belzer, Colleen Davis, Judith A. Levine, Kristine Morrow, and Mary Washington. "How Families Manage Risk and Opportunity in Dangerous Neighborhoods." *Sociology and the Public Agenda* 231–258. Newbury Park, CA: Sage, 1993.

Galler, Janina R., C. P. Bryce, D. Waber, R. S. Hock, N. Exner, D. Eaglesfield, G. Fitzmaurice, and R. Harrison. "Early Childhood Malnutrition Predicts Depressive Symptoms at Ages 11–17." *Journal of Child Psychology and Psychiatry* 51, no. 7 (2010): 789–798.

Gao, Molly, and Marissa Slaven. "Best Practices in Children's Bereavement: A Qualitative Analysis of Needs and Services." *Journal of Pain Management* 10, no. 1 (2017): 119–126.

Garrett, Bob, Gerald Hough, and John Agnew. *Brain and Behavior: An Introduction to Biological Psychology*, 4th ed. Thousand Oaks, CA: Sage Publications, 2014.

Garrett, Greg. *Living with the Living Dead: The Wisdom of the Zombie Apocalypse*. New York: Oxford University Press, 2017.

Gatheridge, Brian J., Raymond G. Miltenberger, Daniel F. Huneke, Melisa J. Satterlund, Amanda R. Mattern, Brigette M. Johnson, and Christopher A. Flessner. "Comparison of Two Programs to Teach Firearm Injury Prevention Skills to 6- and 7-Year-Old Children." *Pediatrics* 114, no. 3 (2004): e294–e299.

Gavidia-Payne, Susana, Bianca Denny, Kate Davis, Andrew Francis, and Merv Jackson. "Parental Resilience: A Neglected Construct in Resilience Research." *Clinical Psychologist* 19, no. 3 (2015): 111–121.

Gershoff, Elizabeth T. "More Harm Than Good: A Summary of Scientific Research on the Intended and Unintended Effects of Corporal Punishment on Children." *Law & Contemporary Problems* 73 (2010): 31–58.

Gershoff, Elizabeth T., and Andrew Grogan-Kaylor. "Spanking and Child Outcomes: Old Controversies and New Meta-Analyses." *Journal of Family Psychology* 30, no. 4 (2016): 453–469.

Gibson, Kyle. "Differential Parental Investment in Families with Both Adopted and Genetic Children." *Evolution and Human Behavior* 30, no. 3 (2009): 184–189.

Glocker, Melanie L., Daniel D. Langleben, Kosha Ruparel, James W. Loughead, Ruben C. Gur, and Norbert Sachser. "Baby Schema in Infant Faces Induces Cuteness Perception and Motivation for Caretaking in Adults." *Ethology* 115, no. 3 (2009): 257–263.

Gordon, Kristina Coop, Michael A. Friedman, Ivan W. Miller, and Lowell Gaertner. "Marital Attributions as Moderators of the Marital Discord–Depression Link." *Journal of Social and Clinical Psychology* 24, no. 6 (2005): 876–893.

Gottman, John M., and Nan Silver. *The Seven Principles for Making Marriage Work*. New York: Crown, 1999.

Grace, Karen Trister, and Christina Fleming. "A Systematic Review of Reproductive Coercion in International Settings." *World Medical & Health Policy* 8, no. 4 (2016): 382–408.

Grahame-Smith, Seth, and Jane Austen. *Pride and Prejudice and Zombies*. Philadelphia: Quirk Books, 2009.

Grant, Mira. *Feed*. New York: Orbit, 2010.

Green, James A., Pamela G. Whitney, and Michael Potegal. "Screaming, Yelling, Whining, and Crying: Categorical and Intensity Differences in Vocal Expressions of Anger and Sadness in Children's Tantrums." *Emotion* 11, no. 5 (2011): 1124–1133.

Grimm, Jacob, Wilhem Grimm, and Maria Tatar. *The Annotated Brothers Grimm*. New York: W. W. Norton, 2004.

Grünebaum, Amos, Laurence B. McCullough, Katherine J. Sapra, Birgit Arabin, and Frank A. Chervenak. "Planned Home Births: The Need for Additional Contraindications." *American Journal of Obstetrics and Gynecology* 216, no. 4 (2017): 401.e1–401.e8.

Hardy, Marjorie S. "Teaching Firearm Safety to Children: Failure of a Program." *Journal of Developmental & Behavioral Pediatrics* 23, no. 2 (2002): 71–76.

Harwood, Anna, Michal Lavidor, and Yuri Rassovsky. "Reducing Aggression with

Martial Arts: A Meta-Analysis of Child and Youth Studies." *Aggression and Violent Behavior* 34 (2017): 96–101.

Hasanović, Mevludin, Osman Sinanović, Zihnet Selimbašić, Izet Pajević, and Esmina Avdibegović. "Psychological Disturbances of War-Traumatized Children from Different Foster and Family Settings in Bosnia and Herzegovina." *Croatian Medical Journal* 47, no. 1 (2006): 85–94.

Hewlett, Barry S., Michael E. Lamb, Donald Shannon, Birgit Leyendecker, and Axel Schölmerich. "Culture and Early Infancy Among Central African Foragers and Farmers." *Developmental Psychology* 34, no. 4 (1998): 653–661.

Hill, Reuben. *Families Under Stress: Adjustment to the Crises of War Separation and Reunion.* New York: Harper & Brothers, 1949.

Himle, Michael B., Raymond G. Miltenberger, Christopher Flessner, and Brian Gatheridge. "Teaching Safety Skills to Children to Prevent Gun Play." *Journal of Applied Behavior Analysis* 37, no. 1 (2004): 1–9.

Hofmann, Wilhelm, Malte Friese, and Fritz Strack. "Impulse and Self-Control from a Dual-Systems Perspective." *Perspectives on Psychological Science* 4, no. 2 (2009): 162–176.

Hooper, Lisa M., Heather M. Moore, and Annie K. Smith. "Parentification in Military Families: Overlapping Constructs and Theoretical Explorations in Family, Clinical, and Military Psychology." *Children and Youth Services Review* 39 (2014): 123–134.

Howse, Robin B., Garrett Lange, Dale C. Farran, and Carolyn D. Boyles. "Motivation and Self-Regulation as Predictors of Achievement in Economically Disadvantaged Young Children." *The Journal of Experimental Education* 71, no. 2 (2003): 151–174.

Hsee, Christopher K., and Bowen Ruan. "The Pandora Effect: The Power and Peril of Curiosity." *Psychological Science* 27, no. 5 (2016): 659–666.

Hystad, Sigurd W., Olav Kjellevold Olsen, Roar Espevik, and Reidar Säfvenbom. "On the Stability of Psychological Hardiness: A Three-Year Longitudinal Study."

Military Psychology 27, no. 3 (2015): 155–168.

Ivey, Paula K. "Cooperative Reproduction in Ituri Forest Hunter-Gatherers: Who Cares for Efe Infants?" *Current Anthropology* 41, no. 5 (2000): 856–866.

Jamison, Tyler B., Lawrence Ganong, and Christine M. Proulx. "Unmarried Coparenting in the Context of Poverty: Understanding the Relationship Between Stress, Family Resource Management, and Resilience." *Journal of Family and Economic Issues* 38, no. 3 (2017): 439–452.

Jaques, M. L., T. L. Weaver, N. L. Weaver, and L. Willoughby. "The Association Between Pediatric Injury Risks and Parenting Behaviours." *Child: Care, Health and Development* 44, no. 2 (2018): 297–303.

Jarrett, Robin L. "Successful Parenting in High-Risk Neighborhoods." *The Future of Children* (1999): 45–50.

Johnston, Deirdre D. "Adolescents' Motivations for Viewing Graphic Horror." *Human Communication Research* 21, no. 4 (1995): 522–552.

Jones, Gerard. *Killing Monsters: Why Children Need Fantasy, Super Heroes, and Make-Believe Violence.* New York: Basic Books, 2002.

Kellett, R. J. "Infanticide and Child Destruction-The Historical, Legal and Pathological Aspects." *Forensic Science International* 53, no. 1 (1992): 1–28.

Keysers, Christian, and Valeria Gazzola. "Expanding the Mirror: Vicarious Activity for Actions, Emotions, and Sensations." *Current Opinion in Neurobiology* 19, no. 6 (2009): 666–671.

Kirsh, Steven J. *Children, Adolescents, and Media Violence: A Critical Look at the Research,* 2d ed. Thousand Oaks, CA: Sage Publications, 2012.

Kirsh, Steven J. *Media and Youth: A Developmental Perspective.* Malden, MA: Blackwell, 2010.

Kirsh, Steven J. "Using Animated Films to Teach Social and Personality Development." *Teaching of Psychology* 25, no. 1 (1998): 49–51.

Kirsh, Steven J., Karen G. Duffy, and Eastwood Atwater. *Psychology for Living: Adjustment, Growth, and Behavior Today,*

11th ed. Upper Saddle River, NJ: Prentice Hall, 2014.

Kobasa, Suzanne C., Salvatore R. Maddi, and Stephen Kahn. "Hardiness and Health: A Prospective Study." *Journal of Personality and Social Psychology* 42, no. 1 (1982): 168–177.

Krishnan, Raman, Paul S. S. Russell, and Sushila Russell. "A Focus Group Study to Explore Grief Experiences Among Parents of Children with Autism Spectrum Disorder." *Journal of the Indian Academy of Applied Psychology* 43, no. 2 (2017): 267–275.

Kübler-Ross, Elisabeth. *On Death and Dying.* New York: Collier Books, 1993.

Lancy, David F. *The Anthropology of Childhood: Cherubs, Chattel, Changelings.* New York: Cambridge University Press, 2008.

Lehrner, Amy, and Rachel Yehuda. "Trauma Across Generations and Paths to Adaptation and Resilience." *Psychological Trauma: Theory, Research, Practice, and Policy* 10, no. 1 (2018): 22–29.

Lis-Turlejska, Maja, Anna Plichta, Aleksandra Luszczynska, and Charles C. Benight. "Jewish and Non-Jewish World War II Child and Adolescent Survivors at 60 Years After War: Effects of Parental Loss and Age at Exposure on Well-Being." *American Journal of Orthopsychiatry* 78, no. 3 (2008): 369–377.

Liu, Richard T. "Childhood Adversities and Depression in Adulthood: Current Findings and Future Directions." *Clinical Psychology: Science and Practice* 24, no. 2 (2017): 140–153.

Lleras, Christy. "Employment, Work Conditions, and the Home Environment in Single-Mother Families." *Journal of Family Issues* 29, no. 10 (2008): 1268–1297.

Lucenko, Barbara A., Irina V. Sharkova, Alice Huber, Ron Jemelka, and David Mancuso. "Childhood Adversity and Behavioral Health Outcomes for Youth: An Investigation Using State Administrative Data." *Child Abuse & Neglect* 47 (2015): 48–58.

Maberry, Jonathan. *Patient Zero: A Joe Ledger Novel.* New York: St. Martin's Griffin, 2009.

Maberry, Jonathan. *Rot & Ruin.* New York: Simon & Schuster, 2010.

Macedonio, Mary F., Thomas D. Parsons, Raymond A. Digiuseppe, Brenda A. Weiderhold, and Albert A. Rizzo. "Immersiveness and Physiological Arousal Within Panoramic Video-Based Virtual Reality." *Cyberpsychology & Behavior* 10, no. 4 (2007): 508–515.

Macksoud, Mona S., and J. Lawrence Aber. "The War Experiences and Psychosocial Development of Children in Lebanon." *Child Development* 67, no. 1 (1996): 70–88.

Madden, Vaishnavee, Jill Domoney, Katie Aumayer, Vaheshta Sethna, Jane Iles, Isabelle Hubbard, Andreas Giannakakis, Lamprini Psychogiou, and Paul Ramchandani. "Intergenerational Transmission of Parenting: Findings from a UK Longitudinal Study." *The European Journal of Public Health* 25, no. 6 (2015): 1030–1035.

Maddi, Salvatore R., Deborah M. Khoshaba, Richard H. Harvey, Mostafa Fazel, and Nephthys Resurreccion. "The Personality Construct of Hardiness, V: Relationships with the Construction of Existential Meaning in Life." *Journal of Humanistic Psychology* 51, no. 3 (2011): 369–388.

Mancini, Jay A., and Karen A. Roberto. *Pathways of Human Development: Explorations of Change.* New York: Lexington Books, 2009.

Marcia, James E. "Development and Validation of Ego-Identity Status." *Journal of Personality and Social Psychology* 3, no. 5 (1966): 551–558.

Masten, Ann S., and Angela J. Narayan. "Child Development in the Context of Disaster, War, and Terrorism: Pathways of Risk and Resilience." *Annual Review of Psychology* 63 (2012): 227–257.

Masten, Ann S., and Auke Tellegen. "Resilience in Developmental Psychopathology: Contributions of the Project Competence Longitudinal Study." *Development and Psychopathology* 24, no. 2 (2012): 345–361.

Mazur, Elizabeth, and Camille L. Mickle. "Online Discourse of the Stressors of Parenting Children with Mental Health Disorders." *Journal of Child and Family Studies* 27, no. 2 (2018): 569–579.

McCabe, Jennifer E. "Maternal Personality

and Psychopathology as Determinants of Parenting Behavior: A Quantitative Integration of Two Parenting Literatures." *Psychological Bulletin* 140, no. 3 (2014): 722–750.

McDougall, Patricia, and Tracy Vaillancourt. "Long-Term Adult Outcomes of Peer Victimization in Childhood and Adolescence: Pathways to Adjustment and Maladjustment." *American Psychologist* 70, no. 4 (2015): 300–310.

McLanahan, Sara, and Audrey N. Beck. "Parental Relationships in Fragile Families." *The Future of Children/Center for the Future of Children, the David and Lucile Packard Foundation* 20, no. 2 (2010): 17–37.

Mendes, Ana Vilela, José Alexandre de Souza Crippa, Roberto Molina Souza, and Sonia Regina Loureiro. "Risk Factors for Mental Health Problems in School-Age Children from a Community Sample." *Maternal and Child Health Journal* 17, no. 10 (2013): 1825–1834.

Meyer, Cheryl L., Michelle Oberman, Kelly White, et al. *Mothers Who Kill Their Children: Understanding the Acts of Moms from Susan Smith to the "Prom Mom."* New York: New York University Press, 2001.

Michel, Frann. "Life and Death and Something in Between: Reviewing Recent Horror Cinema." *Psychoanalysis, Culture & Society* 12, no. 4 (2007): 390–397.

Miller, Shari, Deborah Gorman-Smith, Terri Sullivan, Pamela Orpinas, and Thomas R. Simon. "Parent and Peer Predictors of Physical Dating Violence Perpetration in Early Adolescence: Tests of Moderation and Gender Differences." *Journal of Clinical Child & Adolescent Psychology* 38, no. 4 (2009): 538–550.

Minton, Cheryl, Jerome Kagan, and Janet A. Levine. "Maternal Control and Obedience in the Two-Year-Old." *Child Development* 42 (1971): 1873–1894.

Moed, Anat, Elizabeth T. Gershoff, and Elizabeth H. Bringewatt. "Violence Exposure as a Mediator between Parenting and Adolescent Mental Health." *Child Psychiatry & Human Development* 48, no. 2 (2017): 235–247.

Moore, Janice. "The Behavior of Parasitized Animals." *Bioscience* 45, no. 2 (1995): 89–96.

Moreland, Angela D., Julia W. Felton, Rochelle F. Hanson, Carrie Jackson, and Jean E. Dumas. "The Relation Between Parenting Stress, Locus of Control and Child Outcomes: Predictors of Change in a Parenting Intervention." *Journal of Child and Family Studies* 25, no. 6 (2016): 2046–2054.

Murray, Kantahyanee W., Kathleen M. Dwyer, Kenneth H. Rubin, Sarah Knighton-Wisor, and Cathryn Booth-LaForce. "Parent-Child Relationships, Parental Psychological Control, and Aggression: Maternal and Paternal Relationships." *Journal of Youth and Adolescence* 43, no. 8 (2014): 1361–1373.

Nakaha, Jessica R., L. Michelle Grimes, Cy B. Nadler, and Mark W. Roberts. "A Treatment Selection Model for Sibling Conflict Based on Observational Measurements." *Journal of Child and Family Studies* 25, no. 1 (2016): 124–135.

Norozi, Sultana Ali, and Torill Moen. "Childhood as a Social Construction." *Journal of Educational and Social Research* 6, no. 2 (2016): 75–80.

Nuttall, Amy K., and Kristin Valentino. "An Ecological-Transactional Model of Generational Boundary Dissolution Across Development." *Marriage & Family Review* 53, no. 2 (2017): 105–150.

Oliveira, Paula S., Isabel Soares, Carla Martins, Joana R. Silva, Sofia Marques, Joana Baptista, and Karlen Lyons-Ruth. "Indiscriminate Behavior Observed in the Strange Situation Among Institutionalized Toddlers: Relations to Caregiver Report and to Early Family Risk." *Infant Mental Health Journal* 33, no. 2 (2012): 187–196.

Ong, Anthony D., Cindy S. Bergeman, and Steven M. Boker. "Resilience Comes of Age: Defining Features in Later Adulthood." *Journal of Personality* 77, no. 6 (2009): 1777–1804.

Östberg, Monica, and Berit Hagekull. "A Structural Modeling Approach to the Understanding of Parenting Stress." *Journal of Clinical Child Psychology* 29, no. 4 (2000): 615–625.

Panagiotaki, Georgia, Michelle Hopkins, Gavin Nobes, Emma Ward, and Debra

Griffiths. "Children's and Adults' Understanding of Death: Cognitive, Parental, and Experiential Influences." *Journal of Experimental Child Psychology* 166 (2018): 96–115.

Pargament, Kenneth I., Bruce W. Smith, Harold G. Koenig, and Lisa Perez. "Patterns of Positive and Negative Religious Coping with Major Life Stressors." *Journal for the Scientific Study of Religion* 37 (1998): 710–724.

Parrigon, Kaela Stuart, Kathryn A. Kerns, Mahsa Movahed Abtahi, and Amanda Koehn. "Attachment and Emotion in Middle Childhood and Adolescence." *Psychological Topics* 24, no. 1 (2015): 27–50.

Parritz, Robin H., and Michael F. Troy. *Disorders of Childhood: Development and Psychopathology*, 2d ed. Belmont, CA: Wadsworth, 2014.

Patterson, Joän M. "Understanding Family Resilience." *Journal of Clinical Psychology* 58, no. 3 (2002): 233–246.

Patton, Christina L., Sarah Francis Smith, and Scott O. Lilienfeld. "Psychopathy and Heroism in First Responders: Traits Cut From the Same Cloth?" *Personality Disorders: Theory, Research, and Treatment* 9 no. 4 (2017): 354–368.

Perrin, Robin, Cindy Miller-Perrin, and Jeongbin Song. "Changing Attitudes about Spanking Using Alternative Biblical Interpretations." *International Journal of Behavioral Development* 41, no. 4 (2017): 514–522.

Pescosolido, Bernice A., Peter S. Jensen, Jack K. Martin, Brea L. Perry, Sigrun Olafsdottir, and Danielle Fettes. "Public Knowledge and Assessment of Child Mental Health Problems: Findings from the National Stigma Study-Children." *Journal of the American Academy of Child & Adolescent Psychiatry* 47, no. 3 (2008): 339–349.

Petersen, Jesse. *Married with Zombies*. New York: Orbit, 2010.

Pitt, Steven E., and Erin M. Bale. "Neonaticide, Infanticide, and Filicide: A Review of the Literature." *The Bulletin of the American Academy of Psychiatry and the Law* 23, no. 3 (1995): 375–386.

Prinzie, Peter, Geert Jan JM Stams, Maja Deković, Albert HA Reijntjes, and Jay Belsky. "The Relations Between Parents' Big Five Personality Factors and Parenting: A Meta-Analytic Review." *Journal of Personality and Social Psychology* 97, no. 2 (2009): 351–362.

Pyszczynski, Tom, Jeff Greenberg, and Sheldon Solomon. "A Dual-Process Model of Defense Against Conscious and Unconscious Death-Related Thoughts: An Extension of Terror Management Theory." *Psychological Review* 106, no. 4 (1999): 835–845.

Ridout, Kathryn K., Mateus Levandowski, Samuel J. Ridout, Lindsay Gantz, Kelly Goonan, Daniella Palermo, Lawrence H. Price, and Audrey R. Tyrka. "Early Life Adversity and Telomere Length: A Meta-Analysis." *Molecular Psychiatry* 23, no. 4 (2018): 858–871.

Roberts, Lisa R., and Susanne B. Montgomery. "India's Distorted Sex Ratio: Dire Consequences for Girls." *Journal of Christian Nursing: A Quarterly Publication of Nurses Christian Fellowship* 33, no. 1 (2016): E7-E15.

Roberts, William L., and Janet Strayer. "Parents' Responses to the Emotional Distress of Their Children: Relations with Children's Competence." *Developmental Psychology* 23, no. 3 (1987): 415–422.

Roos, Susan. *Chronic Sorrow: A Living Loss*. New York: Brunner-Routledge, 2002.

Rothbart, Mary K. *Becoming Who We Are: Temperament and Personality in Development*. New York: Guilford Press., 2011.

Rowland, Diana. *My Life as a White Trash Zombie*. New York: Daw Books, 2011.

Rudolph, Karen D., and Megan Flynn. "Childhood Adversity and Youth Depression: Influence of Gender and Pubertal Status." *Development and Psychopathology* 19, no. 2 (2007): 497–521.

Rutter, Michael. "Resilience: Some Conceptual Considerations." *Journal of Adolescent Health* 14 (1993): 626–631.

Sade, Robert M. "Brain Death, Cardiac Death, and the Dead Donor Rule." *Journal of the South Carolina Medical Association* 107, no. 4 (2011):146–149.

Sanders, Catherine M. "A Comparison of Adult Bereavement in the Death of a Spouse, Child, and Parent." *OMEGA—*

Journal of Death and Dying 10, no. 4 (1980): 303–322.

Santayana, George. *The Life of Reason.* Amherst, NY: Prometheus Books, 1998.

Schenck, Laura K., Kiersten M. Eberle, and Jeffrey A. Rings. "Insecure Attachment Styles and Complicated Grief Severity: Applying What We Know to Inform Future Directions." *OMEGA— Journal of Death and Dying* 73, no. 3 (2016): 231–249.

Scheper-Hughes, Nancy. *Death Without Weeping: The Violence of Everyday Life in Brasil.* Berkeley: University of California Press, 1992.

Schiffrin, Holly H., and Miriam Liss. "The Effects of Helicopter Parenting on Academic Motivation." *Journal of Child and Family Studies* 26, no. 5 (2017): 1472–1480.

Schreiber, Joe. *Star Wars: Death Troopers.* New York: Del Rey/Ballantine, 2009.

Scott, James G., Marianne Giørtz Pedersen, Holly E. Erskine, Aida Bikic, Ditte Demontis, John J. McGrath, and Søren Dalsgaard. "Mortality in Individuals with Disruptive Behavior Disorders Diagnosed by Specialist Services—A Nationwide Cohort Study." *Psychiatry Research* 251 (2017): 255–260.

Seligman, Martin E. P. "Phobias and Preparedness." *Behavior Therapy* 2, no. 3 (1971): 307–320.

Shaffer, Anne, and Jelena Obradović. "Unique Contributions of Emotion Regulation and Executive Functions in Predicting the Quality of Parent-Child Interaction Behaviors." *Journal of Family Psychology* 31, no. 2 (2017): 150–159.

Shapero, Benjamin G., Shimrit K. Black, Richard T. Liu, Joshua Klugman, Rachel E. Bender, Lyn Y. Abramson, and Lauren B. Alloy. "Stressful Life Events and Depression Symptoms: The Effect of Childhood Emotional Abuse on Stress Reactivity." *Journal of Clinical Psychology* 70, no. 3 (2014): 209–223.

Sharlach, Lisa. "Rape as Genocide: Bangladesh, the Former Yugoslavia, and Rwanda." *New Political Science* 22, no. 1 (2000): 89–102.

Skinner, Ellen, Sandy Johnson, and Tatiana Snyder. "Six Dimensions of Parenting: A Motivational Model." *Parenting: Science and Practice* 5, no. 2 (2005): 175–235.

Slone, Michelle, and Anat Shoshani. "Children Affected by War and Armed Conflict: Parental Protective Factors and Resistance to Mental Health Symptoms." *Frontiers in Psychology* 8 (2017): 1397.

Smith, Cynthia L., Tracy L. Spinrad, Nancy Eisenberg, Bridget M. Gaertner, Tierney K. Popp, and Elizabeth Maxon. "Maternal Personality: Longitudinal Associations to Parenting Behavior and Maternal Emotional Expressions Toward Toddlers." *Parenting: Science and Practice* 7, no. 3 (2007): 305–329.

Solomon, Andrew. *Far from the Tree: Parents, Children and the Search for Identity.* New York: Scribner/Simon & Schuster, 2012.

Solomon, Zahava, Mark Waysman, Ruth Belkin, Gaby Levy, Mario Mikulincer, and Dan Enoch. "Marital Relations and Combat Stress Reaction: The Wives' Perspective." *Journal of Marriage and the Family* (1992): 316–326.

Specht, Jule, Boris Egloff, and Stefan C. Schmukle. "Stability and Change of Personality Across the Life Course: The Impact of Age and Major Life Events on Mean-Level and Rank-Order Stability of the Big Five." *Journal of Personality and Social Psychology* 101, no. 4 (2011): 862–882.

Story, Lisa B., and Thomas N. Bradbury. "Understanding Marriage and Stress: Essential Questions and Challenges." *Clinical Psychology Review* 23, no. 8 (2004): 1139–1162.

Strong, Jonathan, Christopher Varady, Najla Chahda, Shannon Doocy, and Gilbert Burnham. "Health Status and Health Needs of Older Refugees from Syria in Lebanon." *Conflict and Health* 9, no. 1 (2015): 12.

Sunaga, Yasuyo, Naohiko Kanemura, Masaya Anan, Makoto Takahashi, and Koichi Shinkoda. "Estimation of Inertial Parameters of the Lower Trunk in Pregnant Japanese Women: A Longitudinal Comparative Study and Application to Motion Analysis." *Applied Ergonomics* 55 (2016): 173–182.

Swami, Viren. *Evolutionary Psychology: A*

Critical Introduction. Chichester: Wiley-Blackwell, 2011.

Tao, Ting, Ligang Wang, Chunlei Fan, and Wenbin Gao. "Development of Self-Control in Children Aged 3 to 9 Years: Perspective from a Dual-Systems Model." *Scientific Reports* 4 (2014): 7272.

Tartakovsky, Eugene, and Liat Hamama. "Mothers' Acceptance-Rejection of their Children Infected with HIV: The Role of the Mothers' Social Axioms, Psychological Distress, and Relationships with the Partner." *Journal of Pediatric Psychology* 36, no. 9 (2011): 1030–1042.

Tarullo, Amanda R., Jelena Obradovic, and Megan R. Gunnar. "Self-Control and the Developing Brain." *Zero to Three* 29, no. 3 (2009): 31–37.

ter Kuile, Hagar, and Thomas Ehring. "Predictors of Changes in Religiosity after Trauma: Trauma, Religiosity, and Post-traumatic Stress Disorder." *Psychological Trauma: Theory, Research, Practice, and Policy* 6, no. 4 (2014): 353–360.

Tharp, Andra Teten, Sarah DeGue, Linda Anne Valle, Kathryn A. Brookmeyer, Greta M. Massetti, and Jennifer L. Matjasko. "A Systematic Qualitative Review of Risk and Protective Factors for Sexual Violence Perpetration." *Trauma, Violence, & Abuse* 14, no. 2 (2013): 133–167.

Thomas, Alexander, and Stella Chess. *Temperament and Development*. New York: Brunner/Mazel, 1977.

Tolan, Patrick H., Deborah Gorman-Smith, and David B. Henry. "The Developmental Ecology of Urban Males' Youth Violence." *Developmental Psychology* 39, no. 2 (2003): 274–291.

Tomassetti-Long, Victoria J., Bonnie C. Nicholson, Michael B. Madson, and Eric R. Dahlen. "Hardiness, Parenting Stress, and PTSD Symptomatology in US Afghanistan/Iraq Era Veteran Fathers." *Psychology of Men & Masculinity* 16, no. 3 (2015): 239–245.

Tooley, Greg A., Mari Karakis, Mark Stokes, and Joan Ozanne-Smith. "Generalising the Cinderella Effect to Unintentional Childhood Fatalities." *Evolution and Human Behavior* 27, no. 3 (2006): 224–230.

Turner, Samuel M., Deborah C. Beidel, Roxann Roberson-Nay, and Kari Tervo. "Parenting Behaviors in Parents with Anxiety Disorders." *Behaviour Research and Therapy* 41, no. 5 (2003): 541–554.

Twenge, Jean M., W. Keith Campbell, and Craig A. Foster. "Parenthood and Marital Satisfaction: A Meta-Analytic Review." *Journal of Marriage and Family* 65, no. 3 (2003): 574–583.

Valenzuela, Marta. "Attachment in Chronically Underweight Young Children." *Child Development* 61, no. 6 (1990): 1984–1996.

Van Ijzendoorn, Marinus H., Carlo Schuengel, and Marian J. Bakermans-Kranenburg. "Disorganized Attachment in Early Childhood: Meta-Analysis of Precursors, Concomitants, and Sequelae." *Development and Psychopathology* 11, no. 2 (1999): 225–250.

Vaughn, Brian E., Claire B. Kopp, Joanne B. Krakow, Kim Johnson, and Steven S. Schwartz. "Process Analyses of the Behavior of Very Young Children in Delay Tasks." *Developmental Psychology* 22, no. 6 (1986): 752–759.

Verstynen, Timothy, and Bradley Voytek. *Do Zombies Dream of Undead Sheep? A Neuroscientific View of the Zombie Brain*. Princeton: Princeton University Press, 2014.

Vohs, Kathleen D., and Todd F. Heatherton. "Self-Regulatory Failure: A Resource-Depletion Approach." *Psychological Science* 11, no. 3 (2000): 249–254.

Volling, Brenda L., Annette Mahoney, and Amy J. Rauer. "Sanctification of Parenting, Moral Socialization, and Young Children's Conscience Development." *Psychology of Religion and Spirituality* 1, no. 1 (2009): 53–68.

Vulliez-Coady, Lauriane, Elisabet Solheim, Jeremy P. Nahum, and Karlen Lyons-Ruth. "Role-Confusion in Parent-Child Relationships: Assessing Mother's Representations and its Implications for Counselling and Psychotherapy Practice." *The European Journal of Counselling Psychology* 4, no. 2 (2016): 205–227.

Wagley, Charles. *Welcome of Tears: The Tapirapé Indians of Central Brazil*. Oxford: Oxford University Press, 1977.

Wallace, Maeve E., Donna Hoyert, Corrine Williams, and Pauline Mendola.

"Pregnancy-Associated Homicide and Suicide in 37 US States with Enhanced Pregnancy Surveillance." *American Journal of Obstetrics and Gynecology* 215, no. 3 (2016): 364.e1–364.e10.

Waller, Rebecca, Thomas J. Dishion, Daniel S. Shaw, Frances Gardner, Melvin N. Wilson, and Luke W. Hyde. "Does Early Childhood Callous-Unemotional Behavior Uniquely Predict Behavior Problems or Callous-Unemotional Behavior in Late Childhood?." *Developmental Psychology* 52, no. 11 (2016): 1805–1819.

Wang, L., C. Fan, T. Tao, and W. Gao. "Age and Gender Differences in Self-Control and its Intergenerational Transmission." *Child: Care, Health and Development* 43, no. 2 (2017): 274–280.

Wang, Meifang, and Xiaopei Xing. "Intergenerational Transmission of Parental Corporal Punishment in China: The Moderating Role of Spouse's Corporal Punishment." *Journal of Family Violence* 29, no. 2 (2014): 119–128.

Weiser, Lee. "The Zombie Archetype: Living in a Viral Culture." *Psychological Perspectives* 58, no. 4 (2015): 442–454.

Weissbluth, Marc. *Crybabies.* New York: Arbor House, 1984.

Weyand, Chelsea, Liz O'Laughlin, and Patrick Bennett. "Dimensions of Religiousness That Influence Parenting." *Psychology of Religion and Spirituality* 5, no. 3 (2013): 182–191.

Wilkinson, Paul O., Maciej Trzaskowski, Claire MA Haworth, and Thalia C. Eley. "The Role of Gene-Environment Correlations and Interactions in Middle Childhood Depressive Symptoms." *Development and Psychopathology* 25, no. 1 (2013): 93–104.

Williamson, Hannah C., Benjamin R. Karney, and Thomas N. Bradbury. "Financial Strain and Stressful Events Predict Newlyweds' Negative Communication Independent of Relationship Satisfaction." *Journal of Family Psychology* 27, no. 1 (2013): 65–75.

Wills, Thomas A. "Downward Comparison Principles in Social Psychology." *Psychological Bulletin* 90, no. 2 (1981): 245–271.

Wisman, Arnaud, and Jamie L. Goldenberg. "From the Grave to the Cradle: Evidence that Mortality Salience Engenders a Desire for Offspring." *Journal of Personality and Social Psychology* 89, no. 1 (2005): 46–61.

Woolley, Jacqueline D., Elizabeth A. Boerger, and Arthur B. Markman. "A Visit from the Candy Witch: Factors Influencing Young Children's Belief in a Novel Fantastical Being." *Developmental Science* 7, no. 4 (2004): 456–468.

Woolley, Jacqueline D., and Maliki E. Ghossainy. "Revisiting the Fantasy-Reality Distinction: Children as Naïve Skeptics." *Child Development* 84, no. 5 (2013): 1496–1510.

Wyness, Michael. *Childhood and Society: An Introduction to the Sociology of Childhood.* Houndmills: Palgrave Macmillan, 2006.

Yu, Rongqin, John R. Geddes, and Seena Fazel. "Personality Disorders, Violence, and Antisocial Behavior: A Systematic Review and Meta-Regression Analysis." *Journal of Personality Disorders* 26, no. 5 (2012): 775–792.

Zestcott, Colin A., Uri Lifshin, Peter Helm, and Jeff Greenberg. "He Dies, He Scores: Evidence That Reminders of Death Motivate Improved Performance in Basketball." *Journal of Sport and Exercise Psychology* 38, no. 5 (2016): 470–480.

Zuckerman, Marvin. "Sensation Seeking: A Comparative Approach to a Human Trait." *Behavioral and Brain Sciences* 7, No. 3 (1984): 413–434.

Index